THE BACKGROUND TO SHAKESPEARE'S SONNETS

The Background to Shakespeare's Sonnets

R. J. C. WAIT

SCHOCKEN BOOKS · NEW YORK

Published in U.S.A. in 1972
by Schocken Books Inc.
67 Park Avenue, New York, N.Y. 10016

Printed in Great Britain

Contents

Introduction

SOME three and a half centuries ago there was published in London a small volume entitled *Shake-speare's Sonnets: Never Before Imprinted*. It contains 154 short poems, all except three of which are regular sonnets of fourteen ten-syllable lines, and also a narrative poem called *A Lovers Complaint*. The Sonnets are prefaced by a puzzling dedication 'To the onlie begetter of these insuing sonnets', and many, though perhaps not all, of the poems in it appear to be of a strongly personal character. Most, if not all, of the first 126 are clearly addressed to a young man, and seem to form one sequence, which is terminated by a poem of six couplets, not in sonnet form. Most of the remaining twenty-eight short poems relate to a lady of dark complexion, while the narrative poem tells the story of a girl who has been seduced and abandoned by an attractive but heartless young man.

Many slim volumes more or less of this kind were published towards the end of the sixteenth and the early part of the seventeenth centuries; the special claims to our attention of this one are, first, that some of the sonnets in it are generally thought to be among the finest poetry in the English or any other language, and second, that if some or all of its contents do indeed reflect personal experiences and emotions they represent practically the only personal statement which has been left to us by one of the greatest figures of the world's literature.

After Shakespeare's own time little interest was shown in the Sonnets until the end of the eighteenth century. Though, since then, much has been written on the subject, no one has yet been able to show convincingly whether they do or do not have a preponderantly autobiographical or topical character. Some critics have felt that the Sonnets should be read and enjoyed purely for their intrinsic value as poetry, and that any possible autobiographical background is an irrelevance, if not an illusion. Others have almost ignored the poetry in the attempt to find topical allusions and references to personalities of the time; while yet others have examined every line without reference to its artistic or autobiographical content, but with the sole object of tracing Shakespeare's dependence on other poets.

Taken by themselves, all three of these approaches are too narrow, and betray the proclivities and prejudices of their holders. Thus we find academics who earn their living by literary criticism deriding the approach of the historians and autobiographers, while the historical specialists have little time for the students of prosody and poetics. The immortality which their author claimed for the Sonnets, and about which the modern reader also holds no doubts, is due, not to any key which they may or may not contain to the secrets of Shakespeare's heart,[1] but simply to their quality as poetry; yet, if we were to find in the text a number of personal or topical references which Shakespeare intended to be clear to their first reader, might not our understanding and appreciation even of such supreme poetry be thereby enhanced?

It was at the end of 1963, fired, and a little irritated, by the stream of Shakespeareana which appeared in advance of the celebration the following year of the four hundredth anniversary of the poet's birth, that I decided to examine for myself the language of the Sonnets against the history of the period covered by Shakespeare's adult life up to their publication in 1609. I was moved to do so through a dissatisfaction both with certain theories about the Sonnets then being confidently expressed, and with the attitude of those who took the opposite line that no valid solution to the problem could be found.

The project was conceived while I was employed in the Malaysian Treasury; the research was carried out largely during the spare moments of a period spent in the administration of the finances of Malawi, often during the course of lengthy plane journeys made in pursuit of development finance; the writing was fitted in while I was engaged in advisory financial duties in Afghanistan and Liberia. In such circumstances the method I employed had to be the simplest I could devise.

The Sonnets contain many unusual images of a kind not found in the more conventional poetry of the period; examples are:

> Like widdowed wombes after their Lords decease: 97.6

and

> Yf my deare love were but the childe of state,   124.1–2
> It might for fortune's basterd be unfathered, . . .

Hitherto, no commentator has satisfactorily explained the significance of either of these passages, yet it seemed to me that Shakespeare must have expected them to be clear and meaningful to the audience for whom he was writing. If that was so, there was a good chance that the allusions could be identified today, since we have ample records of the notable events and topics of the period.

My plan, then, was to take as a first hypothesis what seemed to me to be superficially the most likely and least recondite theories as to the order and dating of the Sonnets and the identity of the person to whom they were written, and then to examine this hypothesis against all the available information as to the events of the time and the current activities of the presumed recipient and of Shakespeare himself. If the dating pattern was correct, it should be possible to fill in between these landmarks a number of minor ones which might not be clear enough to stand alone. Of course, one could expect from time to time to encounter blind alleys, which would mean that some part of the working hypothesis would have to be modified and the process begun again.

The reader need not fear that in this book I am going to take him all through the long and, at times, tedious investigation which this method entailed. My working hypothesis in its final form is briefly set out in the first chapter, together with the major landmarks which establish the framework; the remainder of the book sets the Sonnets, according to this framework, against the relevant background of events and personalities of the time, and interprets them in this light. In other words, from the process of investigation only the material which I think valid has been retained; the false starts and the enticing chimaeras have been dropped. What remains I present as being the true dating and context of the Sonnets, from which we can, I think, obtain a picture of the emotional experiences which they reflect and of the circumstances which occasioned them. As in all investigations, not all the pieces of evidence would be equally convincing on their own; but taken together each helps to strengthen the others.

The choice of texts for the quotations both from the Sonnets themselves and from other contemporary works has presented a problem. In many cases I have found that the original orthography and punctuation of the Sonnets convey meanings which no modern-spelling text can do. I have therefore used the original text, with minor amendments such as the sorting out of U's and V's and F's and S's, following the edition of Gerald Willen and V. B. Reed. (In the few Sonnets which ended with a comma in 'Q', I have inserted a full stop instead.)* For other quotations I have modernized where the old spelling offers no advantages, but have retained it when it seems to me to add some additional flavour to the quotations, as with those from George Chapman and also with most of the prose excerpts.

In setting out the background I make no claim to offer new historical material: those familiar with the Elizabethan and Jacobean periods will find here no fresh facts, though they may find a few new interpretations of the facts. Those not so familiar will, I hope, find the information useful and the story as fascinating as I found it myself. More than a hundred works were consulted, some of which are noted at the end of the book; but of these whose authors are still living, I should like to single out for special acknowledgment here G. B. Harrison's *Elizabethan Journals* and *A Jacobean Journal*, which provide an invaluable key to the principal events covered by Shakespeare's working life, and also G. P. V. Akrigg's *Shakespeare and the Earl of Southampton*, and his *Jacobean Pageant*.

I should like also to express my debt to the London Library, particularly to its photocopying service, which enabled rare books to be studied many thousands of miles away; also to the libraries of the Travellers' Club, London, and the British Council, Kabul, each of which contained a surprising amount of essential

---

* Occasional essential amendments to the Q and Willen and Reed text have been footnoted thus; and a few very obvious misprints have been corrected without comment (e.g. 122.1).

reference material. Grateful acknowledgments are also due to Mr Kenneth Barnes of Malawi, who by a chance remark enabled me to establish the dating of Sonnet 97, as well as giving other less dramatic assistance; also to Mr Kenneth Pearson in Kabul and Mr Martin Moynihan and Dr Carl Anonsen in Monrovia, all of whom read the manuscript and gave valuable advice. I should like to pay a special tribute to Mrs K. Farah, my secretary in Kabul, who cheerfully spent her leisure time, when not engaged with the fiscal affairs of Afghanistan, in typing out the whole of the first draft of the book.

CHAPTER I

The Framework

THIS book traces the relationship between William Shakespeare and a younger man who both meant a great deal to him personally and also had an important influence on his career. It is a story which must have been well enough known in Shakespeare's day, but for the last three and a half centuries has been lost in obscurity and incomprehension. To help us unravel it we have not only the sequence of sonnets which Shakespeare addressed to this friend, but also the fruits of the thorough and voluminous work which generations of scholars have done on the historical and literary background of the time. The first questions to be answered are, who was the man to whom the Sonnets were addressed? and, when were the various sonnets written?

William Shakespeare was born in 1564 and became a leading playwright in the early 1590s. From 1594 until shortly before his death in 1616 he was pre-eminent among the dramatists of the time, keeping up a steady flow of new plays for the company in which he was a share-holding partner. In 1593 he published a narrative poem called *Venus and Adonis*, and this was followed the next year by another called *The Rape of Lucrece*. Both of these were prefaced by dedicatory letters addressed to a young nobleman, Henry Wriothesley, Third Earl of Southampton, who was still a minor at the time. These were the only poems of which Shakespeare himself seems to have arranged the publication; a number of short pieces ascribed to him, of which some are certainly not his, were printed under the title *The Passionate Pilgrim* in 1599, and in 1601 a poem on the theme of the Phoenix and Turtle appeared under his signature in a collection of works by various authors which was dedicated to Sir John Salusbury. Finally there appeared the little book entitled *Shakes-peare's Sonnets*.

An entry dated 10th May, 1609, in the Stationers' Register shows that the book was published by one Thomas Thorpe, who is doubtless the 'T. T.' whose initials are printed below the book's dedication. The words 'Never before Imprinted', which appear under the title, seem to carry an implication that the contents had existed in manuscript form for some time. Indeed, two of the sonnets in it, 138 and 144, had appeared with minor variations in *The Passionate Pilgrim* ten years previously. In 1598 Meres had written of Shakespeare's 'sugred sonnets among his private friends'. It seems likely, then, that a number of the sonnets in Thorpe's volume had been written before that date.

The first real puzzle comes no later than the dedication, on the first four words of which, according to Professor Rollins,[1] an entire library has been written. The dedication is set out as if to represent an inscription on a monument; perhaps this a reference to Sonnet 55:

> Not marble, nor the guilded monument,   55.1–2
> Of Princes shall out-live this powrefull rime, . . .

Certainly Thorpe was justified in linking his enterprise with the immortal memory promised in that sonnet; but the syntax of the dedication remains a problem:

TO.THE.ONLIE.BEGETTER.OF.

THESE. INSUING.SONNETS.

MR.W.H. ALL.HAPPINESSE.

AND.THAT.ETERNITIE.

PROMISED.

BY.

OUR.EVERLIVING.POET.

WISHETH.

THE.WELL-WISHING.

ADVENTURER.IN.

SETTING.

FORTH.

T. T.

Rivalrous over who?

Although every possible alternative has been put forward, it seems simplest to regard 'Mr. W. H.' as being the same person as the 'Onlie Begetter'. But the meaning of 'Begetter' is disputed: in ancient times it meant 'obtainer' or 'procurer', though the most usual meaning by Shakespeare's day was that found in the biblical phrase, 'This is my only begotten son'. It is possible that Thorpe was dedicating the book to the procurer of the manuscript, but it is far more likely to my mind that the reference is to the theme of Sonnet 78:

> Yet be most proud of that which I compile,   78.9–10
> Whose influence is thine, and borne of thee, . . .

Furthermore, it does not seem appropriate for Thorpe to wish 'that eternitie promised by our everliving poet' to someone other than the person to whom the poet himself promised it. On the balance of probabilities we may assume that 'Mr. W. H.' is the young man who inspired the sonnets; or, at the least, the first 126 of the series, which are those relating to a young man. That there was only one such inspirer Shakespeare tells us in Sonnet 105:

> Since all alike my songs and praises be   105.3–4
> To one, of one, still such, and ever so.

From the fifth line of Sonnet 37 it seems that the young man was possessed of beauty, birth, wealth and wit, and from two other sonnets that he was a patron of poets and writers:

So oft have I invok'd thee for my Muse,   78.1–4
And found such faire assistance in my verse,
As every *Alien* pen hath got my use,
And under thee their poesie disperse.

I grant thou wert not married to my Muse,   82.1–4
And therefore maiest without attaint ore-looke
The dedicated words which writers use
Of their faire subject, blessing every booke.

In view of what Shakespeare tells us in these sonnets we can safely ignore the attempts which have been made to show that the Sonnets were written to a sea-cook, a boy actor or a little-known law student, as suggested respectively by Samuel Butler, Oscar Wilde and Leslie Hotson. If there were numbers of writers 'dispersing their poesie' under the patronage of characters of that sort it is surprising that we have not heard more about them!

We may also ignore, at least for the time being, the attempts which have been made to tinker with the order of the Sonnets. As published by Thorpe, the first 126 sonnets appear prima facie to be in some sort of logical order, and we should not assume that the order is wrong unless and until our examination provides good reason to come to such a conclusion. Of the remaining twenty-eight, all except 129 and 146, in which the poet moralizes on the themes of lust and of human vanity, appear to have been written either to or about a dark mistress, who seems to be the same woman referred to in 40, 41 and 42, since from both groups it appears that she has seduced the young man behind Shakespeare's back. The dating of the 'dark lady' series will therefore depend largely on that of the related sonnets in the first series, and it is on these 126 that we must concentrate our attention.

The search for a young man of rank who was a patron of literature and known to have extended his patronage to Shakespeare is not a difficult one, particularly when we recall that the first seventeen sonnets are concerned with urging the young man to marry and beget an heir. The only such young men known to have given Shakespeare their patronage were (i) Henry Wriothesley, Third Earl of Southampton, to whom, as we have seen, *Venus and Adonis* and *The Rape of Lucrece* were dedicated, and (ii) and (iii) the 'incomparable pair of brethren', William Herbert, Earl of Pembroke, and his brother Philip, Earl of Montgomery, to whom Shakespeare's fellow-players dedicated the First Folio of his collected plays in 1623:

> But since your LL have been pleased to thinke these trifles some-thing, heeretofore; and have prosequuted both them, and their Authour living, with so much favour: . . .

The chance that Shakespeare had some wholly unknown young patron of rank apart from these can be no more than just a chance; since we are looking only for the most probable hypothesis we need look no further than these three. All three were generous patrons of literature, quite apart from their known connections with Shakespeare.

From the appearance of a version of Sonnet 144 in *The Passionate Pilgrim* in 1599 we know that the triangular affair between Shakespeare, the dark lady and the young man had already occurred at that time. In 1599 Philip Herbert was fifteen years old, and it is thus hardly likely that he was the one involved. His brother William was nineteen and Southampton twenty-six, so both of these are quite possible.

Both Southampton and William Herbert suffered from the unwelcome attempts of their elders to get them suitably married off at an early age. Southampton's guardian, Lord Burghley, started trying to persuade the boy to marry his granddaughter before he had turned seventeen. William Herbert was the subject of marriage negotiations even earlier, when he was still fifteen. In this case the lady was the daughter of Sir George Carey, son of the Lord Chamberlain, who was patron of the company of players in which Shakespeare had become a shareholder the previous year, and with which he remained for the rest of his career. William Herbert again refused marriage in 1601, on this occasion to Mary Fitton, a lady-in-waiting to the Queen, though admitting that he was responsible for her pregnancy.

So far there seems little to choose between the two candidates. Indeed, both to this day have their ardent supporters among critics and commentators. Some, like Sir Sidney Lee, editor of the *Dictionary of National Biography*, and Professor Dover Wilson, editor of the Cambridge *New Shakespeare* series, have supported both candidates equally strongly at different times. Fortunately the matter can be easily settled, at least as between these two front-runners, by an examination of the last poem addressed to the young man, Sonnet 126.

Many people must have been a little disturbed at the opening words of this poem, 'O thou my lovely Boy', which the commentators have assumed to be directly addressed to the young friend. There is no other line addressed to the young man which carries such a sickly flavour, and, as I shall show in more detail in Chapter XXI, this one is no exception. When read with the opening lines of Sonnet 11, the language of No. 126 indicates that a son and heir has at last been born to the friend, and it is this baby that Shakespeare is addressing, as being a perpetuation of the friend's 'sweet selfe'. What more fitting way could be found of bringing the series, which started with seventeen sonnets on this very theme, to a graceful conclusion!

In looking for the person to whom the Sonnets were addressed, then, we must rule out anyone who had not produced a son and heir by 1609, the date when the Sonnets were first published. This requirement immediately catches William Herbert, Earl of Pembroke. Fittingly enough, he made his debut in the controversy within the pages of the *Gentleman's Magazine*, in 1832, at the suggestion of James Boaden. Now, with all the graciousness for which he was noted, he can be allowed to bow himself out. There is no record of any child being born to this earl, apart from his unwanted and short-lived bastard by

Mary Fitton, until 1620, four years after Shakespeare's death, when his wife produced a delicate son who did not long survive. Had there been an earlier one it is inconceivable that no record would remain, even if the child had lived only a few days. The birth of an heir to a great public figure such as the Earl of Pembroke would have been a major event for the gossips and diarists of the time.

And so we are left with Henry Wriothesley, Earl of Southampton, whose claim to be the young man of the Sonnets was first advanced by Dr Nathan Drake in 1817. Southampton married Elizabeth Vernon in 1598, but his first son was not born until 1st March, 1605. The baby was christened James at Greenwich Palace on 26th March, after James I, who acted as one of the godparents.[2]

So much for the first question which I set out at the beginning of this chapter. As regards the second, most of the scholars who have favoured Southampton as the young man have assumed that the Sonnets must have been written round about the time of the dedication to him of *Venus Adonis* and *The Rape of Lucrece*, or not very long thereafter. Apart from similarities between certain phrases in the Sonnets and in these two poems, this is because Sonnet 104 tells us that the seasons have three times changed, from spring through summer and autumn to winter, since the poet and his friend first met. Since *Venus and Adonis* was dedicated and published in 1593, the first 104 sonnets, assuming that the dedication required a meeting between poet and patron and that the Sonnets are more or less in the right order, cannot extend beyond the winter of 1595–6. On the other hand, Sonnet 107 looks as if it carries a reference to the death of Queen Elizabeth and the accession of James I in 1603:

> The mortall Moone hath her eclipse indur'de,   107.5–8
> And the sad Augurs mock their owne presage,
> Incertenties now crowne them-selves assur'de,
> And peace proclaims Olives of endlesse age.

Adherents of the Earl of Pembroke have been happy to accept the date of 1603 for this sonnet. Their candidate was twenty-three at the time, while Southampton was rising thirty. Many of the supporters of Southampton have therefore found reasons for concluding that the sonnet cannot refer to the year 1603, and have decided that the 'eclipse' refers to the dangers of Queen Elizabeth's climacteric year of 1596,[3] or even to the Lopez conspiracy of 1594.[4] However, if No. 126 can be shown, as I have indicated, to refer to an event in March 1605, the reasons for refusing to accept the most obvious interpretation for 107 at once disappear. Southampton was released from his 'confined doom' in the Tower of London by James I in April 1603, and the coronation took place on 25th July. We are, of course, now left with the conclusion that, if Southampton is the person addressed, there must be a very considerable time-gap between Sonnets 104 and 107 to make a date of April–July 1603 possible for the latter. We may reasonably expect to find mention of changes in the young man's appearance in the ensuing sonnets, if this hypothesis is correct, since he could hardly still be the 'world's fresh ornament' of Sonnet 1.

It would be helpful now if we could make a firmer suggestion as to the date of Sonnet 104, since this would enable us to turn the clock back for three revolutions of the seasons and thus arrive at a date for the beginning of the sequence.

Quite near to Sonnet 104, in No. 97, comes the line:

Like widdowed wombes after their Lords decease: ...   97.8

I shall show in Chapter XI that the reference here is to the Countess of Derby, who was left a widow in April 1594, and was later found to be pregnant. This makes the winter of 1594 a strong probability for Sonnet 104; and the sequence must then have begun three springs previously, in 1592:

Three Winters colde,   104.3–8
Have from the forrests shooke three summers pride,
Three beautious springs to yellow *Autumne* turn'd,
In processe of the seasons have I seene,
Three Aprill perfumes in three hot Junes burn'd,
Since first I saw you fresh which yet are greene.

We now have the following time-framework for our investigation:

Sonnets 1 to 104 (and perhaps to 106) — Spring 1592 to Winter 1594.
Sonnets 107 to 126 — Spring 1603 to Spring 1605.

We may add to this that the 'dark lady' sonnets, 127–154, also fall within the first period, in so far as they are linked with 40, 41 and 42.

I have said that the first questions to be answered are 'Who?' and 'When?' There is of course another very important problem, and that is 'Why?' To a large extent the material which provides the answers to the first two questions will help us also to solve this third one; nevertheless there must be a good many readers who have been puzzled to know why poetry of the kind we are considering should have been written by one man to another. It is to be hoped that few nowadays will feel inclined to go as far as George Steevens, who, writing in 1780 about Sonnet 20, found it 'impossible to read this fulsome panegyrick, addressed to a male object, without an equal admixture of disgust and indignation'. Clearly Steevens failed to appreciate, for a start, that the word 'passion' in the second line of that sonnet is used semi-facetiously to mean an emotional poem, like that spoken by Thisbe in *A Midsummer Night's Dream*, of whom Theseus says

Here she comes; and her passion ends the play.   *MND* V.i.323

There are many such differences both in language and manners between the usages of the Elizabethan and Jacobean ages and those of the eighteenth, nineteenth and twentieth centuries. We could not now describe the friendship of Antonio and Bassanio in the words in which it is described throughout the *Merchant of Venice*, or that of David and Jonathan in those used in I *Samuel* xviii. 1, but the language of these two examples is that of the Sonnets. In both cases the relationship is put forward as something to be admired without reservation, free from any of the inhibitions which Freudian psychoanalysts, in their attempts to remove those of the mentally ill, have managed to spread among the otherwise sane.

The lexicographer Eric Partridge has made a very full list of Shakespeare's sexual language in his book *Shakespeare's Bawdy*, and has pointed out that it is overwhelmingly heterosexual. 'Had Shakespeare,' he says, 'so frank and so courageous, been a homosexual, he would have subtly yet irrefutably conveyed the fact.' In Christopher Marlowe, for instance, there are several passages which would make one suspect that he had homosexual inclinations, even if this fact had not been widely known. Shakespeare wrote so much and so quickly that any such concealed tendencies, if they existed, would show up somewhere as in a modern free-association word test. That he approved of deep friendships between men is obvious from many of his plays; that he was sexually attracted by women and repelled by male effeminacy or perversion is equally obvious on the few occasions when these subjects are introduced. Nevertheless he is frequently extremely scathing (or his characters are) about loose women and heterosexual excesses.

To Shakespeare, lawful married love between the sexes and platonic, idealistic love between persons of the same sex were both enjoyable and good, whereas adultery and whoring were pleasurable but bad. Different times have different *mores*, and even at the same period of history different persons have differing moral views; there is thus room for other opinions about these various manifestations of what may or may not be considered as one erotic urge. In this book it is not my intention to say much about these matters, for the sufficient reason that many other persons have already done so.[5] But although my purpose is to treat the Sonnets primarily from the biographical point of view, I do not disagree with Leslie A. Fiedler when he says that

> in the end one reads the complete sequence not as the mere confession of an erotic misadventure but as a study of love itself as understood in Western Europe towards the end of the sixteenth century.[6]

We must indeed be prepared throughout our examination of the Sonnets to consider them as a study of love in the universal sense, as well as of the subjective effect of certain specific loves, 'of comfort and dispaire', on Shakespeare himself.

The framework for our investigation is now ready. We shall proceed to examine the historical and literary background and the activities of Shakespeare and of the Earl of Southampton during the period 1592–1605 against the text of the Sonnets, to see how they all fit in with this working hypothesis, and what further subsidiary material may be brought to light.

B

CHAPTER II

'The Worlds Fresh Ornament'

OUR story starts at the beginning of the year 1592, when Shakespeare was rising twenty-eight and Southampton turned eighteen.[1] The young Earl had taken his degree at St John's, Cambridge, in June 1589, and then begun his legal studies at Gray's Inn, to which his guardian, Lord Burghley, had sponsored his admission the previous year. Though intellectually well advanced, the boy had been slow in developing to physical maturity, as we may easily see from a miniature in the Fitzwilliam Museum, Cambridge, which was painted by Nicholas Hilliard in 1594, when Southampton was twenty. The date and age are clearly written round the edge of the portrait, yet at first glance one might have guessed that the subject was several years younger; perhaps sixteen or seventeen.

In a recent report on an investigation of 'Sex and Marriage in Contemporary England', a well-known anthropologist, Mr Geoffrey Gorer, has established that no less than 23 per cent of the men included in his sample reached puberty over the age of seventeen.[2] This percentage may seem surprisingly large, but both from the Hilliard portrait and from contemporary descriptions of Southampton's youthful appearance it seems very likely that he, at any rate, did not reach maturity any earlier than that. Thus we find that, on the occasion of the Queen's visit to Oxford in September 1592, Southampton's face is described in a Latin poem commemorating the event as 'scarcely yet adorned with a tender down'.[3]

So it was not surprising that, when Lord Burghley in the winter of 1589 had tried to arrange the boy's betrothal to his granddaughter, the Lady Elizabeth Vere, daughter of the Earl of Oxford, the response was the reverse of enthusiastic. Southampton was then sixteen, and the Lady Elizabeth only fourteen. But the right of the Master of the Royal Wards to arrange the marriages of his charges was a valuable perquisite, and Burghley thought it quite adequate to allow the boy 'a further respite of one year to ensure resolution, in respect of his young yeres'. This period was not enough for Southampton to develop any interest either in matrimony in general or in the Lady Elizabeth in particular; yet his immature good looks and precocious intellect were bound to make him a centre of attraction in almost any company. Unable, as yet, through lack of the necessary hormones, to dominate women by his virility, he could easily excel most of them in their own proper quality of personal beauty, while retaining a wholly masculine devotion to athletic and military pursuits and to ideals of courage and honour. Inevitably he tended to compensate for what he lacked by developing too great an esteem for the qualities which he possessed, and too severe standards for judging those of other people; it was not until his thirties that he was able to overcome the vanity and intolerance which, well before then, had brought him to the brink of total disaster.

It could scarcely have been helpful to receive from John Clapham, one of Burghley's secretaries, as the first of the many published works which their authors were to dedicate to Southampton over the years, a Latin poem on the theme of Narcissus,[4] telling how a beautiful and frigid youth came to grief through falling in love with his own reflection—perhaps not the kindest of presents to give to a seventeen-year-old boy who was not yet capable of sexual love, but, to suit the convenience of others, was constantly being urged towards it. For the time being, if they wished to call him Narcissus, then a Narcissus he would be; but when the moment arrived, let the women watch out![5]

The 1591 Christmas season had been celebrated at the Court of Whitehall with festivities which included no less than six plays performed by Lord Strange's company of players.[6] No doubt because of their Court success, this company was given a season by the impresario Henslowe at his theatre, the Rose, from February 19th to June 23rd, 1592. One of the successful productions, which was performed no less than fifteen times during this season, was a play of Henry VI, usually identified as *Part I* of Shakespeare's trilogy. *Parts II* and *III*, which were written earlier, are thought to have been performed by the same company the previous year. As far as is known, Shakespeare had written no other plays by this time, and it is not certain whether he was the sole author of the *Henry VI* plays. There is no doubt, however, that the poet Robert Greene, who died on 3rd September, 1592, was aware that Shakespeare was concerned with *Part III* of the trilogy, since in his literary testament[7] addressed to 'those Gentlemen his Quondam acquaintance, that spend their wits in making plaies', he parodies a line from the play and makes a pun on Shakespeare's name:

> Yes trust them not: for there is an upstart Crow, beautified with our feathers, that with his *Tygers hart wrapt in a Players hyde*, supposes he is as well able to bombast out a blanke verse as the best of you: and being an absolute *Iohannes fac totum*, is in his owne conceit the onely Shake-scene in a countrey.

Now Lord Strange's company contained most of the players who in 1594, after their patron (by then called Lord Derby) had died, joined with Shakespeare in forming the Lord Chamberlain's company, which in 1603, after the accession of James I, emerged as His Majesty's players. It seems probable therefore, as indeed many authorities have thought, that Shakespeare was with Lord Strange's company during the Christmas season at Court in 1591-2, and also for the season at the Rose which followed.

As we shall shortly see, Southampton was also in London at his 'lodging in the Strand' until at least as late as 26th June.

Although Shakespeare had so far written very little, Greene was probably right in implying that he had no illusions about his gifts in this field. He would thus have had good reason at the beginning of 1592 for thinking that he ought to try his hand at becoming a Marlowe or a Daniel, that is to say, a professional poet and dramatist, rather than an actor who fitted in a little play-writing on the side. The life of an actor was a rough and chancy business, and generally thought to be no occupation for a gentleman. There was unsympathetic city authorities and religious bigots to contend with, not to mention the constant threat of the plague, which might at any time cause public gatherings to be forbidden. There was the constant worry of obtaining finance for new productions, as well as the unpredictability of audiences. Although the protection of a prominent aristocrat was essential to avoid molestation by petty officialdom, these patrons gave precious little financial support to their companies. How much better it would be to write poems and plays in a quiet study, preferably under the personal patronage of a discriminating and wealthy noble, and sell them to players and publishers from time to time. Better still to circulate poems privately among the cultivated and tasteful friends of one's patron in return for valuable presents, without having to bother about the uneducated public.

The appearance at the Court performances of a new addition to the ranks of the cultured nobility, willing to add the mantle of Maecenas to his other gracious accoutrements, and as yet uncommitted to any other client poets, would seem to offer a golden opportunity. Furthermore, Southampton's boyish yet sophisticated charm and grace could provide more genuine poetic inspiration than the fading attractions of Sidney's Stella (Lady Rich), or Daniel's Delia (the Countess of Pembroke), who were probably also sitting in the same audience, bedecked with their fashionable wigs and paint. Sonnet sequences had recently become very popular, among them the ones addressed to these ladies, and Shakespeare would naturally wish to try his hand at this form. There was a problem, however, in finding an appropriate subject for a sonnet sequence intended not for a society lady, but for a young man of eighteen.

There were three topics of particular interest and importance to the young Earl at this time. First, there was his inheritance from his father, who had died in 1581, two days before his son's eighth birthday. The estate had been settled by the executors in 1583, and most of the lands were in the hands of the Crown, in trust, until he came of age. Others were out at lease, under the management of the executors. He could thus be expected to have some knowledge of the legal technicalities and accounting procedures of trust management, particularly as he was now a student at Gray's Inn.

Secondly, there was his obligation to marry a bride chosen for him by his guardian. This right of the Master of the Wards was an equally valuable one, whether exercised to secure an alliance between the guardian's own family and that of an aristocratic ward, or to gratify the ambitions of some other parent who was able to pay handsomely to secure a wealthy and distinguished husband for his daughter. For a young man of spirit the thought of being the pawn in such an arrangement must have been quite repugnant.

Thirdly, there was Southampton's idea of his personal image, and the mark he intended to make in the world. At the end of his first year at Cambridge he had been set a Latin essay on the subject, 'Everyone is incited to the pursuit of virtue by hope of reward', but the conclusion he reached at the end of his composition was: 'It is easy therefore to see that everyone is incited to the pursuit of virtue by the hope of glory.'[8] There is no doubt that in his case, at least, this latter sentiment was true. His hero and model was the Earl of Essex, who had earlier also been a ward of Lord Burghley, and both had before them the ideal of the late Sir Philip Sidney, epitome of the virtues of chivalry and master of courtly learning. Their concept of knightly deportment involved, among other things, great attention to their appearance, amounting, indeed, to a high degree of personal vanity. This was offset, however, by the cultivation of polite manners and good temper in dealing with inferior mortals. Rudeness and violence were reserved, when merited, for equals. Praise and flattery were accepted as a natural consequence of their position, and it was thus normal for persons seeking their favour to address them in the most saccharine terms. But with all the vanity, an essential part of this Renaissance image was manliness and courage, with a high degree of proficiency in horsemanship and the more warlike and energetic skills and pastimes. All these various qualities must be placed at the service of the State, in the affairs of which it was the duty and expectation of these brilliant figures to play an important part.

So far I have written as if Shakespeare's motive in beginning to write the Sonnets was wholly an economic one. Of course this was not so, but there is no reason to be contemptuous of economic motives, whether in poets or any other artists, while the guilty goddess, Fortune, is their only provider. It is better to take a realistic attitude at the beginning of the story to that aspect which, in Sonnet 111, Shakespeare is prepared freely to confess. But how the link with Southampton in fact began is graphically described in another sonnet:

> For as you were when first your eye I eyde, 104.2

where the pun on 'eyde' and 'I'd' (meaning 'projected *myself* to') indicates the sudden flash of involvement which passed between them at their first meeting. In spite of this, it was not until the thirteenth sonnet that Shakespeare was able to write with an appropriate degree of intimacy, and then only with difficulty, as he says in Sonnet 23:

> So I for feare of trust, forget to say, 23.5–6
> The perfect ceremony of loves right, . . .

To begin the series Shakespeare must choose a subject that was, as far as he knew, acceptable both to Southampton and to his guardian and relatives. His first seventeen sonnets bring in all three of the preoccupations of the young Earl which I have already described, but their primary concern, following the line of John Clapham's *Narcissus*, is to persuade Southampton to marry and beget an heir. In the first sonnet there is a well-known reference to the Narcissus theme in the lines:

> But thou contracted to thine owne bright eyes, 1.5–7
> Feed'st thy lights flame with selfe substantiall fewell,
> Making a famine where aboundance lies, . . .

Compare this with Ovid's story of Narcissus; in the Loeb translation the relevant lines read:

> I burn with love of myself; I both kindle the flames and suffer them. What shall I do? Shall I be wooed or woo? Why woo at all? What I desire, I have; the very abundance of my riches beggars me.   *Met.* III.464–6

Also in the first sonnet is the description of the young man as 'the worlds fresh ornament, and only herauld to the gaudy spring', an appropriate way of indicating that Southampton had recently made his debut at Court, and also that the time of writing was spring.

In the third sonnet the young man's mother is introduced. A portrait of Mary, Countess of Southampton, exists in Welbeck Abbey, and from this one can easily imagine 'the lovely Aprill of her prime'.

The fourth sonnet speaks of bequests and executors; beauty is not an outright bequest, but must be handed on to satisfy nature's audit. We shall meet this theme again in No. 126, the final envoi to the series addressed to the young man. Southampton's biographer, Professor Akrigg, has described the complications attached to the settling of Southampton's inheritance, from which one may see how appropriate is the imagery of this sonnet.

In the next sonnet comes the first of many reminiscences of another passage of Ovid's *Metamorphoses*, a portion of Pythagoras's speech in Book XV. Excluding passing references to mythological characters such as Narcissus, Adonis, Helen, Saturn and Philomel, Shakespeare uses in the Sonnets only two passages of the *Metamorphoses*, both from the same Book. One is the final envoi (lines 981–95 in the Golding translation and 871–9 in the Latin), of which there are echoes in Sonnets 55, 81 and 107; and the other in lines 196–298 (or thereabouts) in Golding and 176–272 in the Latin. From these hundred-odd lines he draws inspiration for at least eight different sonnets, for they contain the ideas about time and mutability which from one of Shakespeare's main themes:

> For never resting time leads Summer on   5.5–8
> To hidious winter and confounds him there,
> Sap checkt with frost and lustie leav's quite gon.
> Beauty ore-snow'd and barenes every where: . . .

Also in Sonnet 5 Shakespeare makes a reference to Sidney's *Arcadia*, with the simile of the distilled essence imprisoned in glass.[9] Perhaps his object is to show to the young graduate that he is familiar with the fashionable literature of the day, and can make gracious nods to it.

We saw that Sonnets 1 and 3 made mention of spring and April; Sonnets 5 and 6 both speak of the perfumes of summer. We know that Southampton was in London as late as 26th June, 1592, from a letter which he wrote to Lord Burghley's secretary on that day:[10]

> Mr Hyckes, Whereas I am gyven to understand that my manor house at Beaulye, with dyvers parcells of my inheritance there, are lyke to fall in

greate decaye and daunger to be lost thoroughe wante of meanes to supplye the charge of the reparacions during my wardship—I woulde hartely request you to move my Lord Treasurer, accordinge to the note I doe sende, to yealde me his honorable favor in taking such course as shall seeme best to his wisdome whereby the sayd chardges and reparacions may be supplyed; in doing whereof I shall rest most bounde to his Lordship, and wilbe redye to require your curtesye in what I maye, from my lodging in the Strand this 26th of June 1592,

Your loving friend H. Southampton.

A family bereavement soon called the young Earl away from London. This was the death of his mother's brother, Anthony Browne, eldest son of Viscount Montagu, which took place at his house in Cowdray Park on 29th June. A great funeral procession was held at Midhurst on 1st August, in which both the Earl and his mother would have been required to take part. Fortunately his uncle left three sons to carry on the line, the eldest of whom, though four months younger than Southampton, had set him an example by getting married the previous year.

Both this bereavement and Southampton's concern over his Beaulieu property are, I suggest, referred to by Shakespeare and used as examples to support his thesis that the Earl should marry. Is Southampton so moved by the grief of Anthony Browne's widow, the poet seems to be asking in Sonnet 9, that he prefers to stay a bachelor rather than cause similar grief to a widow of his own? This reasoning is quite false, because Mistress Browne has the eyes of her three sons to remind her of her husband. On the other hand, if Southampton dies a bachelor the whole world will weep for him like a widow, both for himself and because he has left no heir behind him. To let his beauty go to waste is far more thriftless than to spend money, because that will pass on and benefit others when spent. So in Sonnet 10 such waste of his beauty is like purposely letting his property go to ruin, when reparations should be his chief concern:

> For thou art so possest with murdrous hate   10.5–8
> That gainst thyself thou stickst not to conspire,
> Seeking that beautious roofe to ruinate
> Which to repaire should be thy chiefe desire:

and the same thought is brought in again to Sonnet 13:

> Who lets so faire a house fall to decay,   13.9–12
> Which husbandry in honour might uphold,
> Against the stormy gusts of winters day
> And barren rage of deaths eternall cold?

This suggests to me that Southampton had earnestly discussed this question of repairs with Shakespeare, and perhaps shown him a copy of his letter to Mr Hicks.

The reason for the termination of the season at the Rose on 23rd June was a general ban on public plays, to last until Michaelmas, on account of the danger of rioting by London apprentices who objected to competition in their trades from European immigrants. Before the ban had expired plague broke out, and because of this public performances continued to be forbidden in London, except for brief periods at Christmas time, until 1594. The companies of players had to tour the provinces to earn a living, but there is no record of Shakespeare having gone with them. He is not listed, for instance in a travelling warrant for Lord Strange's players dated 6th May, 1593. One might guess from Sonnet 12 that, instead, Shakespeare accompanied Southampton to Cowdray to attend Anthony Browne's funeral:

> When lofty trees I see barren of leaves,   12.5–8
> Which erst from heat did canopie the herd
> And Sommers greene all girded up in sheaves
> Borne on the beare with white and bristly beard: . . .

Lofty trees can still be seen canopying the herds in Cowdray Park today, as can at harvest time the wheat all girded up in sheaves. The harvest would have been beginning as the mourners collected for the funeral, and might have given occasion for the lines:

> And nothing gainst Times sieth can make defence   12.13–14
> Save breed to brave him, when he takes the hence.

Anthony Browne's three stalwart sons were there to prove the point.

Up until Sonnet 14 the theme of every sonnet is the exhortation to produce an heir, but then in 15 another idea comes in, that Shakespeare can also perpetuate Southampton's beauty in his poetry:

> And all in war with Time for love of you   15.13–14
> As he takes from you, I ingraft you new.

But 16 goes on to say that it is not enough to rely on this alone, any more than on having his ephemeral beauty captured in portraits:

> But wherefore do not you a mightier waie   16
> Make warre uppon this bloudie tirant time?
> And fortifie your selfe in your decay
> With meanes more blessed then my barren rime?
> Now stand you on the top of happie houres,
> And many maiden gardens yet unset,
> With vertuous wish would beare your living flowers,
> Much liker then your painted counterfeit:
> So should the lines of life that life repaire
> Which this (Times pensel or my pupill pen)
> Neither in inward worth nor outward faire
> Can make you live your selfe in eies of men.

> To give away your selfe, keeps your selfe still,
> And you must live drawne by your owne sweet skill.

In line 10 the word 'this' has two alternative antecedents, which are the final words of the first and second quatrain respectively, 'barren rime' and 'painted counterfeit'. These ideas are repeated in parenthesis to make the meaning quite clear: '(Times pensel or my pupill pen)'. 'Times pensel' is the artist's brush capturing the vision of the fleeting moment, as Shakespeare's 'pupill pen' does in words, but neither can perpetuate the life, as Southampton himself could by procreation.

In Sonnet 17 the two themes of immortality through procreation and through verse are again repeated, but in 18 and 19 the procreation theme drops out and only immortality through verse is mentioned. Time may do his worst, but

> My love shall in my verse ever live young.   19.14

We may surmise that by this time Shakespeare knew the young man well enough to realize that he had had more than his fill of exhortations to marry, however pleasing the verses in which they were expressed.

Sonnet 19 also brings in a new theme, that Southampton is to be:

> . . . beauties patterne to succeding men. . . .   19.12

and this leads us in to the remarkable Sonnet 20:

> A womans face with natures owne hand painted,   20
> Haste thou the Master Mistris of my passion,
> A womans gentle hart but not acquainted
> With shifting change as is false womens fashion,
> An eye more bright then theirs, lesse false in rowling:
> Gilding the object where-upon it gazeth,
> A man in hew all *Hews* in his controwling,
> Which steales mens eyes and womens soules amaseth.
> And for a woman wert thou first created,
> Till nature as she wrought thee fell a dotinge,
> And by addition me of thee defeated,
> By adding one thing to my purpose nothing.
>   But since she prickt thee out for womens pleasure,
>   Mine be thy love and thy loves use their treasure.

The italics and capital letter of the word *Hews* have been thought to indicate some kind of double meaning, and have been used by Samuel Butler and Oscar Wilde as the foundation of giddy edifices of speculation that the young man of the Sonnets must have been a Master Will Hughes. I think it almost certain that there is a name-play here, but of a different kind.

Let us look at other lines that carry the thought 'all hues in his controlling'. In the preceding sonnet we have as already mentioned:

<table>
<tr><td></td><td>For beauties patterne to succeding men.</td><td>19.12</td></tr>
</table>

in 98:

<table>
<tr><td>They weare but sweet, but figures of delight:</td><td>98.11–12</td></tr>
<tr><td>Drawne after you, you patterne of all those.</td><td></td></tr>
</table>

and 53:

<table>
<tr><td>And you in every blessed shape we know.</td><td>53.12–13</td></tr>
<tr><td>In all externall grace you have some part, . . .</td><td></td></tr>
</table>

68:

<table>
<tr><td>And him as for a map doth Nature store,</td><td>68.13–14</td></tr>
<tr><td>To show faulse Art what beauty was of yore.</td><td></td></tr>
</table>

106:

<table>
<tr><td>I see their antique Pen would have exprest,</td><td>106.9–12</td></tr>
<tr><td>Even such a beauty as you maister now.</td><td></td></tr>
<tr><td>So all their praises are but prophesies</td><td></td></tr>
<tr><td>Of this our time, all you prefiguring, . . .</td><td></td></tr>
</table>

The young man, all hues in his controlling, is the master-hue, the platonic Rose, the template of all beauty, the Master-Mistress, and he is Master H? W., the young master of Titchfield, Beaulieu and Holborn, twice Master of Arts, the Master W. H. (with a deceiving inversion of the initials) of the dedication to the Sonnets.

It has often been objected, as far as that puzzling dedication is concerned, that an earl could not be addressed as Master, and of course this is properly so. But might this not be a nickname, or perhaps an alias which Southampton liked to use when sampling the low life, like Prince Hal with Falstaff and his roguish companions? In the cryptic lampoon *Willobie His Avisa*, published in 1594, Southampton appears to be referred to as H. W., while his companion is W. S., the 'old player'. I think that Shakespeare addressed the Sonnets to Master H. W., rather than to the Earl of Southampton, and that this designation probably appeared on the fair copy from which Thorpe published his quarto. If so, how effective a camouflage the simple inversion has proved!

The word 'hue' or 'hew' meant, in Elizabethan times, 'beauty' or 'appearance' as well as 'colour', and so the vocalization of Henry Wriothesley's initials makes an appropriate pun. Leishman[11] tells us that, although many poets declare that the beauty of the person celebrated is a unique and never-to-be-repeated manifestation of what God and Nature can achieve, none of them ever went so far as to declare, like Shakespeare, that the beauty of the person celebrated was the substance, of which all other beauties were but shadows. In other words, that it was the 'master-hue'. Having conceived that notion, how could an Elizabethan fail to seize upon such a perfect pun? It expressed exactly the unique compliment that Shakespeare wished to pay.

CHAPTER III

A Rival Poet and a
Fallen Favourite

THE next sonnet, No. 21, is the first reference to a rival poet who is seeking
Southampton's patronage. We should not jump to the conclusion, however,
that this is the same poet who occasions Sonnets 78 to 86; there are clues which
show us that two different rivals are involved.

First it should be noted that 21 starts a new short group, the important Sonnet
20 having closed the first series. Of this the first fourteen sonnets, as we have
seen, dealt entirely with the 'procreation' theme. Then the concept of immortality through Shakespeare's verse is introduced, and after Sonnet 17 the
procreation theme is dropped. Sonnets 18 and 19 continue the new theme, and
the latter also introduces the further concept of 'beauties patterne', the master-
hue, which is expanded in Sonnet 20. There is thus an unbroken connection of
thought throughout these first twenty sonnets, but no such link can be found
between 20 and 21.

The next thing to notice is that 21, which decries the insincere and flamboyant
language of a rival, is followed shortly afterwards by Sonnet 23, which betrays
misgivings as to whether Shakespeare's own protestations of devotion are
eloquent enough; then by 25, which expresses confidence once more of his place
in his patron's affections; and finally by 26, which is a formal dedicatory poem.
The remarks about the method of his rival seem to be a preliminary to the
presentation by Shakespeare of a work of his own, under cover of this formal
dedication. From this it seems a fair assumption that we should look for a rival
who was also seeking to dedicate his work formally to Shakespeare's patron.
We do not have to look very far; but it will be as well first to consider what it
could be that Shakespeare was presenting under cover of his dedicatory sonnet.

It has been suggested that Sonnet 26 accompanied a fair copy of the preceding
sonnets, or even that the 'written ambassage' mentioned in line three is no more
than the sonnet itself; but surely the very fact that the sonnet is placed so soon
after 21 and 23, with their references to the pretentious work of another poet,
make it out of the question that Shakespeare would attach such a dedication to
so relatively trivial an offering as these few sonnets. To address a single sonnet
in this way would be even more absurd; nor is it possible to believe, as Dover
Wilson[1] suggests, that this dignified yet humble sonnet is 'half-playful':

> Lord of my love, to whome in vassalage   26
> Thy merrit hath my dutie strongly knit;

To thee I send this written ambassage
To witnesse duty, not to shew my wit.
Duty so great, which wit so poore as mine
May make seeme bare, in wanting words to shew it;
But that I hope some good conceipt of thine
In thy soules thought (all naked) will bestow it:
Til whatsoever star that guides my moving,
Points on me gratiously with faire aspect,
And puts apparrell on my tottered loving,
To show me worthy of thy sweet respect,
 Then may I dare to boast how I doe love thee,
 Till then, not show my head where thou maist prove me.

The sonnet bears some resemblance to the prose dedication published at the beginning of *The Rape of Lucrece*, and many of the older editors therefore assumed that it was connected with that poem; in saying this they ignored the important fact that *Venus and Adonis* contains several passages that are very reminiscent of the 'procreation' theme of Sonnets 1–17; compare:

'Is thine own heart to thine own face affected *V&A* 157

with

But thou contracted to thine owne bright eyes, 1.5

and

And so in spite of death thou dost survive, *V&A* 173–4
In that thy likeness still is left alive.'

with

To give away your selfe, keeps your selfe still, 16.13–14
And you must live drawne by your owne sweet skill.

It is difficult not to conclude that these sonnets and *Venus and Adonis* were written close together, or at least in the same phase of the relationship of the poet and his patron. If this is so, it seems more likely that Sonnet 26, following so soon afterwards, relates to the presentation of *Venus and Adonis*:[2] and that Sonnets 21 and 23 refer to another poet who was offering his work to Southampton at about the same date.

Venus and Adonis was entered in the Stationers' Register on 18th April, 1593. The purpose of this procedure was to establish copyright, and it would normally be done as soon as the manuscript reached the printer's hands. Printing and publishing would take several weeks at least, depending on the length of the work. The manuscript would usually also be submitted to potential patrons who might be expected to be willing to sponsor the work; this could be done before or after registration, but usually before. Some poems circulated for long periods in manuscript before being printed, and some were not printed at all, even though of considerable merit. *Venus and Adonis* may thus have been submitted to Southampton under cover of Sonnet 26 before April 1593; from the place of Sonnet 26 in the series we can say that it was some time later than the middle of 1592. When we come to consider Sonnet 25 we shall be able to narrow the dates down rather more than this.

Only one other poet is known to have dedicated work to Southampton in 1592 or 1593, and that is Barnabe Barnes, whose long collection of lyric verse entitled *Parthenophil and Parthenophe*, with dedicatory sonnets to three lords and three ladies, was registered on 10th May, 1593. The lords were the Earls of Northumberland, Essex and Southampton, and the ladies were the Countess of Pembroke, Lady Strange and Lady Bridget Manners. The sonnet to the Earl of Southampton runs as follows:

> To the Right Noble and Virtuous Lord,
> Henry, Earl of Southampton.
> Receive, sweet Lord! with thy thrice sacred hand,
> (Which sacred Muses make their instrument)
> These worthless leaves! which I, to thee present!
> Sprung from a rude and unmanured land)
> That with your countenance graced, they may withstand
> Hundred-eyed Envy's rough encounterment:
> Whose Patronage can give encouragement
> To scorn back-wounding Zoilus his band.
> Vouchsafe, right virtuous Lord! with gracious eyes,
> (Those heavenly lamps which give the Muses light,
> Which give and take, in course, that holy fire)
> To view my Muse with your judicial sight;
> Whom, when time shall have taught, by flight, to rise
> Shall to thy virtues, of much worth, aspire.

Now let us look at Shakespeare's Sonnet 21:

> So is it not with me as with that Muse,   **21**
> Stird by a painted beauty to his verse,
> Who heaven it selfe for ornament doth use,
> And every faire with his faire doth reherse,
> Making a coopelment of proud compare
> With Sunne and Moone, with earth and seas rich gems;
> With Aprills first borne flowers and all things rare,
> That heavens ayre in this huge rondure hems,
> O let me true in love but truly write,
> And then beleeve me, my love is as faire,
> As any mothers childe, though not so bright
> As those gould candells fixt in heavens ayer:
> Let them say more that like of heare-say well,
> I will not prayse that purpose not to sell.

If Barnabe Barnes is the 'Muse' referred to, we shall be able to find in his *Parthenophil and Parthenophe* everything which Shakespeare mentions in the first

eight lines of this sonnet. Leaving out the introductory and dedicatory pages,
Barnes's work occupies 143 pages in Sir Sidney Lee's edition,[3] but we have only
to read through the first 28 of them to come across the following passages:

There had my Zeuxis place and time, to draw   *P&P. Madrigal* 4
   My Mistress' portrait; which, on platane table,
   (With Nature, matching colours), as he saw
   Her leaning on her elbow; though not able,
     He 'gan with vermil, gold, white, and sable
   To shadow forth; and with a skilful knuckle
     Lively set out my fortunes' fable.
On lips a rose; on hand, a honeysuckle.

Imperious Jove, with sweet lipped Mercury;   *P&P. Sonnet* XIX
   Learned Minerva; Phoebus, God of Light;
   Vein-swelling Bacchus; Venus, Queen of Beauty;
   With light-foot Phoebe, Lamp of silent Night:
These have, with divers deities beside,
   Borrowed the shapes of many mortal creature;
   But fair Parthenope, graced with the pride
   Of each of these, sweet Queen of lovely feature!
As though she were, with pearl of all their skill,
   By heaven's chief nature garnished.

But when, in May, my world's bright fiery sun   *P&P. S.* XXXIV
   Had past in Zodiac, with his golden team,
   To place his beams, which in the Twins begun:
   The blazing twin stars of my world's bright beam,
My mistress' Eyes! mine heaven's bright Sun and Moon!

Youth's wanton Spring, when in the raging Bull   *P&P. M.* 7
   My sun was lodged, gave store of flowers,
   With leaves of pleasure, stalks of hours;
Which soon shaked off the leaves, when they were full
Of pleasures, beauty dewed, with April showers.

I wish no rich refined Arabian gold!   *P&P. S.* XLVIII
   Nor orient Indian pearl, rare Nature's wonder!
   No diamonds, th'Egyptian surges under!
   No rubies of America, dear sold!
Nor saphires, which rich Afric sands enfold!
   (Treasures far distant, from this isle asunder)
   Barbarian ivories, in contempt I hold!
   But only this; this only, Venus, grant!
That I, my sweet Parthenophe may get!
   Her hairs, no grace of golden wires want;
   Pure pearls, with perfect rubines are inset;

> True diamonds, in eyes; saphires, in veins!
> Nor can I, that soft ivory skin forget!
> England, in one small subject, such contains!

Now it is true that these images and hyperboles are the common material of the conventional sonneteers, borrowed from the poets of Italy and France, and can be found scattered about the works of Lodge, Watson, Constable, Daniel and others. Nevertheless, I do not think it is possible to find any work where the items listed by Shakespeare can be so closely matched, and in almost the identical order. Certainly there is no other such work bearing a dedication to Southampton.

Mention of Barnes's dedication to Southampton brings us to the last six lines of Shakespeare's sonnet. The first eight dealt with the subject of Barnes's poem, the 'painted beauty', Parthenophe, who seems to be merely a creature of the poet's imagination; in the dedicatory Sonnet to Lady Bridget Manners, Barnes says she will find

> . . . all the secret powers
> Of thine, and such like beauties, here set down! . . .

a clear enough indication that no specific lady is described. Shakespeare's last six lines deal with Southampton:

> . . . my love is as faire,
> As any mothers childe, though not so bright
> As those gould candells fixed in heavens ayer:

and it would therefore be appropriate if the mention of 'gould candells' were a reference to the rival poet's specific description of the same person. Sure enough, in Barnes's dedicatory Sonnet to Southampton, we have the lines:

> Vouchsafe, right virtuous Lord! with gracious eyes,
> (Those heavenly lamps which give the Muses light,
> Which give and take, in course, that holy fire)
> To view my Muse with your judicial sight; . . .

'Gold candles' are surely close enough to 'lamps which give and take fire' to support the view that Sonnet 21 refers to Barnes's *Parthenophil and Parthenophe*. Shakespeare here seems confident enough that no one could really relish the insincere hyperboles of the conventional poet more than his own sincere and direct protestations of his love. Nevertheless in 23 he feels it necessary to excuse his inability to use all the flattering language which someone like Barnes can command:

> O let my books be then the eloquence,   23.9–12
> And domb presagers of my speaking brest,
> Who pleade for love, and look for recompence,
> More then that tonge that more hath more exprest.

The last line is a compressed way of saying 'hath expressed more and done so more expressively'. Shakespeare's modest tone in referring here to the florid compliments poured out by his rival seems to indicate that Southampton may not after all have found them too sickly for his taste; at any rate the presence of the dedicatory sonnet in Barnes's published book suggests that he did not withhold the customary reward. But as for Shakespeare himself, he will let his own 'books' speak his love without the addition of flattering personal addresses to his patron. So his dedicatory sonnet, No. 26 (thus identified as relating to a 'book'), is a model of restrained language.

We shall see in the next chapter that Shakespeare wrote some more sonnets relating to *Venus and Adonis* a little later on, when the book appeared in print, and certain other links with Barnes's *Parthenophil and Parthenophe* will be discernible then. In the meantime we must look at the three sonnets which are interspersed with 21, 23 and 26, that is to say, 22, 24, and 25.

Sonnets 22 and 24 are both on conventional themes, of hearts and eyes, which are to be found over and over again in the works of the sonneteers of the time. No. 22 is a very much finer treatment of the 'exchange of hearts' theme than is to be found in Barnes or any of the others of his ilk. No. 24 is little above the common conventional level. They seem to me to be included here because Shakespeare wants to show his patron that he is quite capable of turning out this run-of-the-mill, artificial stuff to a standard as high or higher than that of Barnes, although his own preference is for a more sincere and original kind of sonnet, such as 23 or 25, neither of which could possibly have been written by anyone but Shakespeare.

Sonnet 25 contains some important dating material and demands a thorough examination in the light of the events of the time, which, as we have seen above, must be somewhere between the middle of 1592 and April 1593.

In August of 1592 the Earl of Southampton, already a Master of Arts of Cambridge University, became M.A. of Oxford by incorporation. This was in preparation for the Queen's visit to Oxford from September 22nd to 28th, when Southampton appeared for the first time as one of her official attendants, together with Lord Burghley, the Earl of Essex and other great peers of the realm. The poet who celebrated the visit in Latin verse waxed almost as lyrical as Shakespeare in his description of the young Earl as he appeared at this time. Having described the Earl of Essex he goes on:

> After him followed a Prince of a distinguished race, who (rich in her right) Southampton blazons as a great hero. No youth there present was more beautiful or more brilliant in the learned arts than this young prince of Hampshire, although his face was scarcely yet adorned by a tender down.[4]

It could well be that Shakespeare was present at this glittering occasion and that Sonnet 25 refers to it:

> Let those who are in favor with their stars,   25.1-4
> Of publike honour and proud titles bost,
> Whilst I whome fortune of such tryumph bars
> Unlookt for joy in that I honour most; . . .

He is himself unlooked for as he stands in the midst of the crowd, and his joy is unlooked for in that no one could have expected to find a patron who would provide him with such a feeling of personal exaltation.

The rest of the sonnet contrasts the insecurity of a royal favourite with Shakespeare's confidence in the love of his own patron. Rowse[5] tells us that it is 'obvious' that the favourite in question is Sir Walter Raleigh, who had been sent to the Tower the previous June for the dreadful offence of marrying one of the Queen's ladies-in-waiting without her permission. He was released during the Oxford visit so that he could go down to Dartmouth with Sir Robert Cecil to prevent the cargo of a captured Portuguese carrack, the *Madre di Dios*, from being looted before the Queen and the other partners in the prize expedition could receive their shares. This expedition had in fact been organized by Raleigh before his fall from grace, and he was recalled from it to be flung in the Tower. It seems to me that there is direct evidence connecting Raleigh with Shakespeare's Sonnet 25 in a poem which was discovered only a hundred years ago among the Cecil Papers at Hatfield House. It is called *The 11th and last booke of the Ocean to Scinthia* and is an abject plea to the Queen about his woeful plight. 'Ocean' is a nickname for Raleigh derived from the resemblance of his name Walter to 'water', while Cynthia, as often in poetry, represents Queen Elizabeth. A comparison of this poem with Sonnet 25 will, I think, show beyond reasonable doubt that Shakespeare had seen it and is intentionally alluding to it. Shakespeare writes:

> Great Princes favorites their fair leaves spread,   25.5-14
> But as the Marygold at the suns eye,
> And in them-selves their pride lies buried,
> For at a frowne they in their glory die.
> The painefull warrier famosed for worth,
> After a thousand victories once foild,
> Is from the booke of honour rased quite,
> And all the rest forgot for which he toild:
> > Then happy I that love and am beloved
> > Where I may not remove, nor be removed.

I will quote from Raleigh's long poem those lines that seem to me to be relevant to the sonnet:[6]

> Sufficeth it to you, my joys interred,
> In simple words that I my woes complain,
> You that then died when first my fancy erred,
> Joys under dust that never live again . . .

C

Twelve years entire I wasted in this war,
Twelve years of my most happy younger days,
But I in them, and they now wasted are,
'Of all which past the sorrow only stays' . . .

Such is of women's love the careful charge,

Held, and maintained with multitude of woes,
Of long erections such the sudden fall,
One hour diverts, one instant overthrows
For which our life's, for which our fortune's, thrall.

So many years those joys have dearly bought,
Of which when our fond hopes do most assure
All is dissolved; our labours come to nought,
Nor any mark thereof there doth endure; . . .

So of affection which our youth presented.
When she that from the sun reves power and light
Did but decline her beams as discontented
Converting sweetest days to saddest night:

All droops, all dies, all trodden under dust . . .

Those thoughts so full of pleasure and content
That in our absence were affection's food
Are razèd out and from the fancy rent
In highest grace and heart's dear care that stood,

Are cast for prey to hatred, and to scorn. . . .

So shall thy painful labours be perused
And draw on rest, which sometime had regard. . . .

So to thy error have her ears inclined,

And have forgotten all thy past deserving,
Holding in mind but only thine offence;
And only now affecteth thy depraving,
And thinks all vain that pleadeth thy defence . . .

Whose life once livèd in her pearl-like breast,
Whose joys were drawn but from her happiness,
Whose heart's high pleasure, and whose mind's true rest

Proceeded from her fortune's blessedness, . . .
Though of the same now buried be the joy, . . .

It is interesting that Shakespeare keeps the notion of burial from the first line of Raleigh's poem (repeated in the last line quoted); but where Raleigh is apostrophizing his dead joys, for Shakespeare it is Raleigh's pride that lies buried. Raleigh was notorious for pride; in a lampoon which appeared in 1601 we find the lines:[7]

> Raleigh doth time bestride
> he sits 'twixt wind and tide
> yet up hill he cannot ride,
> for all his bloody pride.

In his plaintive poem Raleigh swallows all his pride in the hope of moving the Queen's hard heart.

For the rest, Shakespeare's few lines are a masterly précis of Raleigh's rambling poem. The lines:

> When she that from the sun reves power and light
> Did but decline her beams as discontented . . .
> All droops, all dies, all trodden under dust . . .

become

> Great Princes favorites their faire leaves spread,
> But as the Marygold at the suns eye, . . .
> For at a frowne they in their glory die.

and

> Twelve years entire I wasted in this war,
> Those thoughts . . .
> Are razed out and from the fancy rent
> In highest grace and heart's dear care that stood, . . .
> So shall thy painful labour be perused. . . .
> So to thy error have her ears inclined,
> And have forgotten all thy past deserving, . . .

become

> The painefull warrior famosed for worth,
> After a thousand victories once foild,
> Is from the booke of honour rased forth,
> And all the rest forgot for which he toild: . . .

and indeed these few lines of Shakespeare's contain, in effect, almost everything that Raleigh says in his 468. The last couplet of the sonnet compares the security of Shakespeare's position in his patron's affections with the collapse of the favourite whose life was once, but is no longer, lived in the Queen's 'pearl-like breast'.

It will be observed that in quoting line 11 of Shakespeare's sonnet for the second time I have corrected 'rased quite', which does not rhyme with 'famosed for worth' in line 9, to 'rased forth'. Other emendations which have been proposed are the substitution of 'fight' or 'might' for 'worth' at the end of line 9. From Raleigh's poem it seems at last possible to know what Shakespeare intended to write. Surely the phrase was suggested to Shakespeare by Raleigh's words:

> Are razed out and from the fancy rent . . .

Shakespeare frequently used 'forth' in the sense of 'out': cf. 'Wherefore didst thou lock me forth' (*Comedy of Errors* IV. iv. 97). Furthermore, the war in which Raleigh claims to have wasted twelve years is the courtly war for Elizabeth's favour, so it is unlikely that Shakespeare had the word 'fight' or 'might' in mind for line 9 of his sonnet. The word 'worth' has two main connotations in Shakespearian usage, (i) wealth or magnificence, and (ii) deservingness.[8] Raleigh was certainly renowned for ostentatious magnificence whenever he was in favour, and in his poem it is his 'past deservinge' that he claims has been forgotten. In addition, the 'worth/forth' coupling is surely necessary to complete the beautiful pattern of *f*'s and *w*'s in this quatrain.

Although it has been generally thought that Raleigh's poem must have been written during his imprisonment in 1592, there has been no firm evidence of this. The linking of it with this sonnet could make the dating certain. Lord Burghley perhaps had it with him at the Privy Council held at Merton College, Oxford, on 25th September, when Sir Robert Cecil's letter from Dartmouth came up for consideration, reporting the efforts of Raleigh and himself in securing the cargo of the *Madre di Dios*. Afterwards Burghley might have passed it to that budding connoisseur of literature, his young ward Southampton, who showed it to Shakespeare.

Two days later, on 27th September, the Queen heard a 'copious and eloquent oration' from the Bishop of Hereford at St Mary's Church, on the question 'Whether it be lawful in a Christian commonwealth to feign in the cause of religion'. The Queen twice sent to cut him short, because she wanted to make a speech herself. But he either would not or could not shorten it, 'for fear lest he should have marred it all and perhaps confounded his memory'. By the time he finished the Queen was too tired to make her speech. The next day the Queen made a speech in Latin thanking the heads of the Colleges for their hospitality, and purposely stopped in the middle to call for a stool for Lord Burghley, afterwards proceeding with her speech without losing the thread for a moment, as if to shame the Bishop of Hereford. It was perhaps the nervous Bishop that Shakespeare had in mind in this passage in *A Midsummer Night's Dream*:

> Where I have come great clerks have purposed   *MND* V.i.
> To greet me with premeditated welcomes;   93–105
> Where I have seen them shiver and look pale,
> Make periods in the midst of sentences,
> Throttle their practis'd accent in their fears,
> And, in conclusion, dumbly have broke off,
> Not paying me a welcome. Trust me, sweet,
> Out of this silence yet I pick'd a welcome;

And in the modesty of fearful duty
I read as much as from the rattling tongue
Of saucy and audacious eloquence.
Love, therefore, and tongue-tied simplicity
In least speak most to my capacity.

Theseus in the play claims to have taken just the kindly attitude to persons overwhelmed with 'feare of trust' (that is to say, of their responsibility) that Shakespeare asks his patron to take to him in Sonnet 23; the passage, though probably written in 1594, is in fact a close echo of that sonnet and helps us to understand what inspired it.

After making her speech the Queen returned to London,[9] but it is unlikely that Southampton went with her, because a proclamation was issued on 12th October saying that, because of the plague, no one should repair to London, or the suburbs or places within two miles of the city, even for their ordinary attendance on the Queen's person, without special licence in writing. It may be that Southampton and Shakespeare both stayed in Oxford until 6th October, the Earl's nineteenth birthday, when a performance was given there by Lord Strange's players. But another family bereavement soon called Southampton to Cowdray again. His grandfather, Viscount Montagu, died on 19th October, and the great public funeral was fixed for 6th December. His tomb can still be seen in Easebourne church, just a short distance from Cowdray Park, where the burnt-out shell of his house (Southampton's birthplace) still draws an occasional glance from the crowds who come every summer to watch the polo.

And what of Raleigh? As a result of his laborious efforts in Dartmouth, which earned high praise from Sir Robert Cecil, much of the cargo was saved, but the Queen was very niggardly in apportioning it, thriftily keeping the main proceeds for the exchequer. The signed award of the Commissioners allowed Raleigh £15,900 out of a total value salved of £150,000. He had had to borrow £11,000 at interest to finance the expedition, so there was little remaining after this had been paid back. He was not sent back to prison, but remained banished from court, though nominally retaining his title of Captain of the Guard. He was out of favour for five years more. During this period he did not lose the friendship of Sir Robert Cecil, and the Queen was prevailed upon to let him sail to Guiana and to take part in the sacking of Cadiz even though he was forbidden her presence until June 1597. As early as July 1594 he was required to raise pioneers in Cornwall to be sent with a force of soldiers to seize Brest.

When was it then, that Barnabe Barnes disturbed Shakespeare by approaching Southampton to be one of the sponsors of *Parthenophil and Parthenophe*? By virtue of Sonnet 25, with its reference to Southampton's public honour and titles, as well as to Raleigh's fall from favour, we can put the earliest date as that of the Queen's visit to Oxford in September 1592. The latest will be about April 1593, when *Venus and Adonis* was registered. There is a report from May 1593 of rumours having been in circulation that Southampton was to be made a Knight of the Garter that year,[10] which would have been a further reason to mention 'proud titles'. Now *Venus and Adonis* must have taken quite a long time to write, and it must have been ready when Shakespeare disparaged Barnes's dedication in Sonnets 21 and 23 and offered his own in Sonnet 26. With a rival preparing to go into print it is likely that Shakespeare wasted no time in getting his printer to register the proposed book and start the work of printing it. He already had his sponsor, and there was no need to delay publication while he sought patronage, as Barnes was doing.

I take the Sonnet group 21–26, including the two conventional Sonnets 22 and 24, to have been written and presented more or less at the same time, for the purpose of securing Southampton's formal agreement to the dedication, and also of warding off any unfavourable comparisons with Barnabe Barnes's offerings. If Sonnet 25 does indeed carry a reference to the rumour about the Order of the Garter, a date very shortly before the registration of *Venus and Adonis* is likely, in April 1593. Barnabe Barnes would thus have approached Southampton a little earlier, as indicated in Sonnet 21, though he was not able to complete his registration until May.

It is interesting to see that in an introductory poem to *Parthenophil and Parthenophe* Barnes apparently makes a reference to Shakespeare having been slandered by Robert Greene, as we noted in Chapter II. In December 1592, about three months after Greene's death, Robert Chettle, who had published the offensive work, made generous amends to Shakespeare in the 'Epistle' to a book called *Kind-Harts Dreame*:

> ... for that as I have moderated the heat of living writers, and might have used my own discretion (especially in such a case) the Author being dead, that I did not, I am as sorry as if the original fault had been my fault, because myself have seen his demeanour no less civil than he excellent in the quality he professes: Besides, divers of worship have reported his uprightness of dealing, which argues his honesty, and his facetious grace in writing, that approves his Art.

In his poem, which is addressed to his book, Barnes says:

> Some good man, that shall think thee witty,
> Will be thy Patron! and take pity;
> And when some men shall call thee base
> He, for thy sake, shall them disgrace!
> Then, with his countenance backed, thou shalt
> Excuse the nature of thy fault.

It seems most likely that Barnes is here referring to the championing of Shakespeare by Southampton, who could be expected to be one of the 'divers of worship' mentioned by Chettle. There is another passage in the same introductory poem which links Barnes with the Sonnets:

> And if I chance, un'wares to meet thee,
> Neither acknowledge me, nor greet me!
> Admit I blush (perchance I shall),
> Pass by! regard me not at all!

Compare this with Sonnet 36:

> I may not ever-more acknowledge thee,
> Least my bewailed guilt should do thee shame, . . .

36.9–10

CHAPTER IV

The Death of Marlowe

THE plague continued at full force in London until the end of 1592, and between March and 11th December, 503 people were reckoned to have died from it. The Michaelmas law term was held at Hertford, much to the dismay of the Lord Mayor and Aldermen of London. For the Christmas season the Court took up residence at the palace of Hampton Court, where five plays were given, three by the servants of Lord Strange and two by a new company, Lord Pembroke's men. By 30th December the plague was considered to have abated sufficiently for the impresario Henslowe to put on a season at the Rose, with Lord Strange's players, until 1st February; but then the theatres were again closed down. The Lord Mayor and Aldermen were sharply rebuked by the Queen for not taking sufficient steps to reduce the spread of the plague, and she threatened to hold the February session of Parliament outside London. However, in the end it was held at Westminster as usual.

Shakespeare was not the only playwright who thought to fill in the time while the theatres were closed by writing poetry. The leading dramatist of the day, Christopher Marlowe, spent the spring with his friend and patron, Thomas Walsingham, second cousin of Sir Francis Walsingham, Queen Elizabeth's Secretary of State and founder of her secret service, who had died in 1590. The Walsingham estate was near Chislehurst, well out of the range of the plague but nevertheless conveniently near London. Here Marlowe was writing his poem *Hero and Leander*, which was left unfinished at his sudden death on 30th May. There are indications in this poem that Marlowe was in touch with Shakespeare's work at this time: in particular there are the lines,

> Where Venus in her naked glory strove   *H&L* I.12–14
> To please the careless and disdainful eyes
> Of proud Adonis that before her lies.

The concept of Adonis as proud and disdainful of Venus's charms is not in the classical story in Book X of Ovid's *Metamorphoses*. There she has no difficulty in reclining with her head in Adonis's lap while she tells a long story interspersed with kisses. Shakespeare drew the disdain from the story of Hermaphroditus and Salmacis in Ovid's Fourth Book and added it to his description of Adonis; this was presumably to suit the character to that of the Southampton described in the sonnets of 1592. It is Shakespeare's Adonis, not that of Ovid or any other poet, that Marlowe portrays.

Southampton had occasion to be in London during March 1593, since the

Privy Council was deliberating about his claim to prize-money for one of the ships captured by Sir Martin Frobisher in the grand freebooting expedition organized by the unfortunate Raleigh the previous year. Like many others of the nobility, Southampton had joined in a syndicate to fit out one of the ships taking part, his partners being Raleigh's brother, Carew, and Mr Ralph Bowes. Their ship captured a vessel laden with sugar from Brazil, but as commander of the expedition Frobisher disputed their title to the prize-money on behalf of the Queen.[1]

That *Venus and Adonis* was registered on 18th April indicates that Shakespeare was probably in London at this time; he may have stayed there after the end of Henslowe's season at the Rose to finish off his poem and see it through the press. But next come some sonnets which show that Shakespeare and Southampton were again far apart:

> Weary with toil I hast me to my bed,   27.1–2
> The deare repose for lims with travaill tired, . . .

Shakespeare is working hard in a place far from his friend, and he is kept awake by the nightly journey which his thoughts make to the place where his friend is. How can he return happily from this mental journey when it means a sleepless night?

> How can I then returne in happy plight   28.1–4
> That am debard the benefit of rest?
> When daies oppression is not eazd by night,
> But day by night and night by day oprest.

The reason for his journeying would be that with the theatres in London closed by the plague he had no source of income there. The players had now split themselves up into smaller groups for touring purposes, and companies were on the road under the sponsorship of the Lord Admiral, Lord Strange, Lord Sussex and Lord Pembroke. Henslowe shared out the same stock of playbooks amongst them all, so Shakespeare may perhaps have visited more than one to rehearse his plays with them. Receipts were poor and the cost of travel high. The atmosphere of depression is intense in these sonnets which fall between the completion of *Venus and Adonis* and its publication, but the quality of the poetry is high.

In Sonnet 27 there may be an echo of a line from Marlowe's *Hero and Leander*:

> Rich jewels in the dark are soonest spied. . . .

Shakespeare uses the same notion:

> Which like a jewell (hunge in gastly night)   27.11–12
> Makes blacke night beautious, and her old face new.

Further and more tragic reminiscences of Marlowe may be seen in Sonnets 30, 31 and 32. It will be remembered that Marlowe was killed in a private room of a tavern in Deptford on 30th May, 1593.[2] According to the evidence at the coroner's inquest, a quarrel broke out between him and his fellow diners over the reckoning, during which he pulled out the dagger worn by one of them, Ingram Frizer, and cut the man's head with it. Frizer in retaliation forced Marlowe's hand back, so that the point of the dagger entered his head just over the right eyeball, piercing the brain. That Shakespeare knew of the quarrel over the reckoning can be deduced from a line in *As You Like It*:

> It strikes a man more dead than a great reckoning in a little room.   *AYLI*
> III.iii.16

This is generally thought to be a reference to Marlowe's own line in the *Jew of Malta*:

> Infinite riches in a little room . . .

as well as to the circumstances of his death.

It is striking that in Sonnet 30 the images are all to do with reckoning:

> Then can I drowne an eye (un-us'd to flow)   30.5-12
> For precious friends hid in deaths dateles night,
> And weepe afresh loves long since canceld woe,
> And mone th' expence of many a vannisht sight.
> Then can I greeve at greevances fore-gon,
> And heavily from woe to woe tell ore
> The sad account of fore-bemoned mone,
> Which I new pay, as if not payd before.

Cancelled, expense, tell, account, pay—this choice of metaphor is surely intended to convey a message. In the sonnet dead friends are spoken of in the plural, and of course plenty of people were dying in this plague period. Another friend, the poet Thomas Watson, had died the previous year in a brawl. Nevertheless, the use of the plural when it was desired to allude to a single person without naming him was at least as common in Shakespeare's time as it is now, and several other instances are referred to in the present book. It seems to me that Marlowe alone is intended here.

In Sonnet 32 Shakespeare applies to himself, in the event of Southampton outliving him, sentiments which might well have been suggested by Marlowe's death. Although only two months older than Shakespeare, Marlowe had already written several highly successful plays, his 'mighty line' had already transformed English blank verse. On the other hand, if Shakespeare had died the same day he would have died almost unknown. Yet he knew well enough that his Muse was capable of growing 'with this growing age', and that his genius would give birth to much greater things 'to march in ranks of better equipage'.

The intervening Sonnet 31, in which Shakespeare finds in Southampton's bosom the hearts of his dead and buried friends (containing parts of Shakespeare himself), becomes more poignant if, in fact, Marlowe had been intending to dedicate *Hero and Leander* to Southampton. His description of Leander's long hair, so reminiscent of the portraits of Southampton, strongly suggests that this was so:

> His dangling tresses that were never shorn,
> Had they been cut and unto Colchos borne,
> Would have allured the venturous youth of Greece
> To hazard more than for the Golden Fleece.[3]

CHAPTER V

Venus and Adonis and an Anagram

THE next group of sonnets, 33–42, is remarkable for dealing with two entirely different themes, and also for containing the only instance where there seems clearly to be something wrong with the 1609 order. Let us deal first with the order, because misunderstanding of the subject-matter will be avoided if that is put right first.

The first two lines of No. 36 read:

> Let me confesse that we two must be twaine,   36.1–2
> Although our undevided loves are one: . . .

The last lines of No. 42, however, tell us:

> But here's the joy, my friend and I are one,   42.13–14
> Sweete flattery, then she loves but me alone.

Sonnets 33–35 and 40–42 all deal with a wrong done to the poet by his friend. The nature of the wrong is made clear in the last two lines of 35 read with Sonnet 40:

> That I an accessary needs must be,   35.13–14
> To that sweete theefe which sourely robs from me.

> Take all my loves, my love, yea take them all,   40.1–10
> What hast thou then more then thou hadst before?
> No love, my love, that thou maist true love call,
> All mine was thine, before thou hadst this more:
> Then if for my love, thou my love receivest,
> I cannot blame thee, for my love thou usest,
> But yet be blam'd, if thou this selfe deceavest
> By wilfull taste of what thy selfe refusest.
> I doe forgive thy robb'rie gentle theefe
> Although thou steale thee all my poverty: . . .

The young earl has stolen the poet's mistress. In the intervening Sonnets 36–39, however, there is no mention of this. They are all about his relations with the young man as patron of his verse, and they stress the social barrier between them which must not be publicly breached by too much familiarity. Their separateness, acknowledged in the first line of 36, is again stressed in 39:

> Even for this, let us devided live,   39.5–8
> And our deare love loose name of single one,
> That by this seperation I may give:
> That due to thee which thou deserv'st alone: . . .

It is thus absurd for Sonnet 42 to bring back the notion:

> But here's the joy, my friend and I are one, . . .   42.13

This idea has already been killed dead.

The difficulty is completely removed if we take out Sonnets 36–39 and insert them again between 42 and 43. Sonnet 40 then naturally follows upon 35 as it does in my excerpt above, while after the final couplet of 42, with its fanciful conceit of the two friends rolled into one person, we get the return to hard reality:

> Let me confesse that we two must be twaine,   36.1

after which there is no more mention of the wanton mistress. How this misplacing occurred we can only speculate; if the four Sonnets 36–39 were originally written on both sides of a single sheet of paper this might have happened quite easily. When we come to consider the subject-matter, the possibility becomes even easier to envisage.

It has long been recognized that Sonnets 33–35 and 40–42 refer to the same lady as do numbers 127–154, the so-called Dark Lady of the Sonnets. It will therefore be convenient to leave these six sonnets to be dealt with in Chapter XIII, only noting here that they come, in time, just before Sonnets 36–39. The subject-matter of this misplaced quartet is of great importance in confirming the dating of the sequence if, as I believe, it was written to accompany the publication of *Venus and Adonis*.

As we have noted, *Venus and Adonis* was entered in the register of the Stationers' Company on 18th April, and it is likely that it was published some weeks later. It was prefaced by a dedication, as follows:

To The Right Honorable
Henrie Wriothesley, Earle of Southampton,
and Baron of Titchfield.

Right Honourable, I know not how I shall offend in dedicating my unpolisht lines to your Lordship, nor how the worlde will censure mee for choosing so strong a proppe to support so weake a burthen, onlye if your Honour seeme but pleased, I account myselfe highly praised, and vowe to take advantage of all idle houres, till I have honoured you with some graver labour. But if the first heire of my invention prove deformed, I shall be sorie it had so noble a god-father: and never after eare so barren a land, for feare it yeeld me still so bad a harvest, I leave it to your Honourable survey, and your Honor to your hearts content, which I wish may alwaies answere your owne wish, and the worlds hopefull expectation.

Your Honors in all dutie,

William Shakespeare.

Now this is an extremely formal and humble dedication from one who was at the time such an intimate friend as Shakespeare appears from the Sonnets to have become. Is it really addressed to the same person to whom Shakespeare has just been saying:

> Those pretty wrongs that liberty commits,   41.1–4
> When I am some-time absent from thy heart,
> Thy beautie, and thy yeares full well befits,
> For still temptation followes where thou art.   ?

Looking back at Sonnet 26, we recollect that at that time Shakespeare was not going to show his head where his patron could prove him; in other words, he had no poetry ready then which he was prepared to publish under Southampton's sponsorship. In Sonnet 38, however, he says:

> If my slight Muse doe please these curious daies,   38.13–14
> The paine be mine, but thine shall be the praise.

Clearly he is speaking of work which is being laid before the critical public —'these curious daies'.

The Adonis of Shakespeare's first published poem bears a strong resemblance to the Southampton of the sonnets of 1592, the young Narcissus with, as yet, no time for girls. Ironically, just at the time *Venus and Adonis* is due to be published, he shows that he has now developed some interest in the opposite sex, in fact he experiments with Shakespeare's own girl friend. Shakespeare does not want to draw attention to their close relationship and perhaps bring disrepute upon the young Earl. So he explains in Sonnet 36 the need for discretion and for his restrained letter of dedication:

> Let me confesse that we two must be twaine,   36.1–14
> Although our undevided loves are one:
> So shall those blots that do with me remaine,
> Without thy helpe, by me be borne alone.
> In our two loves there is but one respect,
> Though in our lives a seperable spight,
> Which though it alter not loves sole effect,
> Yet doth it steale sweet houres from loves delight,
> I may not ever-more acknowledge thee,
> Least my bewailed guilt should do thee shame,
> Nor thou with publike kindnesse honour me,
> Unlesse thou take that honour from thy name:

> But doe not so, I love thee in such sort,
> As thou being mine, mine is thy good report.

In lines 11 and 12 there appears to be a reference to Southampton's style of Right Honourable. 'If you publicly favour a low character like me, you will lose the honour which attaches to your name.' The reference is the more appropriate in that the dedicatory letter to *Venus and Adonis* is full of 'Honours' and 'Honourables'. The particular 'bewailed guilt' referred to in line 10 perhaps has reference to Shakespeare's position as inadvertent pander, in bringing together the young nobleman and the 'woman collour'd il', and not merely to his inferior social position.

Dover Wilson, who, following Beeching and Pooler, notices that Sonnets 36-39 are misplaced (though he wants to put them after 25), has pointed out[1] that they are linked together by an elaborate rhyme pattern, the couplet at the end of 39 repeating the rhymes at the beginning of 36:

36.	1 twaine	3 remaine	37.	1 delight	3 spight
	2 one	4 alone		10 give	12 live
	6 spight	8 delight		13 thee	14 me
	9 thee	11 me			
38.	5 me	7 thee	39.	2 me	4 thee
	6 sight	8 light		5 live	7 give
				6 one	8 alone
				13 twaine	14 remaine

It is difficult to be sure that this means anything, as some of these rhymes are common to many sonnets. However, there is another clear link between the first and last of the four. The first quatrain of 39 is, in a sense, the mirror-image of that of 36:

> Oh how thy worth with manners may I singe,   39.1-4
> When thou art all the better part of me?
> What can mine owne praise to mine owne selfe bring;
> And what is't but mine owne when I praise thee, . . .

In 36 the poet says that the two friends must 'be twaine' so that all the blots can remain with Shakespeare, and Southampton be free from shame; in 39 they must 'devided live' so that Shakespeare can praise his patron without at the same time praising himself. In the one case the purpose is to let all the faults remain with Shakespeare, in the other to let all the virtues remain with Southampton.

There is another reference in Sonnet 39, to appreciate which we must look again at Barnabe Barnes's *Parthenophil and Parthenophe*. We have seen that one of the dedicatory poems accompanying this was addressed to the Lady Bridget Manners. This young lady was the sister of Southampton's close friend (also a ward of Lord Burghley), the Earl of Rutland, and we know from a letter written the following year to her mother that she had been thought of as a possible wife for Southampton.

Southampton and Lady Bridget were the only unmarried persons in the group to whom Barnes addressed his fulsome poems. Here is the one to the girl:

> To the beautiful Lady,
>   The Lady Bridget Manners.
>
> Rose of that Garland! fairest and sweetest
>   Of all those sweet and fair flowers!
>   Pride of chaste Cynthia's rich crown!
>   Receive this Verse, thy matchless beauty meetest!
> Behold thy graces which thou greetest,
>   And all the secret powers
> Of thine such like beauties, here set down
>   Here shalt thou find thy frown!
>   Here, thy sunny smiling!
> Fame's plumes fly with thy Love's, which should be fleetest!
>   Here, my loves' tempests and showers!
>   These read, sweet Beauty! whom my Muse shall crown!
>   Who for thee! such a Garland is compiling,
>   Of so divine scents and colours,
>   As is immortal, Time beguiling!

Shakespeare had not put anything like this in his *Venus and Adonis*. Nor could he ever, if the conceit of his patron and himself being one person were to be maintained, for he would merely be praising himself:

> Oh how thy worth with MANNERS' may I singe,
>   When thou art all the better part of me?

It is difficult to see how, if we are right about the timing, anyone who read this in 1593 could fail to take the pun, since everyone who had access to the sonnet would know that Barnabe Barnes was just then praising Southampton's worth together with that of Lady Bridget Manners! Those who would read it were all young, quick-witted and ready to be amused, and puns were held in higher esteem than they are now.

Sonnet 38 perhaps also makes a back-handed reference to Barnabe Barnes's Sonnet to Southampton:

> How can my Muse want subject to invent   38.1–4
>   While thou dost breath that poor'st into my verse,
> Thine own sweet argument, to excellent,
>   For every vulgar paper to rehearse: . . .

There is certainly a sting in that fourth line. Shakespeare kept his flattery for his unpublished papers. We may also remark in passing that 'these curious daies' in line 13 of Shakespeare's sonnet means much the same as 'Zoilus his band' in that addressed to Southampton by Barnabe Barnes (see Chapter III). Zoilus, a Greek grammarian who attacked Homer, was the prototype of the captious critic.

I have left till last in this group of sonnets No. 37, because it is one which has a special importance.

> As a decrepit father takes delight,   37.1–14
> To see his active childe do deeds of youth,
> So I, made lame my Fortunes dearest spight
> Take all my comfort of thy worth and truth.
> For whether beauty, birth, or wealth, or wit,
> Or any of these all, or all, or more
> Intitled in their parts, do crowned sit,
> I make my love ingrafted to this store:
> So then I am not lame, poore, nor dispis'd,
> Whilst that this shadow doth such substance give,
> That I in thy abundance am suffic'd,
> And by a part of all thy glory live:
>   Looke what is best, that best I wish in thee,
>   This wish I have, then ten times happy me.

The theme follows on that of 36: Shakespeare does not seek public kindness from his patron; he is satisfied to glory in the brilliance and success of the young Earl and to obtain inspiration from his private friendship. The publication of *Venus and Adonis* might seem the right moment to recall Sonnet 26:

> Then may I dare to boast how I doe love thee,   26.13

but it has become clear to Shakespeare, perhaps as a result of the incident with his mistress, that this would be dangerous to the reputation of the thoughtless and headstrong youth. Let their relationship be privately intimate, but publicly at arm's length. Vicariously Shakespeare will obtain everything that he would have if it were indeed true that 'my friend and I are one':

> Looke what is best, that best I wish in thee,   37.13–14
> This wish I have, then ten times happy me.

But there is something more hidden in this sonnet, and it is related to the qualities of 'worth and truth' which are, for Shakespeare, Southampton's pre-eminent virtues.

It was a common practice[2] for authors to look for complimentary anagrams

D

on the names and titles of their patrons, and I think there is a reference to one here. The title:

> Henry Wriothesley Third Earle of Southampton

gives the anagram:

> *Thy worth and truth, Rose, are my life's onlie hope.*

This could, of course, be dismissed as sheer coincidence, were it not that the sentiment expressed in the anagram is repeated over and over again in the Sonnets.

First of all, lines 3 and 4 of the sonnet are a close paraphrase of the same thought:

So I, . . .   37.3–8
Take all my comfort of thy worth and truth.
For whether beauty, birth, or wealth, or wit,
Or any of these, or all, or more
Intitled in their parts, do crowned sit,
I make my love ingrafted to this store: . . .

By engrafting his love to Southampton's worth and truth, that is to say, to his virtue and constancy (*whether or not* he also possesses good looks, nobility, riches, learning or other qualities), Shakespeare is sufficed and able to live. The existence of any qualities in Southampton other than worth and truth is irrelevant, because these two give him *all* his comfort.

The line 'Intitled in their parts do crowned sit' evokes the image of rows of titled and coroneted peers sitting in their due places in the House of Lords, as they had when the Queen ceremonially opened Parliament on 19th February that year. But it also suggests the anagram of Southampton's title: 'For whether or not any more qualities can be found out of your title, it is your worth and truth which command my love and enable me to live.'

The same ideas come again in Sonnets 91 and 92:

Thy love is better than high birth to me,   91.9–14
Richer than wealth, prouder than garments cost,
Of more delight then Hawkes or Horses bee:
And having thee, of all mens pride I boast.
   Wretched in this alone, that thou maist take,
   All this away, and me most wretched make.

But doe thy worst to steale thy selfe away,   92.1–12
For tearme of life thou art assured mine,
And life no longer then thy love will stay,
For it depends upon that love of thine.
Then need I not to feare the worst of wrongs,
When in the least of them my life hath end,

> I see, a better state to me belongs
> Then that, which on thy humor both doth depend.
> Thou canst not vex me with inconstant minde,
> Since that my life on thy revolt doth lie,
> Oh what a happy title do I finde,
> Happy to have thy love, happy to die!

Why does Shakespeare speak of finding a happy 'title'? It is the 'better state' which 'belongs' to him, as he says in line 7, but he finds it in the anagram of Southampton's title of Sonnet 37:

> *Thy worth and truth, Rose, are my life's onlie hope.*

If he is deprived of them, he will die. But in that case he will have nothing more to fear; therefore he will be equally happy alive or dead. 'Truth' means constancy of love; thus Sonnet 93 begins,

> So shall I live, supposing thou art true, . . .   93.1

In Sonnet 52, before Southampton's constancy came under suspicion, the accent was on his 'worth':

> Blessed are you whose worthiness gives skope,   52.13–14
> Being had to tryomphe, being lackt to hope.

Again the themes of worth, truth and hope are put together in Sonnet 60:

> Time doth transfixe the florish set on youth,   60.9–14
> And delves the paralels in beauties brow,
> Feeds on the rarities of natures truth,
> And nothing stands but for his sieth to mow.
>   And yet to times in hope, my verse shall stand
>   Praising thy worth, dispight his cruell hand.

Nature's truth means not only genuine natural beauty, but constancy of heart, the perfume in the Rose:

> Oh how much more doth beautie beautious seeme   54.1–4
> By that sweet ornament which truth doth give,   and 11–14
> The Rose lookes faire, but fairer we it deeme
> For that sweet odor, which doth in it live: . . .
> Of their sweet deathes, are sweetest odours made:
>   And so of you, beautious and lovely youth,
>   When that shall vade, by verse distils your truth.

Much later, in Sonnet 109, Shakespeare gives us yet another paraphrase of the 'happy title' he has found:

> For nothing this wide Universe I call,   109.13–14
> Save thou my Rose, in it thou art my all.

This is so close in sense to what the anagram says that it is hard to believe that the connection could be accidental.

CHAPTER VI

'In Sequent Toile'

DURING the second half of 1593 the plague continued to strike with increasing vigour: by September about a thousand deaths a week were being reported in London, and some five hundred outside. There was no question of any theatres being allowed to operate in London, and the companies continued to tour the provinces. One, Lord Pembroke's men, which had only started the previous Christmas, found that its takings did not cover its costs and by August was having to pawn its costumes. But, with both Greene and Marlowe recently dead there was a shortage of playwrights, and after the success of his published poem Shakespeare's work was in demand. He somehow found time between 1592 and 1594 to write *Richard III, The Comedy of Errors, Titus Andronicus, The Taming of the Shrew, Two Gentlemen of Verona, Love's Labour's Lost* and, very probably, *Romeo and Juliet.* Apart from *Titus Andronicus* and *The Taming of the Shrew*, which were based on existing plays and written with a public audience chiefly in mind, and from *Richard III*, which was a sequel to the *Henry VI* trilogy, these plays probably had their premières in noble households, particularly, of course, the houses of Southampton and his friends, all keen students of Italian and French and likely to be interested in stories set in those countries. With such a heavy programme of writing to occupy him it is unlikely that Shakespeare did much, if any, acting during this period, but no doubt he had to travel a good deal in order to discuss his plays with the actors and perhaps help with the production.

During these journeys he found time to keep up a steady flow of sonnets to his friend and patron. Many of this series, which starts with No. 43, are somewhat conventional in style, weaving typical conceits round the theme of yearning for the beloved. Although these sonnets fulfil a definite purpose as letters to maintain contact with his friend, many of them lack the specifically personal flavour of most of the earlier sonnets. There is much display of verbal virtuosity:

> Then thou whose shaddow shaddowes doth make bright,   43.5–8
> How would thy shadowes forme, forme happy show,
> To the cleere day with thy much cleerer light,
> When to un-seeing eyes thy shade shines so?

There are displays of erudition, such as the basing of sonnets 44 and 45 on the following lines of Golding's translation of Ovid:

> This endlesse world conteynes therin I say
> Fowre substances of which all things are gendred. Of theis fower
> The Earth and Water for theyr masse and weyght are sunken lower.

The other cowple Aire and Fyre, the purer of the twayne,
Mount up, and nought can keepe them downe.

(Golding, Met. XV 263–7)

There are exercises on conventional sonneteering conceits, such as the strife between eye and heart over the beloved's picture in Sonnets 46 and 47. All these are beautifully done, but they could have been addressed to anyone, since they lack any of the topical references which individualize so many of the sonnets we have examined earlier.

Sonnets 50 and 51 introduce a more specific note with the mention of a journey on horseback, perhaps to deliver a play to one of the travelling companies. Then in 53 we have this:

> Describe *Adonis* and the counterfet,   53.5–8
> Is poorely immitated after you,
> On *Hellens* cheeke all art of beautie set,
> And you in *Grecian* tires are painted new: . . .

The mention of Adonis reminds us that *Venus and Adonis* had not long been offered to Southampton, and of Helen that the main character of his next poem was to be a heroine rather than a hero. The theme, however, was as yet undecided, or at least was still secret. It would have been easy otherwise to write:

> On *Lucrece'* cheeke all art of beautie set,
> And you in *Roman* tires are painted new.

Whatever lady Shakespeare chose, her beauty would be patterned after that of his patron.

Sonnet 55, which is based on the concluding lines of Ovid's *Metamorphoses*, reads as if written to round off a sequence of sonnets. This would presumably be the dozen poems from 43 to 54, a pretty enough little collection. What the 'guilded monuments of Princes' looked like can now once more be seen in Westminster Abbey, where the former bright colours of the memorial effigies have all been restored. It is clearly an equestrian statue that Shakespeare has in mind as being outlasted by his 'powrefull rime':

> Gainst death, and all oblivious enmity   55.10–11
> Shall you pace forth, . . .

Shakespeare has already once referred to Southampton's love of horsemanship by placing Adonis on a horse, although no such thing is mentioned in Ovid's story. He refers to it again in Sonnet 91 and also, in more detail, in *A Lover's Complaint*, lines 106–12.* So it is natural in the present sonnet that Southampton should be pictured as riding out eternally against death and oblivion by means of Shakespeare's verse.

* See p. 137.

In this short sequence the merest trace of uneasiness begins to make itself felt. In Sonnet 48 Shakespeare is worried that in his absence his patron has been:

> . . . left the prey of every vulgar theefe.   48.8

The next sonnet foreshadows a time when Southampton will frown on his defects, and so the poet prepares

> Against that time when thou shalt strangely passe,   49.5–6
> And scarcely greete me with that sunne thine eye,

by thinking up all the reasons why he deserves to be thrown over. But this line of thought must not be carried too far, and in 53 and 54, to reassure himself, he stresses the young man's truth and constancy.

A new short sequence begins with 56:

> Sweet love renew thy force, . . .   56.1

and, making a virtue out of necessity, Shakespeare finds that enforced separation makes reunion sweeter. There is a brief reminiscence of Hero and Leander, separated by the Hellespont:

> Let this said *Intrim* like the Ocean be   56.9–12
> Which parts the shore, where two contracted new
> Come daily to the banckes, that when they see:
> Returne of love, more blest may be the view.

This is another reminder that the year is still 1593, and Marlowe fresh in mind. But the next two sonnets show that the absence is involuntary only on Shakespeare's side. Southampton is purposely neglecting him for dubious pleasures with others:

> That God forbid, that made me first your slave,   58.1–4
> I should in thought controule your times of pleasure,
> Or at your hand th' account of houres to crave,
> Being your vassail bound to staie your leisure.

This is the bitterest outburst yet, in which the sincere self-denigratory humility of some of the earlier sonnets has become an ironic mock humility:

> Be where you list, your charter is so strong,   58.9–14
> That you your selfe may priviledge your time
> To what you will, to you it doth belong,
> Your selfe to pardon of selfe-doing crime.
>   I am to waite, though waiting so be hell,
>   Not blame your pleasure be it ill or well.

As so often happens, love has brought with it an overwhelming temptation to preach when the loved one fails to live up to the idealistic image which has been created in the mind of the lover. But this is a very dangerous line to take if the relationship is to survive, and for most of the sonnets which close this little group Shakespeare is wise enough to return to the safe ground of Golding's translation of Ovid. Sonnets 63, 64 and 65 are all on the subject of change and decay as they affect the loved one:

> When I have seen such interchange of state,   64.9–14
> Or state itself confounded, to decay,
> Ruine hath taught me thus to ruminate
> That Time will come and take my love away.
>   This thought is as a death which cannot choose
> But weepe to have, that wich it fears to loose.

Ostensibly it is death that is the enemy, but there is an underlying feeling that Time may work on love in the abstract as well as on the person of the beloved. We are reminded of Ulysses' speech to Achilles in *Troilus and Cressida*:

> For beauty, wit,
> High birth, vigour of bone, desert in service,
> Love, friendship, charity, are subjects all
> To envious and calumniating time.

There is really nothing that the miracles wrought by 'black inck' may do about this. It is the same misgiving which we saw in Sonnet 49:

> Against that time when thou shalt strangely passe,   49.5–6
> And scarcely greete me with that sunne thine eye, . . .

Unfortunately that time was not so far distant.

It seems most likely to me that Sonnet 65 was composed before Christmas and that it was the last one to be written in the year 1593. On 26th December Henslowe was able to open a season at the Rose with the Earl of Sussex's players. Their repertory consisted largely of old plays, but there was one new one, *Titus Andronicus*. There is no doubt that this was written at least partly by Shakespeare, as it contains many parallels with *The Rape of Lucrece* which Shakespeare may also have been working on at this time, since it was published in 1594. The play is probably a revision of an older one, *Titus and Vespacia*, which had been performed by Lord Strange's company in their two previous London seasons, and probably also by Lord Pembroke's players. The names of these two companies, as well as that of the Earl of Sussex, are given on the title page of the quarto edition of *Titus Andronicus*, which came out in 1594, the first of Shakespeare's plays to be published. (By that time Lord Strange had become the Earl of Derby, and is so referred to.) Whether or not Shakespeare also acted in some of the plays during this season, he was probably busy with other commissions to produce plays for Henslowe, in the expectation that a good long season would be required. It would not be surprising, therefore, if he had little time for sonneteering. As we shall see, the next sonnet was not written until February 1594.

CHAPTER VII

'And Strength by Limping Sway Disabled'

AT COURT there was no season of plays for the Christmas of 1593. Because of the ferocity of the plague in London the Queen had taken up residence at Windsor in June, and she stayed there until the following February. Great precautions were taken to see that no unnecessary visitors from plague-stricken areas came near the court, and certainly no common players could be allowed. For those who did have business at court and could hear its gossip, the news was frequently of the efforts of the Earl of Essex to increase his influence in the face of determined opposition from the Cecil family.

Essex, like his devoted admirer Southampton, had been left fatherless at an early age, and, as a royal ward, had similarly been committed to the care of Lord Burghley.[1] His mother, after two years of widowhood, married the Earl of Leicester, the dominant figure at the English court. At the age of eighteen Essex was appointed General of the Horse in his stepfather's Netherlands campaign, and performed with distinction at the battle of Zutphen, where Sir Philip Sidney met his death. Before he died Sidney handed over his sword to Essex, and a few years later, as if to emphasize his right to Sidney's place in the popular imagination, Essex married his widow, the daughter of the Queen's Secretary of State, Sir Francis Walsingham. Handsome, cultured, high-born and ambitious, Essex seemed to have every opportunity of becoming not only the most brilliant but also the most powerful figure in the realm. After the deaths of Leicester in 1588 and Walsingham in 1590, however, the reins of power were all gathered into the hands of the ageing Lord Burghley. The old man was determined that no glamorous courtier should interfere with what he considered to be the natural succession in the handling of serious matters of state. He had brought up his able young hunchbacked son to this end, and Robert Cecil was already unofficially assisting him in carrying on the duties of the vacant office of Secretary of State in addition to those of his own as Lord Treasurer. By and large the Queen, although very taken with the charms of young Essex, who was already putting another brilliant man of action, Sir Walter Raleigh, in the shade, agreed that there were many matters where a deeper and more reliable type of character was called for, and it was this that the unromantic Cecil family possessed.

On Walsingham's death Essex had tried to get his friend William Davison appointed Secretary. Davison had fallen from grace in 1587, when he was made the scapegoat for the beheading of Mary, Queen of Scots. The warrant had been duly signed by Queen Elizabeth, but she maintained that Davison, who was then acting for Walsingham as Secretary, should not have passed it on to the Council for action. For this he was sent for eighteen months to the Tower. The Queen had no intention of reinstating Davison, but she preferred to keep everyone waiting rather than snub Essex directly. In May 1591 she knighted Robert Cecil, but refrained from officially appointing him to the Secretary's post until 1596, when Essex was away at sea. All this time he carried out the Secretary's duties, in fact if not in name, and from August 1591 he was a Privy Councillor, while Essex had to wait until February 1593 to receive this honour.

One of Walsingham's achievements had been to set up an efficient secret service network from which the Queen derived valuable information about the intentions of foreign governments, and about the plots against her which were constantly being devised both at home and on the Continent. With Essex's failure to secure the appointment of a Secretary of State of his own choosing, the control of this organization naturally passed to Burghley and his son, thus further strengthening their influence with the Queen. Nothing daunted, Essex decided to establish a rival intelligence organization of his own, which would show up the Cecils as incompetent bunglers and make apparent his own indispensability.

Lord Burghley had two nephews on his wife's side, Anthony and Francis Bacon,[2] who felt that their uncle's obsession with the prospects of his son had deprived them of the help which they had a right to expect from such an influential relative. In 1592 both brothers were in their thirties. Anthony had spent the last eleven years travelling in Europe, and had become a useful though ill-paid intelligence agent of Walsingham and Burghley. Francis during this time had been serving as a Member of Parliament and exercising his literary talents from his chambers in Gray's Inn. Though a learned lawyer, he did not practise at the bar, for, as he wrote in a letter to his uncle:

> I ever bare in mind to serve her Majesty, not as a man born under Sol, that loveth honour, nor under Jupiter, that loveth business (for the contemplative planet carrieth me away wholly). I confess that I have as vast contemplative ends as I have moderate civil ends, for I have taken all knowledge to be my province.

In short, he expected to be financed by Burghley in order to pursue an academic life, through the medium of a lucrative government position. The Lord Treasurer was not disposed to fall in with this notion.

Since their uncle would do nothing for them the brothers decided to turn to his young and ambitious rival. For Essex they were just the right people to form the nucleus of his private Department of State. When he became a Privy Councillor he was able to offer foreign intelligence to the Queen from his own network of agents, and policy memoranda beautifully prepared by his own political staff. For a time he appeared to be having considerable success.

Then the Attorney-General, Sir Thomas Egerton, was nominated to the vacant post of Master of the Rolls and his own appointment became vacant.

Essex immediately proposed Francis Bacon for the post, even though he had no court experience and, moreover, had just infuriated the Queen by vigorously opposing a bill for subsidies in the House of Commons. The obvious candidate was the Solicitor-General, Edward Coke,[3] who had years of experience at the bar and was, in addition, Speaker of the House of Commons. Once again the Queen had no intention of appointing Essex's candidate, and once again she prevaricated and left the position open rather than over-ride Essex directly.

One of Essex's ideas for getting the better of the Cecils was to secure secret information about the intentions of the Spaniards, who were still meditating ways and means of overthrowing Elizabeth and returning England to Catholicism. Essex had suspicions that at this time the Cecils were not averse to the thought of a Spanish succession to the English throne, whereas he himself supported the claims of James VI of Scotland. He therefore conceived the plan of using a Portuguese physician called Roderigo Lopez as a double agent. This Lopez had settled in England and become one of the leading doctors of the day.[4] In addition to holding the post of house physician at St Bartholomew's Hospital he had been appointed personal physician to the Queen. He was also highly thought of by the King of Spain. The suggestion was that Lopez should offer his services as a secret agent to certain of his friends in Spain and Portugal, and so gain information from them which could be passed to Essex.

Without telling Essex, Lopez talked the proposal over with the Queen, who gave him permission to go ahead; but with the condition that all the information he gained should be first given to herself, and only then made known to Essex. This Lopez faithfully did. When, therefore, Essex came hotfoot to the Queen to tell her of the latest piece of secret intelligence which his private organization had ferreted out, the Queen would take the words out of his mouth and laugh at him for producing stale news.

Essex could never stand being made a fool of, particularly in front of the Queen. When he learned that, to cap it all, Lopez had been gossiping amongst his cronies about having treated Essex for embarrassing diseases, he determined to get rid of the man. At the beginning of 1594 the opportunity seemed to present itself, when an unsavoury Portuguese calling himself Tinoco arrived in England with a story involving Lopez in a plot on behalf of the King of Spain.

Tinoco first told his story to Sir Robert Cecil. Then Essex insisted on examining him further, and the story he got out of him was a great deal more lurid. The Queen then appointed a joint commission of Burghley, Cecil and Essex to get to the bottom of the matter, and Tinoco was again interrogated on 24th January. After the hearing Sir Robert Cecil posted rapidly to Windsor to get his version of the story in first. This was to the effect that there was nothing which could be held against Dr Lopez.

The Cecils as well as the Queen were well aware of Lopez's role as a double agent and were convinced that Essex was taking the opportunity to frame him in revenge for having been made a fool of. It is probable that this was at least partly so, but there is no doubt that Essex had managed fully to convince himself that Lopez was a dangerous Spanish spy. When he finally reached the Queen he was incensed to be told that he was 'a rash and temerarious youth to enter into a matter against the poor man which he could not prove'. Essex stalked to the door, threw it open, and shut himself away in his own room for an hour. After that he refused to talk to anyone but the Lord Admiral, who acted as a go-between until such time as ruffled pride was more or less smoothed down.

Essex's vehemence eventually convinced the Queen and even the Cecils that there might be something in the story. It appeared that Dr Lopez had been receiving a pension from the King of Spain for the last seven years and that, at the very least, further investigations should be carried out. Lopez, who had been detained at Essex House, was on Tuesday 29th January committed to the Tower,[5] and the Earl of Essex continued working night and day to establish the evidence against him.

The following day Dr Lopez was again examined before the Earl of Essex and Sir Robert Cecil and was considered to have confessed enough to justify prosecution. After the hearing Essex and Cecil travelled back in the same coach and Sir Robert mentioned that the Queen had resolved within five days to make an appointment to the vacant office of Attorney-General. He asked Essex whom he would favour for the post. Essex replied that he wondered Sir Robert should ask him that question seeing that it could not be unknown to him that he favoured Francis Bacon. 'Good Lord,' replied Sir Robert, 'I wonder your Lordship should go about to spend your strength in so unlikely or impossible a manner.' After further talk passed between them, Sir Robert said, 'If at least your Lordship had spoken of the Solicitorship, that might be of easier digestion to her Majesty.'

The Earl replied in characteristic vein, 'Digest me no digestions; for the Attorneyship for Francis is that I must have, and in that will I spend all my power, might, authority and annuity, and with tooth and nail defend and procure the same for him against whosoever; and that whosoever getteth this office out of my hand for another, before he have it, it shall cost him the coming by, and of this be you assured of, Sir Robert, I think it strange both of my Lord Treasurer and you that can have the mind to seek the preference of a stranger before so near a kinsman. For if you weigh in a balance the parts every way of his competitor and him, only excepting five poor years of admitting to a house of court before Francis, you shall find in all other respects whatsoever, no comparison between them.'

Late in the evening of the day after this conversation, Thursday 31st January, Essex saw the Queen, who told him 'that she had been straitly urg'd to the nomination of Coke to be her attorney-general, and of Sir Robert Cecil and Sir Edward Stafford to be her secretaries, and of two other officers in her household; and all these to be plac'd on Candlemass-day, or the Sunday following at the farthest' (i.e. February 2nd or 3rd). One of Essex's followers, the secret agent Anthony Standen, wrote to Anthony Bacon reporting what Essex had told him about this interview, and went on to say that the Lord Keeper and many others had gone to court

> to be the news-bringers hither: and this is here so full, as all stand gaping for it with open mouth: yea, so far forth, that the old man and the son do believe the same. *Mais nostre bon pullet chante de tout autre façon: et s'en est rie & gausse avec moy a pleine gorge*, as you shall understand farther by the event; for none of all these shall be, to the end a couple thrust not in, whom he nothing liketh, and saith the honest gentleman, no less noise shall we likewise hear at Shrovetide: *ma allora come prima tanto di naso.**

Essex, the *bon pullet*, may have been in high good humour about this, but all that it meant was that the Queen was prepared to prevaricate a little longer. By March he had given up the struggle for the Attorneyship and was urging the Queen to make Bacon Solicitor-General. Eventually she appointed Coke to the one post and Serjeant Fleming to the other. The 'old man and the son' had won after all.

On February 6th[6] an event took place which was as galling for Shakespeare as were the frustrations over Lopez and Francis Bacon for Essex and his friends. Because of renewed incidence of plague, the Lord Mayor was instructed by the Privy Council that no plays or interludes should be 'exercised' by any company within the compass of five miles of the City, and accordingly the theatre season at the Rose, which had commenced on 26th December, was summarily ended. The closing play was Shakespeare's *Titus Andronicus*, which had been presented for the first time during this season and ran for four successful performances. There was no indication when playing might resume, and Shakespeare must have been left with no source of income, except the bounty of his patron, until better times returned. It was time to write some more sonnets.

Sonnet 66, unlike all the others, seems at first glance to be composed in single lines, which makes the logical connection difficult to grasp. Since the Shakespearian sonnet normally consists of three quatrains followed by a closing couplet, with a stronger break in the thought between the second and third quatrains than between the first and second, let us set the Sonnet out to indicate this, even though there is nothing in the punctuation to assist us.

> Tyr'd with all these for restfull death I cry,   66
> As to behold desert a begger borne,
> And needie Nothing trimd in jollitie,
> And purest faith unhappily forsworne,
>
> And gilded honor shamefully misplast,
> And maiden vertue rudely strumpeted,
> And right perfection wrongfully disgrac'd,
> And strength by limping sway disabled,

* But then as before there will be disappointment.

> And arte made tung-tide by authoritie,
> And Folly (Doctor-like) controuling skill,
> And simple-Truth miscalde Simplicitie,
> And captive-good attending Captaine ill.
>
>   Tyr'd with all these, from these would I be gone,
>   Save that to dye, I leave my love alone.

Taking the second quatrain first, and remembering the point of history we appear to have reached in our progress through the Sonnets, it is difficult to avoid seeing a reference to the struggle for power between Essex and the Cecils; on the one hand the brilliant and gallant young nobleman, on the other the gout-lamed old counsellor and his hunchbacked son:

> And right perfection wrongfully disgrac'd   66.7–8
> And strength by limping sway disabled, . . .

The third quatrain appears to turn to the poet's own troubles, for surely the line,

> And arte made tung-tide by authoritie,   66.9

refers to the premature closing of the theatre season. With these landmarks it is easy to see how the second and third lines,

> And to behold desert a begger borne,
> And needie Nothing trimd in jollitie,

could refer to the rival candidatures for the Attorneyship of Francis Bacon and Edward Coke.

Francis Bacon, who I think is referred to in the first of these lines, was the son of a Lord Keeper of the Great Seal and nephew of the Lord Treasurer of England. As a child he had mingled with all the aristocrats of the court in the great houses of Gorhambury and Theobalds in Hertfordshire, and York House and Cecil House in London. He had early been noticed by the Queen and nicknamed her 'Young Lord Keeper'. After attending Cambridge for three years he spent another three at the Paris Embassy, by which time he was still only eighteen. Then his father died, and it transpired that, while his elder brothers were well provided for, Francis was left with an income of only £300 a year and some small properties. From then on he was constantly in debt, yet he had very little idea of doing anything to improve his fortunes. He read for the bar at Gray's Inn, but after qualifying in 1584 he made no attempt to practise. A seat in Parliament was found for him, but, as frequent letters to Burghley begging for a Government appointment failed to produce any results except the promise of the reversion of a clerkship after the retirement of the present holder, he continued to believe that the world owed him a living, and a very good one at that. Unfortunately only Essex and his entourage, including, of course, the Earl of Southampton, could be persuaded that this was so.

Edward Coke, though coming from a respectable Norfolk family, was no more than the son of a practising barrister and of the daughter of a Norwich attorney. After qualifying at the Temple in 1578 he is said to have started on his career as a barrister with no possessions beyond a horse, a rapier, ten pounds, and a ring set with three rose diamonds and bearing the motto 'O Prepare'.[7] Then, unlike Bacon, he committed what Essex no doubt regarded as the vulgar solecism of successfully earning his own living. As if his lucrative practice was not enough he was favoured with public appointments: in 1586 Recorder of Coventry and Norwich, and Justice of the Peace for Norfolk, in 1591 Recorder of London and in 1592 Solicitor-General. He sat in Parliament in 1586 and 1593, and in the latter year was appointed Speaker of the House of Commons. This is how he is described by his biographer, Mrs Catherine Drinker Bowen, as he addressed the Queen from the bar of the House of Lords at the state opening of Parliament:

> His eyes, large, dark and brilliant, bore the watchful look of a man ambitious and self-contained. He wore the heavy Speaker's robe with style; for one with a scholar's reputation Coke was remarkably well turned out. The ruff at his neck was wide, meticulously fluted and starched uncomfortably high; when he lifted his hand the gown fell back to show a sleeve fashionably puffed and quilted. On his left thumb he wore a heavy gold ring.[8]

This description, which is based on a portrait of Coke in 1593 appearing in Mrs Bowen's book, tells us clearly enough how the self-made Coke, 'trimd in jollitie', must have looked to Shakespeare, as compared with the well-born and fastidious Bacon, the prey of the money-lenders, whose only robe of office was the black woollen gown of an outer barrister. With what masterly succinctness the contrast, as seen through the eyes of Essex and Southampton, is summed up!

Of course, Bacon felt himself the victim of treachery when the Queen did not immediately recognize his pre-eminent merits. On 10th November, 1593, he had written to Essex:

> My Lord,
>
> I thought it not amiss to inform your lordship of that, which I gather partly by conjecture, and partly by advertisement of the late recover'd man, that is so much at your devotion; of whom I have some cause to think, that he worketh for the *Huddler* under hand . . .
>
> Your lordship's in most
faithful duty.
>
> I pray, Sir, let not my jargon privilege my letter from burning, because it is not such, but the light sheweth through.[9]

The 'Huddler' is generally understood to be Bacon's nickname for his rival, Edward Coke. The word carried, according to the Oxford Dictionary, the meanings of 'hustle' and 'muddle' as well as the modern sense of huddling, and probably refers to Coke's hectoring and undisciplined style of forensic oratory, later to become so famous in the trials of Essex and Southampton and of Sir Walter Raleigh. 'The late recover'd man, that is so much at your devotion', is a reference to Lord Burghley, who made a show of regard for Essex, and had recently been ill. Another member of the Essex entourage, the secret agent Anthony Standen, in commenting the next day upon Essex's reception of this letter, wrote that the opinion was at court that the Lord Treasurer, 'was amended in health, tho' his sons denied it'. A few days before he had had a severe attack of gout and on that account had been visited by the Queen in his lodgings.

Burghley had some reason to preserve good relations with Essex at this time, since it was largely due to the latter's opposition that the Queen had so far refused to confirm Sir Robert Cecil in the appointment of Secretary. On 27th September 1593 Burghley had written to Francis Bacon:

> Nephew,
>
> I have no leisure to write much; but for answer, I have attempted to place you; but her majesty hath required the lord keeper to give her the names of diverse lawyers to be preferred; wherewith he made me acquainted, and I did name you as a meet man, whom his lordship allowed in way of friendship for your father's sake; but he made scruple to equal you with certain, whom he named, as Brograve and Branthwayt, whom he specially commendeth. But I will continue the remembrance of you to her majesty, and implore my Lord of Essex's help.
>
> Your loving uncle,
W. Burghley.

Clearly what Bacon had asked him to do was to support him for the Attorney-ship, but there is little doubt that Coke was Burghley's nomination from the start, and that he never intended that Bacon should get more than the Solicitor-ship. Towards the end of October the Queen condemned Essex's judgment in thinking Bacon fittest to be Attorney 'whom his own uncle did name but to a second place'. Bacon was right in thinking that Burghley would trust to his 'art and finesse' to keep Essex's good opinion while serving his own ends. It therefore seems likely that it is Burghley who is so harshly referred to in the line,

And purest faith unhappily forsworne, . . .   66.4

The second quatrain seems to refer to the incident on 24th January, 1594, when Essex was called a "rash and temerarious youth' by the Queen, as a result of the report of Lopez's innocence made to her by Sir Robert Cecil. The line,

And gilded honor shamefully misplast,   66.5

would then be the honour wrongly conferred on Cecil, who was acting as Secretary and likely in the general opinion soon to be confirmed in the post.

And maiden vertue rudely strumpeted,   66.6

perhaps refers to the misleading of the Queen into rounding upon Essex and wrongfully disgracing his 'right perfection'. Behind all is the 'limping sway' of the apparently obsequious and physically lame Burghley, who could hamper Essex's firmest intentions even from his sick-bed, and of his deformed son.

For the third quatrain we should expect some change of subject, or at least some different reflection on the subject, and sure enough we find Shakespeare turning from Essex's frustrations to others which are more personal to him and Southampton.

The lines,

> And Folly (Doctor-like) controuling skill,   66.10–11
> And simple-Truth miscalde Simplicitie,

take us forward to Sonnet 82, where Shakespeare's complaint on this score is fully spelled out:

> Thou art as faire in knowledge as in hew,   82.5–12
> Finding thy worth a limmit past my praise,
> And therefore art inforc'd to seeke anew,
> Some fresher stampe of the time bettering dayes.
> And do so love, yet when they have devisde,
> What strained touches Rhethorick can lend,
> Thou truly faire, wert truly simpathizde,
> In true plaine words, by thy true telling friend.

In short, there is a rival who is trying to undermine Shakespeare's position as Southampton's poet by saying that his style is that of a simpleton. There will be more to say about this subject shortly.

The next line of this jam-packed Sonnet,

> And captive-good attending Captaine ill   66.12

must be read with the first quatrain of the following one:

> Ah wherefore with infection should he live,   67.1–4
> And with his presence grace impietie,
> That sinne by him advantage should atchive,
> And lace it selfe with his societie?

and it indicates that Southampton has been getting into some company of which Shakespeare does not approve. The key is in the second line of Sonnet 67, for 'impietie' is a specific kind of sin, not to be confused with the petty debaucheries of a young man sowing his wild oats. Once again, the subject is a very topical one.

CHAPTER VIII

The Shadow of Atheism

IN 1592 there was circulated in England a Latin pamphlet called the *Responsio*, by Andreas Philopater.[1] It was an answer to Elizabeth's Proclamation of 1591 against Jesuits and seminary priests, and was in reality written by Father Parsons, leader of the Jesuit Mission to reconvert England to Catholicism. Amongst other attacks on notabilities of the court it included the following paragraph about Raleigh:

> There is a flourishing and well known School of Atheism which Sir Walter Raleigh runs in his house, with a certain necromancer-astronomer as teacher, where noble youths are taught to make witty jests about the ancient law of Moses and the new law of Christ; but if this School should grow in strength and proceed a little further with atheism and Raleigh himself were to be promoted to the Privy Council to preside over affairs of the state—which seeing he holds first place in the Queen's favour after Leicester and Hatton, is very possible—then one day there might some edict appear in the Queen's name, drawn up by that magician and Epicure, Raleigh's teacher, in which belief in Divinity, in the immortality of the soul and in a future life would be openly denied—a doctrine which appears to those who pursue the lusts of the flesh—while those who voiced their disapproval would be accused of *lèse majesté*.

Since Leicester had died in 1588 and Hatton in 1591 it would seem likely that this part of the pamphlet had been written some time earlier; nevertheless, Raleigh had sufficient enemies in 1592 for any such titbits to be eagerly snapped up and repeated. The reputation for atheism was to dog Raleigh all his life, or at least until the publication of his *History of the World*, in which he took pains to refute it.

The term 'atheism' was at this time used in a very broad sense, covering any kind of disbelief in or questioning of accepted Christian belief. It was therefore natural that anyone interested in scientific speculation should incur such suspicion, and Raleigh since 1580 had had the astronomer and mathematician Harriot lodging in his house. Most of the astronomers of the day were also interested in astrology, alchemy, spiritualism and magic, all subjects that sat ill with orthodox Christianity; yet even the Queen encouraged the savant John Dee in his researches into them. Raleigh liked to keep abreast of all new thought; as he said at his trial, speaking of his library, 'it is well known that there comes out nothing in these times but I have it'. Harriot held dangerous opinions about the Bible; Anthony à Wood tells us that 'notwithstanding his great skill in mathematics he had strange thoughts of the Scriptures and always undervalued the old story of the Creation of the World, and could never believe that trite position, *ex nihilo nihil fit*. He made a Philosophical theology wherein he cast off the Old Testament, so that consequently the New would have no foundation.' Christopher Marlowe, Walter Warner the mathematician, Matthew Roydon the poet and friend of Chapman, Adrian Gilbert (Raleigh's half-brother) and Carew Raleigh (his full brother) were other members of the circle. There were also noblemen such as the Earls of Derby and Northumberland, who were perhaps the 'noble youths' mentioned by Father Parsons.

The arrest of Thomas Kyd, who had been Marlowe's room-mate in 1593, on suspicion of having written inflammatory placards about Flemish immigrants, led to an enquiry into 'Marlowe's monstrous opinions' concerning atheism. Kyd accused him in a letter to the Lord Keeper of consorting with 'Harriot, Warner, Roydon and some stationers in Paules Churchyard' to carry on their blasphemous conversations. Marlowe was also reported to have persuaded 'with men of quality to go unto the King of Scots', a highly treasonable proceeding at this time. However, before Marlowe could be properly examined on the subject he was (perhaps conveniently) killed in the tavern brawl.

We have already noted* that the Earl of Southampton was a partner with Carew Raleigh and Ralph Bowes in fitting out one of the ships for Raleigh's expedition in 1592, and that he was subsequently involved in a dispute with the Crown over the prize-money due for the capture of the *St Malo* laden with sugar from Brazil. This indicates fairly close involvement with the Raleigh family at that time, since it is not likely that at the age of eighteen he would have joined Carew in a business venture unless he knew him well. Southampton retained all his life a deep concern with maritime expeditions and explorations, and it is reasonable to suppose that he took the opportunity to join in the discussions of the two Raleighs, Harriot, Lawrence Keymis, Humphrey and Adrian Gilbert, Frobisher and Grenville about problems of navigation and astronomy. It would be difficult to avoid getting involved with the other subjects which were of such great interest to the Raleigh household at this time, particularly if, as Professor Akrigg suggests, Southampton was already turning away from the Catholic beliefs which his family held so strongly.[2]

During 1593 and early 1594 the scandalous rumours about atheism and other blasphemous practices at Raleigh's country house and elsewhere continued to increase. On 8th September, 1593, a book by Thomas Nashe was registered, entitled *Christ's Tears over Jerusalem*. This compares the wickedness of London with that of Jerusalem, which refused to accept Christ and forty years afterwards was sacked and destroyed. One of the deadly sins said by Nashe to be excessively prevalent was that of atheism:

* See p. 41.

The third sonne of Pride is Atheisme, which is when a man is so tim-
paniz'd with prosperity, and entranced from himselfe with Wealth,
Ambition, and Vaine-glory, that he forgets he had a Maker, or that there
is a Heaven above him which controules him. To much ioy of this world
hath made him drunke. . . .

In our Saviours time there were *Saduces*, that denyed the Resurrection;
what are these Atheists but Saducaean sectaries that deny the resurrection?
They believe they must die, though they believe not the Dietie. By no
meanes may they avoid what they will not admitte. In the very houre of
death shall appeare to them a God and a devill. . . .

Of Atheists this age affordeth two sorts, the inwarde and the outward;
The inwarde Atheist is he that devoures widowes houses under pretence
of long prayers, that (like the Panther) hideth his face in a hood of Religion, when he goeth about his pray. He wold professe himself an Atheist
openly but that (like the Pharisies) he feareth the multitude. Because
the multitude favours Religion, he runnes with the streame, and favours
Religion; only for he woulde be Captaine of a multitude. To be the God
of gold, he cares not how many gods he entertaines. . . .[3]

Sir John Harington wrote several epigrams on Raleigh's atheism, giving him
the name of Paulus. Although these were not printed until 1605, when Raleigh
was safely in jail, some of them clearly derive from this period, and are probably
based on Nashe's own book. Here is one:

> Lewd Paulus, led by Sadducees' infection
> Doth not believe the body's resurrection,
> And holds them all in scorn and deep derision
> That tell of Saints' or Angels' apparition,
> And swears such things are fables all and fancies
> Of lunatics or fools possessed with franzies,
> I have, (said he) travelled both near and far
> By sea, by land, in time of peace and war
> Yet never met I sprite or ghost or elf
> Or aught (as is the phrase) worse than myself;
> Well Paulus, this I now believe indeed,
> For who, in all or part, denies his creed
> Went he to sea, land, hell, I would agree
> A fiend worse than himself shall never see.

Passages about the Sadducees denying the resurrection, referred to by both
Nashe and Harington, are to be found in the Gospels and in the Acts of the
Apostles, ch. 23 v. 8. It is probable that Harington took the name Paulus also
from the Acts of the Apostles. We are told in chapter 13 that Sergius Paulus,
the Deputy of Cyprus, had with him 'a certain sorcerer, a fallen prophet' whose

name was Bar-jesus or Elymas. When Barnabas and Saul came to preach to Sergius Paulus, they found him willing to listen: 'But Elymas the sorcerer (for so is his name by interpretation) withstood them, seeking to turn away the deputy from the faith.' Elymas the sorcerer is therefore reminiscent of Thomas Harriot, the astronomer-magician kept by Sir Walter Raleigh, though Sir John Harington has blackened the character of Sergius Paulus to suit his purpose.

During the summer of 1593 the Privy Council extended its enquiries about atheism from London to Dorset, where Raleigh occupied Sherborne Castle. Information was obtained about a supper party held by Sir George Trenchard, one of the two deputy Lieutenants of the county, which was attended by the two Raleigh brothers and several other guests. Carew Raleigh and Sir Walter interrogated Mr Roger Ironside, the minister of neighbouring Winterborne Abbas, on the nature of the soul. The evidence did not add up to any offence of atheism by Raleigh, but it was decided to set up a commission to investigate the matter at Cerne Abbas on 21st March, 1594.

There is no evidence at all that any suspicion of being mixed up in these affairs fell on the Earl of Southampton, except that contained in the first quatrain of Sonnet 67. Once we have seen, however, that the preceding sonnet is likely to have been written around February 1594, it is difficult to imagine that the first four lines of 67 can have any other interpretation but that there appeared to be a risk that the current atheism enquiries might disclose some involvement of the young Earl:

> Ah wherefore with infection should he live,   67.1-4
> And with his presence grace impietie,
> That sinne by him advantage should atchive,
> And lace it selfe with his societie?

It is interesting to see that Sir John Harington also uses the word 'infection' in exactly the same sense. Atheism was regarded as a dangerous and fast-spreading disease which might well lead to contempt not only for religion but for the established order of society; indeed, to everything comprised in the word 'impiety'. To the Privy Council, it was a disease which might easily develop into sedition.

Largely because of Father Parsons' pamphlet, it was Sir Walter Raleigh, Captain of the Queen's Guard, who was regarded as leader of the cult of atheism, although he was never proved to have made the same kind of blasphemous statements as did many others. Nashe describes him as the inward sort of atheist, too clever to strike against the stream of the multitude who favour religion, because 'he would be Captaine of a multitude'. The thought is very close to that of Shakespeare in Sonnet 66,

> And captive-good attending Captaine ill.   66.12

Fortunately, the danger seems soon to have passed, for in Sonnet 70 South-ampton is told:

> Thou hast past by the ambush of young daies,   70.9–10
> Either not assayld, or victor beeing charg'd, . . .

But let us first finish with Sonnet 67.

After the reference to the infection of impiety, the rest of the sonnet, together with the following one, is concerned with the old theme of Southampton as the pattern of all beauty, the 'master-hue'. His fresh and genuine complexion is contrasted with that of the so-called beauties of the court, who find it necessary to paint roses on their cheeks and to wear wigs made from the hair of corpses. Such a one was the Countess of Pembroke, Sir Philip Sidney's sister, who, as Fulke Greville tells us, when young,

> Adorn'd her head with golden borrowed haire
> (*Caelica*, Sonnet LVIII)

though in later life she reverted to her natural brunette. But the reference in 68 may well be to the Queen herself, who wore wigs of the same colour as that of Southampton's natural hair.

These two flattering sonnets form a tactful introduction to number 69, which indicates that Southampton's behaviour has not altogether been measuring up to his looks.

Sonnet 69 is the first one which clearly and distinctly makes allusion to George Chapman, the rival playwright whose first poems were just now being pub-lished. 'Skia Nuktos, or the Shadow of Night, containing two poetical hymns, devised by Mr George Chapman' was entered in the Stationers' Register on 31st December, 1593, and published by William Ponsonby with the date 1594. The book is dedicated 'To My Deare and Most Worthy Friend Master Mathew Roydon', and in the dedication there is reference to 'most ingenious Darbie, deepe searching Northumberland, and skill-imbracing heire of Hunsdon'. Now Ferdinando, 5th Earl of Derby, the Amyntas of Spenser's *Colin Clout Comes Home Again*, died on 16th April, 1594, and mention would certainly not be made of the new Earl (if he were the one intended) without some reference to this. It can be taken, therefore, that the book was printed some time between 25th March (when under the calendar in force at the time the year 1593 gave place to 1594) and 16th April. It may well have been passed round in manuscript before that, as was normal custom, and perhaps submitted to possible patrons. Both Southampton and Shakespeare may thus have had the chance of reading it before it was officially published.

The connection between *The Shadow of Night* and the Sonnets was pointed out by William Minto in 1874 and Arthur Acheson in 1903.[4] Unfortunately the latter damaged his case by trying to carry it too far, but it would be wrong to ignore it because of that. There are good reasons for thinking that, in Sonnet

69, Shakespeare is saying something about a reference to Southampton in Chapman's 'poetical hymns':

> Those parts of thee that the worlds eye doth view 69.
> Want nothing that the thought of hearts can mend:
> All toungs (the voice of soules) give thee that due,★
> Uttring bare truth, even so as foes Commend.
> Thy★ outward thus with outward praise is crownd,
> But those same toungs that give thee so thine owne,
> In other accents doe this praise confound
> By seeing farther then the eye hath showne.
> They looke into the beauty of thy mind,
> And that in guesse they measure by thy deeds,
> Then churls their thoughts (although their eies were kind)
> To thy faire flower ad the rancke smell of weeds,
> But why thy odor matcheth not thy show,
> The soyle★ is this, that thou doest common grow.

In the third line the plural is used, as so often in literary polemics, to indicate a single and specific person. The words in brackets in line 3 indicate whose 'tongue' is referred to, for the first 'hymn' in the *Shadow of Night*, the 'Hymnus in Noctem', begins with this invocation:

> Great Goddesse to whose throne in Cynthian fires, *HN.* 1-2
> This earthlie Alter endlesse fumes exspires. . . . and 10-17
> . . . .; now let humor give
> Seas to mine eyes, that I may quicklie weepe
> The shipwrecke of the world: or let soft sleepe
> (Binding my sences) lose my working soule,
> That in her highest pitch, she may controule
> The court of skill, compact of misterie,
> Wanting but franchisement and memorie
> To reach all secrets: then in blissfull trance,
> Raise her (deare Night) to that perseverance,
> That in my torture, she all earths may sing, ...[5]

It is Chapman's 'working soule', loosed by soft sleep, that is to sing earth's tortures. Hence his tongue, singing forth his poem, is the voice of his soul, a sufficient identification for Shakespeare's purpose of the poet referred to. The voice of Chapman's austere soul is contrasted in Shakespeare's preceding line with 'the thought of hearts', that is to say, of warm sympathetic friends, such as Shakespeare himself.

Chapman's first 'hymn' is concerned with urging men of good wit to shun the gross temptations of the day and dedicate themselves to night. The second, con-

---

★ In the first Quarto edition (Q) and Willen and Reed's edition: end, Their and solye.

taining the passage which, according to Shakespeare, churlishly casts aspersions on Southampton, consists of a poem in praise of Cynthia ('Hymnus in Cynthiam') representing the moon, goddess of the night, and also representing Elizabeth, the Virgin Queen. Cynthia, in order to take the pleasures of the day, decides to institute a hunt. She creates out of a meteor a nymph called Euthimya (meaning gaiety), to be the quarry. She also creates hunters and hounds. They start off from Ortygia, or Delos, the birthplace of Diana. Euthimya has the power of changing her shape, and turns into a panther, which was supposed in legend to have a very sweet breath with which it enticed its prey. The hunt arrives at

> a fruitful Iland sited by,   *HC.* 366–7
> Full of all wealth, delight and Emperie, ...

which seems to be England. Euthimya changes from a panther into a boar, and leads the chase through mansions, gardens and groves. At the end of the day the goddess 'blew retraite', and all was dispersed; then she

> mounts into her Sphere,   *HC.* 398–9
> And leaves us miserable creatures here.

The poet then implores her to come back and build her Ephesian temple here, with its 'virgine-chamber' tended by chaste 'Elisian Ladies'. There seems to be a direct reference to Queen Elizabeth's ladies-in-waiting, whose chastity was always in danger of seduction by rakish courtiers, to the scandal and fury of the Queen, which was increased rather than decreased by the subsequent marriage of the offending parties: Thomas Shirley and Frances Vavasour in 1591, Raleigh and Elizabeth Throckmorton in 1592, and subsequently Tyrwhitt and Lady Bridget Manners in the summer of 1594 and the Earl of Southampton and Elizabeth Vernon in 1598—all incurred the Queen's severe displeasure and were successively clapped in jail, but they never seemed to learn.

Chapman's stern message is that what is important, both for ladies of the 'virgine-chamber' and for handsome young gentlemen ('sweet Ganemedes') is not beauty of the body but beauty of the mind. In the case of the ladies they may keep their outward adornments, but the jewels set on their foreheads should reflect the virtues of their minds. In the case of the young gentlemen, they should realize that the Ganymede whom Jupiter, disguised as an eagle, snatched up to heaven to be his cup-bearer was a personification of the mind, and it was beauty of the mind, not the 'bodies pride', that attracted Jupiter and caused him to set Ganymede in the stars as the constellation Aquarius. (Chapman does not explain why, in that case, Juno should have been so annoyed about it!)

> And that minde most is bewtifull and hye,   *HC.* 467–71
> And nearest comes to a Divinitie,
> That furthest is from spot of earths delight,
> Pleasures that lose their substance with their sight,
> Such one, Saturnius ravisheth to love,
> And fills the cup of all content to Jove.

If those sweet Ganymedes shall only find, he goes on, that wisdom is the mind's true beauty, and that such beauty shines in virtuous men . . . and then there is a tantalizing hiatus; at least one line, if not three or more, has been left out, as is shown by the rhyme:

> If wisdome be the mindes true bewtie then,   HC. 472–6
> And that such bewtie shines in vertuous men,
> If those sweet Ganemedes shall onely finde,
>
> *   *   *   *
>
> Love of Olimpius, are those wizerds wise,
> That nought but gold, and his dyjections prise?

Shakespeare tells us that it is Southampton that Chapman is lecturing here:

> But those same toungs that give thee so thine owne,   69.6

(i.e., ascribe to you the beauty of Ganymede),

> In other accents doe this praise confound   69.7–10
> By seeing farther than the eye hath showne
> They look into the *beauty of thy mind.**
> And that in guesse they measure by thy deeds,

It is tempting to think with Acheson that the hiatus in Chapman's poem was caused by a deliberate cut of a passage more directly offensive to Southampton; whether or not this is so, sufficient is left for us to understand what Shakespeare was referring to. Chapman rubs home what kind of behaviour he is inveighing against by returning again after the Ganymede passage to the ladies of the virgin-chamber:

> Thy virgin chamber then that sacred is   HC. 509–14
> No more let hold, an idle Salmacis,
> Nor let more sleights, Cydippe injurie:
> Nor let black Jove possest in Scicilie,
> Ravish more maids, but maids subdue his might,
> With well-steeld lances of thy watchfull sight.

Let us have no more ladies-in-waiting, he says, that ensnare handsome young men, as the nymph Salmacis trapped Hermaphroditus, and no more who are themselves trapped by young men, as Cydippe was deceived into marrying Acontius; and let the ladies take care not to be carried off by force, as Pluto (black Jove) ravished Proserpine.

In the next sonnet Shakespeare goes on to say that Southampton need not be upset by these criticisms:

> That thou art blam'd shall not be thy defect,   70.1–2
> For slanders marke was ever yet the faire, . . .

* My italics.

One is inclined to think that he is at pains to rub in, in case Southampton has not paid sufficient attention to it, the fact that Chapman has had the temerity to lecture him. But there is a sincere point to be made as well; up to this time Southampton had not incurred the wrath of Queen Elizabeth, whereas her current favourite, the Earl of Essex, had many times exasperated her and was in danger of losing his privileged position. The following year Sir Henry Wotton was to write that Sir Fulke Greville, seeing in the Queen 'some weariness or perhaps some wariness' towards Essex, 'almost superinduced into favour the Earl of Southampton.[6] There was clearly a good opportunity for Southampton to establish himself, perhaps even with the support of his friend Essex, as the Queen's chief favourite. The important thing was, not that his conduct should be exemplary, but that he should not be caught out by the Queen in anything that she disapproved of. There were always tale-bearers anxious to slander any-one who was so much in the public eye:

> So thou be good, slander doth but approve,   70.5–14
> Thy worth the greater being woo'd of time,
> For Canker vice the sweetest buds doth love,
> And thou present'st a pure unstayned prime.
> Thou has past by the ambush of young daies,
> Either not assayld, or victor beeing charg'd,
> Yet this thy praise cannot be soe thy praise,
> To tye up envy, evermore inlarged,
>> If some suspect of ill maskt not thy show,
>> Then thou alone kingdomes of hearts shouldst owe.

Seymour-Smith describes the closing couplet of this sonnet as 'a curiously weak and obscure ending'.[7] But the message is really a direct and powerful one: 'if the Queen could be sure that your character matched your appearance, you alone could have her favour to yourself and so rule over all hearts'. The key to the meaning is in the word 'kingdomes'.

But it does not seem that Southampton took any notice of Shakespeare's advice, and he was probably not particularly upset about Chapman's aspersions either. In fact, after having had to put up with so many comments on his reluctance to have anything to do with women up to the previous year, he may well have felt flattered now, at the age of twenty, to be earning the reputation of a lady-killer. The Queen's prudish ideas no doubt carried less weight than the plaudits of his contemporaries.

At any rate, in the next four sonnets Shakespeare desists from proffering advice and dilates on his own worthlessness and inadequacy as a poet. There is nothing of any value in his life except the spirit embodied in his verses which is consecrated to Southampton.

But the 'thought of hearts' made no more impression on Southampton than the 'voice of soules'. Shakespeare's next four sonnets are humble bids for affection, cast in tones of deepest gloom. Indeed the despondent atmosphere seems to catch the note of Chapman's 'Hymnus in Noctem'. Says Chapman:

> There will I furnish up my funerall bed,   *HN.* 276–9
> Strewd with the bones and relickes of the dead.
> Atlas shall let th'Olympick burthen fall,
> To cover my untombed face withall.

If the poetry of melancholy is the order of the day, Shakespeare will try his hand at it too:

> Noe longer mourne for me when I am dead,   71.1–4
> Than you shall heare the surly sullen bell
> Give warning to the world that I am fled
> From this vile world with vildest wormes to dwell: . . .

But whereas Chapman arrogantly maintains the virtues of his unappreciated work and the stupidity of those who are blind to them, Shakespeare adopts a contrasting line of extravagant humility:

> My name be buried where my body is,   72.11–14
> And live no more to shame nor me, nor you.
> For I am shamd by that which I bring forth,
> And so should you, to love things nothing worth.

Chapman's advice is quite different:

> Ye living spirits then, if any live,   *HN.* 288–9
> Whom like extreames, do like affections give, . . .

> Thunder your wrongs, your miseries and hells,   *HN.* 306–14
> And with the dismall accents of your knells,
> Revive the dead, and make the living dye
> In truth and terror of your torturie:
> Still all the powre of Art into your grones,
> Scorning your triviall and remissive mones,
> Compact of fiction, and hyperboles,
> (Like wanton mourners, cloyd with too much ease)
> Should leave the glasses of the hearers eyes
> Unbroken, counting all but vanities.

'Triviall and remissive mones, compact of fiction and hyperboles.' That is certainly how Chapman would have described Sonnets 71–74. Perhaps he had in fact seen these very ones before the final version of *The Shadow of Night* was printed.

> In me thou seest the glowing of such fire,   73.9–14
> That on the ashes of his youth doth lye,
> As the death bed, whereon it must expire,
> Consum'd with that which it was nurrisht by.

> This thou percev'st, which makes thy love more strong,
> To love that well, which thou must leave ere long.

Since Shakespeare had still not completed his thirtieth year, this description of him certainly qualifies to be called a 'hyperbole'.

The whole of Sonnet 73 derives inspiration from the 15th book of Ovid's *Metamorphoses*, lines 199–213. Here are lines 221–35 of Golding's translation:[8]

> What? Seest thou not how that the yeere as representing playne
> The age of man, departes itself in quarters fowre? First bayne
> And tender in the spring it is, even like a sucking babe.
> Then greene, and voyd of strength, and lush, and foggye, is the blade,
> And cheeres the husbandman with hope. Then all things florish gay.
> The earth with flowres of sundry hew then seemeth for to play,
> And vertue small or none to herbes there dooth as yit belong.
> The yeere from springtyde passing foorth to sommer, wexeth strong,
> Becommeth lyke a lusty youth. For in our lyfe through out
> There is no tyme more plentifull, more lusty, hote and stout.
> Then followeth Harvest when the heate of youth growes sumwhat cold,
> Rype, meeld, disposed meane betwixt a yoongman and an old,
> And sumwhat sprent with grayish heare. Then ugly winter last
> Like age steales on with trembling steppes, all bald, or overcast
> With shirle thinne heare as whyght as snowe.

Notice that Shakespeare does not adopt exactly any of the seasons described by Ovid. He places himself somewhere between 'Harvest' and 'Winter':

> That time of yeeare thou maist in me behold,   73.1–4
> When yellow leaves, or none, or few doe hange
> Upon those boughes which shake against the could,
> Bare ruin'd quiers, where late the sweet birds sang.

It is interesting also to see that in this passage Shakespeare is not merely relying on Golding's translation. The line:

> When yellow leaves, or none, or few doe hange

seems to be derived directly from Ovid's line 213:

> *aut spoliata suos, aut, quos habet, alba capillos.*

The fact that in the Latin it is winter's hair that is referred to, shows us that Shakespeare is referring to his own hair when he speaks of 'yellow leaves'. Because of his balding head, Shakespeare seems to feel that he cannot claim merely to be

> Rype, meeld, disposed meane betwixt a yoongman and an old,
> And sumwhat sprent with grayish heare.

yet he has not reached full winter. He thus gives himself a place at the very end of autumn when almost all the leaves have fallen and the branches of the trees stand out starkly like the ruined vaulting of a despoiled church. Perhaps he had seen the ruined choir of the Abbey Church at Beaulieu, which had been destroyed by the First Earl, our Southampton's grandfather, when he purchased the property after the dissolution of the monastery in 1538.

The next four lines of the sonnet are suggested by lines 186–90 of the same book of Ovid, which Golding (lines 206–10) translates as follows:

> Wee see that after day commes nyght and darks the sky
> And after nyght the lyghtsum Sunne succeedeth orderly.
> Like colour is not in the heaven when all things weery lye
> At midnyght sound asleepe, as when the daystarre cleere and bryght
> Commes foorth uppon his milkwhyght steed.

Shakespeare, however, gives more space to night and speaks of it in a more complimentary way than usual. Could this be in recognition of the impression made by Chapman's poem?—

> In me thou seest the twi-light of such day,   73.5–8
> As after Sun-set fadeth in the West,
> Which by and by blacke night doth take away,
> Deaths second selfe that seals up all in rest.

Sonnet 74 continues the same dismal theme, but makes the point that after Shakespeare's death Southampton will still have left 'the better part' of him, namely his verses, the foundation of which is the inspiration of Southampton himself:

> My spirit is thine the better part of me,   74.8–14
> So then thou hast but lost the dregs of life,
> The pray of wormes, my body being dead,
> The coward conquest of a wretches knife,
> To base of thee to be remembred,
>   The worth of that, is that which it containes,
>   And that is this, and this with thee remaines.

The mention of 'The coward conquest of a wretches knife' is interesting. Primarily the reference must be to Sonnet 63:

> For such a time do I now fortifie   63.9–12
> Against confounding Ages cruell knife,
> That he shall never cut from memory
> My sweet loves beauty, though my lovers life.

but it is difficult to imagine that there is not an intentional reminiscence of the 'wretches knife' which put an end to Christopher Marlowe the previous year.

CHAPTER IX

'A Better Spirit Doth Use
Your Name'

WE have seen in the last chapter the impact made upon Shakespeare's relations with Southampton by the appearance of Chapman's two hymns, together entitled *The Shadow of Night*. The Sonnets from 75 to 96 are directly concerned with the sad rift which now developed between the poet and his patron.

Sonnet 75 is a conventional description of Shakespeare's yearning for his friend, uncoloured by any particular topical circumstances. Because of this some critics have thought that it is out of place; it is little more than a reworking of the theme of Sonnet 52, and indeed the resemblance is emphasized by the construction of the first lines of the two sonnets:

> So am I as the rich whose blessed key,   52.1

and Sonnet 75:

> So are you to my thoughts as food to life, . . .   75.1

The suggestion therefore has been that the two sonnets were written together as a pair. But Sonnet 76 tells us that there is nothing wrong with the order. The resemblance gives the occasion for some rhetorical questions about the sameness of Shakespeare's writing, which he proceeds to answer:

> Why is my verse so barren of new pride?   76
> So far from variation or quicke change?
> Why with the time do I not glance aside
> To new found methods, and to compounds strange?
> Why write I still all one, ever the same,
> And keepe invention in a noted weed,
> That every word doth almost tell* my name,
> Shewing their birth, and where they did proceed?
> O know sweet love I alwaies write of you,
> And you and love are still my argument:
> So all my best is dressing old words new,
> Spending againe what is already spent:
>   For as the Sun is daily new and old,
>   So is my love still telling what is told.

> * In Q and Willen and Reed: fel

It is amply clear that Shakespeare's patron has shown interest in the style of a new poet and that Shakespeare feels it necessary to explain why his own style appears to be stereotyped. From Sonnet 77, it seems that he has offered Southampton a present of a blank notebook with a mirror and a sundial on the covers. No stone must be left unturned to keep his name in Southampton's mind.

The next sonnet is of particular interest because it is made the subject of a riposte in the dedication to the Earl of Southampton by Thomas Nashe of his picaresque novel *The Unfortunate Traveller or The Life of Jack Wilton*. This work was entered in the Stationers' Register on 17th September, 1593, but was not published, as we can see from the date on the title page, until 1594 (i.e., as I have pointed out before, not before 25th March, 1594, the date on which the new year began under the Old Style calendar). In the meantime, no doubt, the manuscript or proof copy had been submitted to possible patrons.

Shakespeare now clearly recognizes that Southampton is giving assistance to one or more rivals:

> So oft have I invok'd thee for my Muse,   78
> And found such faire assistance in my verse,
> As every *Alien* pen hath got my use,
> And under thee their poesie disperse.
> Thine eyes, that taught the dumbe on high to sing,
> And heavie ignorance aloft to flie,
> Have added fethers to the learneds wing,
> And given grace a double Majestie.
> Yet be most proud of that which I compile,
> Whose influence is thine, and borne of thee,
> In others workes thou doost but mend the stile,
> And Arts with thy sweete graces graced be.
>   But thou art all my art, and doost advance
>   As high as learning, my rude ignorance.

In Thomas Nashe's dedication we find the following passage:

> Unrepriveably perisheth that book whatsoever to wast paper which on the diamond rock of your judgement, disasterly chanceth to be shipwrackt. A dere lover and cherisher you are, as well of the lovers of Poets, as of Poets themselves. Amongst their sacred number, I dare not ascribe my selfe, though now and then I speak English: that smal braine I have to no further use I convert, save to be kinde to my frends and fatall to my enemies. A new brain, a new wit, a new stile, a new soule will I get mee, to canonize your name to posteritie, if in this, my first attempt I be not taxed of presumption. Of your gracious favor I despaire not, for I am not altogether Fame's out-cast.[1]

Nashe does not dare to number himself among the poets whom Southampton cherishes though, as he says, 'now and then I speak English'. There is no apparent explanation for this remark until we look at Shakespeare's Sonnet 78:

> As every *Alien* pen hath got my use,   78.3–4
> And under thee their poesie disperse.

Nashe is saying that although he is not one of those poets who are 'dispersing' their poesy under Southampton, nevertheless there is no reason to call his an '*alien* pen'. Notice also that in the first sentence of the passage quoted above, Thomas Nashe uses a metaphor of shipwreck which recalls the following lines of Sonnet 80:

> Your shallowest helpe will hold me up a floate,   80.9–12
> Whilst he upon your soundlesse deepe doth ride,
> Or (being wrackt) I am a worthlesse bote,
> He of tall building, and of goodly pride.

If Nashe had seen Sonnet 78, he probably saw this one also. In both cases the shipwreck is envisaged as a consequence of Southampton's unfavourable judgment of the writer's work.

Knowing Thomas Nashe's satirical wit, it seems not unlikely that there is also a hit at Shakespeare in the sentence in which he describes Southampton as a dear lover and cherisher 'as well of the lovers of Poets, as of Poets themselves.' Ostensibly this means that Southampton cherishes those who love and appreciate poetry, but can it not also imply that the young Earl is paying his attentions to a poet's mistress?

This dedication does not appear in any edition of Thomas Nashe's book except the first. It may be therefore, as Mrs Stopes has suggested,[2] that either Shakespeare or Southampton took exception to it and that the Earl consequently insisted on its removal.

Before we leave Sonnet 78 we should glance at the lines:

> Thine eyes, that taught the dumbe on high to sing,   78.5–8
> And heavie ignorance aloft to flie,
> Have added fethers to the learneds wing,
> And given grace a double Majestie.

'The dumbe', as the final couplet of the sonnet makes clear, is Shakespeare himself, as is also 'heavie ignorance'. The 'learneds wing' represents another poet to whom Southampton has given inspiration. The contrast between ignorance and learning is one that is constantly being made by Chapman; it forms, for instance, the theme of his dedication of *The Shadow of Night*. The last line of the quatrain is a little puzzling, however. What is the significance of 'Majestie'? It might be thought that there is a reference to Southampton's two degrees of Master of Arts, at Cambridge and Oxford, because 'grace' is a term used for the decree authorizing the conferring of a degree.[3] But 'Majestie' is still not right. Why should Southampton's two eyes confer majesty?

The usual abbreviation for 'majestie' in Shakespeare's time was 'mãtie'. The word can be seen in several places in that part of the manuscript of the play *Sir Thomas More* which is believed by many scholars to be in Shakespeare's own hand. (Sometimes the contraction mark is omitted so that the word appears as 'matie'.) But it seems more likely to me that Shakespeare wrote, not Mãtie, but Mãtrie‹ in Sonnet 78, and that the word was misread by the compositor. The line should thus read:

> And given grace a double Magistrie.

We would then have a clear reference to the double degree of *Magister Artium*, which is reinforced by line 12, with its capital A to match the capital M of line 8:

> And Arts with thy sweete graces graced be.   78.12

But there is more to it than this: 'magistery' also meant, in alchemy, a transmuting agent, such as the philosopher's stone which was supposed to be able to turn dross into gold. Now let us look at the last six lines:

> Yet be most proud of that which I compile,   78.7–14
> Whose influence is thine, and borne of thee,
> In others workes thou doost but mend the stile,
> And Arts with thy sweete graces graced be.
>   But thou art all my art, and doost advance
>   As high as learning, my rude ignorance.

'Influence' is another occult word, meaning in astrology the etherial fluid which flowed from the stars and acted upon men:

> Whereon the Stars in secret influence comment.   15.4

In line 13 'thou art all my art' now becomes a reference to *ars magica*, as when Glendower in *Henry the Fourth*, Part I, says:

> And bring him out that is but woman's son   I *H.IV.*
> Can trace me in the tedious ways of art   iii.1.47–9
> And hold me pace in deep experiments.

Thus we are to understand that Southampton's eyes provide him with a double transmuting power, which can both make the dumb sing and add feathers to the learned's wing. But we must not forget that these eyes are also stars:

> But from thine eies my knowledge I derive,   14.9–10
> And constant stars in them I read such art . . .

So they are a source of astrological inspiration and knowledge. While Chapman (Doctor-like) controls the Court of Skill, compact of mistery, and at the same time collects extra assistance from the scholarly Southampton, Shakespeare's mystic art is dependent entirely on Southampton, whose eyes are his magisteries and sources of occult influence. This is the whole theme of the sonnet, but it is made immensely more powerful by the introduction of the word magistery or *magisterium*, meaning all at once the state of being a *Magister Artium*, the office of or capacity for being a teacher, and the philosopher's stone,[4] all three of which are attributes of Shakespeare's patron.

In the next eight sonnets, Shakespeare makes it clear that the competition which is worrying him is coming from a single poet:

> Whilst I alone did call upon thy ayde,   79.1-4
> My verse alone had all thy gentle grace,
> But now my gracious numbers are decayde,
> And my sick Muse doth give an other place.

It appears that this poet has addressed some direct flattery to Southampton:

> I grant (sweet love) thy lovely argument   79.5-8
> Deserves the travaile of a worthier pen,
> Yet what of thee thy Poet doth invent,
> He robs thee of, and payes it thee againe,

and Sonnet 80:

> O how I faint when I of you do write,   80.1-4
> Knowing a better spirit doth use your name,
> And in the praise thereof spends all his might,
> To make me toung-tide speaking of your fame.

It is this which has caused uncertainty as to the identity of the poet referred to. There is nothing in Chapman's *The Shadow of Night*, as published, to justify Shakespeare's comments, nor have we any other offerings from other poets to Southampton which can be described as more fulsome in their praise than Shakespeare's own. However, Sonnet 82 tells us that this flattery was not contained in the body of the poem but in a dedication:

> I grant thou wert not married to my Muse,   82
> And therefore maiest without attaint ore-looke
> The dedicated words which writers use
> Of their faire subject, blessing every booke,
> Thou art as faire in knowledge as in hew,
> Finding thy worth a limmit past my praise,
> And therefore art inforc'd to seeke anew,
> Some fresher stampe of the time bettering dayes.
> And do so love, yet when they have devisde,
> What strained touches Rhethorick can lend,
> Thou truly faire, wert truly simpathizde,
> In true plaine words, by thy true telling friend.

F

> And their grosse painting might be better us'd,
> Where cheekes need blood, in thee it is abus'd.

The line:

> What strained touches Rhethorick can lend

reminds us immediately of the kind of language Chapman uses in his dedications; but none of these is addressed to the Earl of Southampton. *The Shadow of Night* is in fact, dedicated, as we have seen, to Matthew Roydon, another poet and a member of Raleigh's philosophical discussion group. From the embittered tone of this dedication it appears only too likely that Chapman had hoped to dedicate it to someone else, but had had his hopes dashed:

> How then may a man stay his marvailing to see passion-driven men,
> reading but to curtoll a tedious houre, and altogether hidebownd with affec-
> tion to great mens fancies, take upon them as killing censures as if they were
> judgements Butchers, or as if the life of truth lay tottering in their verdits.

It seems likely that in the end Shakespeare prevailed and Southampton did not give his patronage to Chapman. This is perhaps what is referred to in lines 296-9 of the 'Hymnus in Noctem':

> But you that ne'er had birth, nor ever prov'd,
> How deare a blessing tis to be belov'd,
> Whose friends idolatrous desire of gold,
> To scorne, and ruine have your freedome sold: . . .

In this case it would be Shakespeare's 'idolatrous desire of gold' which Chapman says has brought him to scorn and ruin. However, if this is so, Shakespeare does not seem to have achieved success in cutting out his rival at least until after he had written Sonnet 90, if not later still.

In Sonnets 83 and 84, Shakespeare finds it necessary to explain why he does not accompany his offerings to Southampton with fulsome letters of dedication. As we have seen earlier, the dedication accompanying *Venus and Adonis* was extremely restrained in character. However, Shakespeare gave some explanation of this in Sonnets 36 and 39. He now sees that other writers who had not exercised any such restraint appear to be finding favour with Southampton. Sonnet 84 is interesting also in that it is inspired by a punning sonnet addressed by Sir Philip Sidney to Lady Rich:

> What may words say, or what may words not say;   S. XXXV
>   Where truth itself must speak like flattery?
>   Within what bounds, can one his liking stay;
>   Where Nature doth with infinite agree?
>   What NESTOR'S counsel can my flames allay,
>   Since REASON'S self doth blow the coal in me?
> And ah! what hope that hope should once see day,
>   Where CUPID is sworn page to CHASTITY?

> HONOUR is honoured, that thou dost possess
> Him as thy slave; and now long needy FAME
> Doth even grow rich, naming my STELLA's name.
> Wit learns in thee perfection to express;
> Not thou by praise, but PRAISE in thee is raised.
> It is a praise to praise, where thou art praised.[5]

In Sonnet 84 Shakespeare gracefully acknowledges his debt to Sidney with a similar pun:

> Who is it that sayes most, which can say more,   84.1–4
> Then this rich praise, that you alone, are you,
> In whose confine immured is the store,
> Which should example where your equall grew, . . .

To say that 'you alone are you' is 'rich praise' not only because it is in itself flattery, but also because it is praise that has been addressed to Lady Rich by another poet.

Sonnet 84 goes on:

> Leane penurie within that Pen doth dwell,   84.5–14
> That to his subject lends not some small glory,
> But he that writes of you, if he can tell,
> That you are you, so dignifies his story.
> Let him but coppy what in you is writ,
> Not making worse what nature made so cleere,
> And such a counter-part shall fame his wit,
> Making his stile admired every where.
> You to your beautious blessings adde a curse,
> Being fond on praise, which makes your praises worse.

The word 'worse' at the end of the last line picks up that in line 10:

> Not making worse what nature made so cleere,

so the 'curse' which is added to Southampton's 'beautious blessings' is that the praise which he receives cannot measure up to the excellence of what is being praised. The couplet is often read as if it means that Southampton's fondness for praise causes him to receive base sycophantic flattery. While this was no doubt true, if Shakespeare intended this implication at all, it is likely that it was as a satirical secondary meaning to an apparent compliment.

In Sonnet 85 there is a further direct reference to Chapman:

> I thinke good thoughts, whilst other write good wordes,   85.5–8
> And like unlettered clarke still crie Amen,
> To every Himne that able spirit affords,
> In polisht forme of well refined pen.

The 'Hymnus in Noctem' and the 'Hymnus in Cynthiam' which together make up *The Shadow of Night* are plainly referred to here. Shakespeare ironically likens himself to an illiterate assistant at a church service who can do no more than utter the Amens to such erudite works.

The great Sonnet 86 sums up Shakespeare's discontent over Southampton's apparent intention to favour Chapman:

> Was it the proud full saile of his great verse,   86
> Bound for the prize of (all-to-precious) you,
> That did my ripe thoughts in my braine inhearce,
> Making their tombe the wombe wherein they grew?
> Was it his spirit, by spirits taught to write,
> Above a mortall pitch, that struck me dead?
> No, neither he, nor his compiers by night
> Giving him ayde, my verse astonished.
> He nor that affable familiar ghost
> Which nightly gulls him with intelligence,
> As victors of my silence cannot boast,
> I was not sick of any feare from thence.
>   But when your countinance fild up his line,
>   Then lackt I matter, that infeebled mine.

In considering this sonnet, we must look back to these two lines of Sonnet 66:

> And Folly (Doctor-like) countrouling skill,   66.10–11
> And simple-Truth miscalde Simplicitie, . . .

We have already glanced at the second of these lines in Chapter VII, and seen how Shakespeare expanded his case in Sonnet 82. The first line of the pair takes us back to the beginning of the 'Hymnus in Noctem', which we have already looked at in connection with Sonnet 69:

> or let soft sleepe   *HN.* 10–13
> (Binding my sences) lose my working soule,
> That in her highest pitch, she may controule
> The court of skill . . .

Chapman's 'working soule' controlling the 'court of skill' is written off by Shakespeare as 'Folly (Doctor-like) controuling skill'. 'Doctor-like' seems to be a reference to Dr Faustus, who vainly obtained control of supernatural powers in exchange for his soul. Christopher Marlowe's famous play on this subject was presented for the first time the following October and may, perhaps, already have been in rehearsal when the theatres were closed by the plague. In any case, the story on which the play was based had also been published in 1592 as a chap-book and was widely known.[6]

Chapman's description of how he goes into some kind of trance and obtains release, in return for drops of his soul, of all the secrets which are necessary for his poetry, is indeed reminiscent of *Dr Faustus*. It has been strongly suggested that Chapman was the poet of Raleigh's school of atheism, which, as we have seen, was thought to carry on all kinds of supernatural investigations and activities. Chapman's phrase 'the court of skill' has in fact been identified by M. C. Bradbrook[7] with the 'school of night' referred to in Shakespeare's play *Love's Labour's Lost*. I do not propose to go into this question except to suggest that the third quatrain of Sonnet 66 may perhaps be a pointer to such a link between the metaphysical activities of Raleigh and Chapman. Shakespeare's antipathy to Chapman's poetical methods may thus be accentuated by his fear of the consequences of Southampton's coming into contact with the infection of impiety, as described in the first quatrain of Sonnet 67.

Lines 10–17 of 'Hymnus in Noctem'* are in themselves sufficient explanation of what Shakespeare has in mind in Sonnet 86; but Chapman enlarges further on the subject in lines 370–7:

> All you possess with indepressed spirits,
> Indu'd with nimble, and aspiring wits,
> Come consecrate with me, to sacred Night
> Your whole endevours, and detest the light.
> Sweete Peaces richest crowne is made of starres,
> Most certaine guides of honord Marinars,
> No pen can any thing eternall wright,
> That is not steept in humor of the Night.

and also in a passage of the dedication to *The Shadow of Night*:

> Now what a supererogation in wit this is, to thinke skill so mightilie pierst with their loves, that she should prostitutely shew them her secrets, when she will scarcely be lookt upon by others but with invocation, fasting, watching; yea not without having drops of their soules like an heavenly familiar.

In the light of these passages it is scarcely necessary, as some have done, to take into account Chapman's further claim to have been inspired by the spirit of Homer, which he did not make any public mention of until 1609, since there is no evidence that Shakespeare had heard of it in 1594.

There is no reason to suppose that Shakespeare's phrase 'his compiers by night' refers to any human collaborators such as those who might have made up the postulated 'school of night'; 'compiers' are the supernatural assistants to Chapman's 'working soule'. The 'affable familiar ghost' is, as Chapman tells us in the above-quoted lines of his dedication, 'Skill' who shows him secrets in return for drops of his soul, and it is 'Skill's court' that Chapman, with the help of Sleep and Night, is able to control.

There have been differences of opinion amongst critics as to whether Shakespeare is sincere in speaking about the 'proud full saile' of Chapman's 'great

* Quoted on p. 70.

verse' in the first line of Sonnet 86. That the apparent compliment is not sincere is shown clearly enough by line 10 of Sonnet 66, once the connection has been grasped:

> And Folly (Doctor-like) controuling skill, . . .

Shakespeare is saying in Sonnet 86 that he has no fears of the merits of Chapman's poetry, but only of the effect of Southampton's sponsorship of it:

> But when your countinance fild up his line,   86.13–14
> Then lackt I matter, that infeebled mine.

We see in Sonnet 87 that the affair has now assumed crisis proportions; not only does Southampton prefer the poetry of Chapman, but he apparently thinks that Shakespeare's is no longer worth supporting. At any rate, that is how Shakespeare chooses to interpret the situation.[8]

CHAPTER X

'Farewell Thou Art Too Deare
For My Possessing'

ALTHOUGH I have chosen to end my chapter about Shakespeare's rivalry with
Chapman with Sonnet 86, because it sums up the reasons for the final crisis, the
break in sense is really at the end of 85. Between Sonnet 76 and 85 Shakespeare
is putting the case for his own style of poetry and endeavouring to show that
Chapman's is pretentious and obscure and his flattering dedication strained and
insincere. With 86 all attempt to fight the battle further is dropped. From 86–90
the tone is one of weary resignation. Shakespeare admits and even insists that
he has no claim on Southampton's good will. He heaps coals of fire on his
patron's head:

> When thou shalt be dispode to set me light,　　　　　88.1–8
> And place my merrit in the eie of skorne,
> Upon thy side, against my selfe ile right,
> And prove thee virtuous, tho thou art forsworne:
> With mine owne weaknesse being best acquainted,
> Upon thy part I can set downe a story
> Of faults conceald, wherein I am attainted:
> That thou in losing me, shall win much glory: . . .

Sonnet 90 looks back to line 9 of 66:

> And arte made tung-tide by authoritie,

with its invitation to hit him when he is down:

> Then hate me when thou wilt, if ever, now,　　　　　90.1–4
> Now while the world is bent my deeds to crosse,
> Joyne with the spight of fortune, make me bow,
> And doe not drop in for an after losse:

but this tone of savage despair soon softens. In Sonnets 91–96 Shakespeare
admits that he cannot face the thought that he may really have lost Southampton's love. Sonnets 91 and 92 return to the theme of Sonnet 37:

> Thy love is better   then high birth to me,　　　　　91.9–10
> Richer than wealth, prouder then garments cost, . . .

　　　　　* In Q and Willen and Reed: bitter.

These lines recall the quatrain:

> For whether beauty, birth or wealth, or wit, 37.5–8
> Or any of these all, or all, or more
> Intitled in their parts, do crowned sit,
> I make my love ingrafted to this store:

and in doing so recall the anagram concealed in that sonnet, which Shakespeare now refers to in Sonnet 92:

> Thou canst not vex me with inconstant minde, 92.9–12
> Since that my life on thy revolt doth lie,
> Oh what a happy title do I finde,
> Happy to have thy love, happy to die!

It will be remembered that the 'happy title' was:

> *Thy worth and truth, Rose, are my life's onlie hope.*

Whether or not Southampton has really deserted him, Shakespeare proposes to go on believing in his worth and truth:

> So shall I live, supposing thou art true, 93.1–4
> Like a deceived husband, so loves face,
> May still seeme love to me, though alter'd new:
> Thy lookes with me, thy heart in other place.

The four Sonnets 93–96 are the last to be written before the substantial gap in the relations of Shakespeare and Southampton about which we are told in Sonnets 97 and 98. Shakespeare takes the opportunity in these four Sonnets to read Southampton a lecture about his character and behaviour, which is of great interest both because it paints such a clear picture of the young man at this time, and also because it is clothed in very striking verse. It is interesting in another way also, in that it provides a plain link with the poem *A Lover's Complaint*, which was published in 1609 in the same volume as the first edition of the Sonnets. The young man portrayed in *A Lover's Complaint* so closely resembles the person described in Sonnets 93–96, that one cannot help feeling certain that the *Complaint* was written almost at the same time as these sonnets; perhaps very soon after them.

Sonnets 93 and 94 describe a person with a deceptively sweet face who nevertheless is inwardly cold and unmoved by those who are attracted to him:

> But heaven in thy creation did decree 93.9–14
> That in thy face sweet love should ever dwell,
> What ere thy thoughts, or thy hearts workings be,
> Thy lookes should nothing thence, but sweetnesse tell.
> How like Eaves apple doth thy beauty grow,
> If thy sweet vertue answere not thy show.

> They that have powre to hurt, and will doe none,   94.1–4
> That doe not do the thing, they most do showe,
> Who moving others, are themselves as stone,
> Unmooved, could, and to temptation slow: . . .

The young man is a person who hurts others without having any intention of doing so, because he does not act in the loving way which the appearance of his face seems to promise. 'The thing they most do showe' is the 'sweet love' which heaven has decreed should always dwell in the young man's face, whatever he might feel in his heart. In the *Complaint* the young man is made to tell us the same thing:

> 'Among the many that mine eyes have seen,   *LC.* 190–6
> Not one whose flame my heart so much as warmed,
> Or my affection put to th'smallest teen,
> Or any of my leisures ever charmed.
> Harm have I done to them, but ne'er was harmed;
> Kept hearts in liveries, but mine own was free,
> And reigned commanding in his monarchy.

People like him are 'the Lords and owners of their faces' of Sonnet 94; in other words, their hearts reign commanding in their monarchy, as line 196 of the *Complaint* says.

There is an even more striking link with *A Lover's Complaint* in the next two lines of Sonnet 94:

> The sommers flowre is to the sommer sweet,   94.9–10
> Though to it selfe, it onely live and die, . . .

The unhappy young lady of the *Complaint* says that she might have remained as unmarked by emotion as the young man of Sonnet 94:

> 'Father,' she says, 'though in me you behold   *LC.* 71–7
> The injury of many a blasting hour,
> Let it not tell your judgement I am old:
> Not age, but sorrow, over me hath power.
> I might as yet have been a spreading flower,
> Fresh to myself, if I had self-applied
> Love to myself, and to no love beside.

The words 'Fresh to myself' in line 76 of the *Complaint* recall the words 'Though to it selfe . . .' in line 10 of the sonnet. By using in the *Complaint* the image of the flower blossoming only for itself, Shakespeare seems to be making an intentional reference to Sonnet 94 in order to indicate the contrast between the cold young exquisite and the warm-hearted girl over whom he has trampled. She completes the metaphor in lines 146 and 147 of the *Complaint* when she tells us that she

> Threw my affections in his charmed power,   *LC.* 146–7
> Reserved the stalk and gave him all my flower.

It is remarkable that, in spite of the close and obvious connection between *A Lover's Complaint* and these sonnets, a number of critics should have doubted the authorship of the *Complaint*. For instance, M. M. Reese in his excellent book, *Shakespeare, His World and his Work* states: 'The theme and sentiments are Shakespearean but the imagery is not.'[1] But a great authority on Shakespeare imagery, Dr Caroline Spurgeon, tells us that[2]

> Shakespeare's tendency to have a similar group of ideas called up by some one single word or idea is a very marked feature of his thought and imagination.

In some cases the groups of ideas which recur together

> are so apparently unrelated that it is difficult to trace more than a thread of meaning in them. Such a group is the association of death, cannon, eyeball, eye-socket of skull (a hollow thing), tears, vault, mouth (sometimes teeth), womb, and back to death again. The association is so vivid that whenever Shakespeare speaks of death he seems immediately conscious of the hollows in the skull where the eyes have been:

> > And I will kiss thy [Death's] detestable bones
> > And put my *eyeballs* in thy *vaulty* brows,   *KJ*. III.iv.29

> cries Constance in *King John*. In the Dauphin's speech to Salisbury about war (i.e. *death*), the whole series is seen: Salisbury has been moved to *tears*, and the Dauphin says,

> > But this effusion of such manly drops,   V.ii.49
> > This shower, blown up [cannon?] by tempest of the soul,
> > Startles mine *eyes*, and makes me more amazed
> > Than I had seen the *vaulty* top of heaven
> > Figured quite o'er with burning meteors.

Dr Spurgeon goes on to quote many more examples from other plays. Now, if we look at *A Lover's Complaint* we shall find the whole of this syndrome of ideas in the first four stanzas; hollow womb, death, heaven's raging vault, eye-sockets, briny tears, shrieking mouth, staring eye-balls and the cannon's roar:

> From off a hill whose *concave womb* reworded   *LC*. 1-28
> A plaintful story from a sist'ring vale,
> My spirits to attend this double voice accorded,
> And down I laid to list the sad-tun'd tale;
> Ere long espied a fickle maid full pale,
> Tearing of papers, breaking rings a-twain,
> Storming her world with *sorrow's wind and rain*.

> Upon her head a plaited hive of straw,
> Which fortified her visage from the sun,
> Whereon the thought might think sometime it saw
> The *carcase* of a beauty *spent* and *done*.
> Time had not scythed all that youth begun,
> Nor youth all quit; but, spite of *heaven's fell rage*,
> Some beauty peeped through *lattice of sear'd age*.
>
> Oft did she heave her napkin to her *eyne*,
> Which on it had conceited characters,
> Laund'ring the silken figures in the *brine*
> That seasoned woe had pelleted in *tears*,
> And often reading what contents it bears;
> As often *shrieking* undistinguishe'd woe,
> In clamours of all size, both high and low.
>
> Sometimes her *levell'd eyes* their *carriage* ride,
> As they did *battery* to the spheres intend;
> Sometimes diverted their poor *balls* are tied
> To the orbed earth; sometimes they do extend
> Their view right on; anon their gazes lend
> To every place at once, and nowhere fix'd,
> The mind and sight distractedly commix'd.

Perhaps Dr Spurgeon's most striking image group is that of dogs fawning and licking up sweetmeats:

> The hearts   *A&C.* IV.xii.20
> That *spaniel'd* me at *heels*, to whom I gave
> Their wishes, do *discandy*, melt their *sweets*
> On blossoming Caesar.

This is one of half a dozen examples she quotes, showing that the same picture keeps on recurring in Shakespeare's mind when the subject of fawning flattery arises. Now there is no mention of dogs in *A Lover's Complaint*, but the picture of 'hearts that spaniel'd me at heels' is close to the surface in this stanza:

> 'That he did in the general bosom reign   *LC.* 127–33
> Of young, of old, and sexes both enchanted
> To dwell with him in thoughts, or to remain
> *In personal duty, following where he haunted.*
> Consents bewitch'd for him what he would say,
> Ask'd their own wills, and made their wills obey.

And, a few stanzas later:

> 'Nor gives it satisfaction to our blood   *LC.* 162–8
> That we must curb it upon others' proof,

To be forbod the *sweets* that seem so good
For fear of harms that preach in our behoof.
O *appetite*, from judgement stand aloof!
The one a palate hath that needs will *taste*,
Though Reason weep, and cry "It is thy last".

To quote Dr Spurgeon again,

> This curious group of images illustrates better, I think, than any other, Shakespeare's strong and individual tendency to return under similar emotional stimulus to a similar picture or group of associated ideas, and it is obvious at once that it forms an extraordinarily reliable test of authorship.

Although one may thus concede that in imagery as well as in theme and sentiment the *Complaint* is thoroughly Shakespearean, there remains the fact that it is not up to the standard of *Venus and Adonis* or *The Rape of Lucrece*. But of course that is one reason why Shakespeare did not attempt to publish it until it was printed with the Sonnets in 1609. The other reason is that, like the Sonnets, it deals with too personal a subject, and one which could readily be identified at the time.

In Chapter VIII we found Chapman telling us what had been going on amongst Queen Elizabeth's ladies-in-waiting. There were ladies who brazenly ensnared young men, and others who allowed themselves to be deceived and seduced. Shakespeare makes the lady in *A Lover's Complaint* tell us the same story:

> 'Yet did I not, as some my equals did,   LC. 148–51
> Demand of him, nor being desired yielded;
> Finding myself in honour so forbid,
> With safest distance I mine honour shielded. . . .

> 'For lo, his passion, but an art of craft,   LC. 295–301
> Even there resolved my reason into tears;
> There my white stole of chastity I daffed,
> Shook off my sober guards and civil fears;
> Appear to him as he to me appears,
> All melting, though our drops this diff'rence bore:
> His poisoned me, and mine did him restore.

Sonnet 95 refers to some writer who had written a description of Southampton's activities:

> That tongue that tells the story of thy daies,   95.5–8
> (Making lascivious comments on thy sport)
> Cannot dispraise, but in a kinde of praise,
> Naming thy name, blesses an ill report.

It may be that this refers to Chapman's remarks on the subject in the 'Hymnus in Cynthiam' which we have already looked at, particularly if the hiatus after line 474 of that poem was originally filled with some more 'lascivious comments' on the young Earl's behaviour. However that may be, it seems possible that, while writing Sonnet 95, Shakespeare conceived the notion of himself telling the story of Southampton's philandering activities in the form of a conventional 'complaint' poem, after the style of Daniel's *Complaint of Rosamund*. Whether or not he had the courage to send it to Southampton one can only guess. It bears the marks of a hurriedly composed poem which has not been fully revised; such banal lines as:

> In clamours of all size, both high and low   *LC.* 21

and such strange verbal forms as 'sawn' instead of seen in line 91, apparently used merely in order to make a rhyme, fall short of Shakespeare's usual standard. I would think that, having let off steam by writing the poem, he then put it away until it later turned up with the Sonnets in the edition of 1609.

There is little doubt that under the guise of expressing the feelings of the ruined maid, Shakespeare is also expressing his own:

> 'Thus merely with the garment of a Grace   *LC.* 316–22
> The naked and concealed fiend he covered,
> That th'unexperient gave the temper place,
> Which, like a cherubin, above them hovered.
> Who, young and simple, would not be so lovered?
> Ay me, I fell, and yet do question make
> What I should do again for such a sake.

Shakespeare, like the young lady of the *Complaint*, is also prepared to be exploited all over again.

Sonnet 96 is, if anything, even more closely related to *A Lover's Complaint* than the preceding sonnets in this series:

> Some say thy fault is youth, some wantonesse,   96.1–4
> Some say thy grace is youth and gentle sport,
> Both grace and faults are lov'd of more and lesse:
> Thou makst faults graces, that to thee resort:

> How many gazers mighst thou lead away,   96.11–12
> If thou wouldst use the strength of all thy state?

and this sonnet is particularly valuable because it contains some of those strikingly unusual images which we have learnt to recognize as indicating a topical reference:

> As on the finger of a throned Queene,   96.5–10
> The basest Jewell wil be well esteem'd:
> So are those errors that in thee are seene,
> To truths translated, and for true things deem'd.
> How many Lambs might the sterne Wolfe betray,
> If like a Lambe he could his lookes translate.

Clearly there is something behind this talk of jewels and wolves, and we do not have to search very far to discover what it is.

In Chapter VII we saw how Dr Lopez, the Queen's physician, was arrested at the insistence of the Earl of Essex on a charge of treason. On 28th February Lopez was put on trial, and in the evidence the following story came out.[3] In 1591 one Andrada, an emissary from King Philip's Secretary of State, had brought Dr Lopez a diamond and ruby ring, from amongst the 'old jewels from his Majesty's casket', which was ostensibly a present for his daughter. In fact it was almost certainly intended to be offered to the Queen in the course of Dr Lopez's negotiations with her for peace with King Philip and the confinement or expulsion of the pretender to the Spanish throne, Don Antonio, who was living in England. Lopez did so offer it, and it was refused. After Lopez's conviction, however, the Queen retained this ring from his property, although most of the rest of his goods were returned as an act of clemency to his widow. The Queen delayed signature of the death warrant for three months, and Lopez was not finally executed until 7th June. His name had become a byword for the most extreme villainy, and frequent mention is made of him in contemporary literature, often with a play on the meaning of his name, which was 'wolf' (from the Latin 'lupus').

The Queen is said to have worn the notorious jewel until her death. In 1601, Sir Thomas Egerton, then Lord Keeper, referred to this foible in a speech in the House of Lords:

> I would be loth to speak of the dead, much more to slander the dead. I have seen her Majesty wear at her Girdle the price of her blood; I mean Jewels which have been given to her physicians to have done that unto her, which I hope God will ever keep from her; but she hath rather worn them in Triumph than for the price, which hath not been greatly valuable.[4]

At the time of the Lopez trial Sir Thomas Egerton, although already nominated for promotion to Master of the Rolls, was still Attorney-General, and took a leading part in the preparation of the case against him.

After Lopez's trial and conviction London would have been buzzing with the story, and it is not surprising to find Shakespeare making a reference both to the jewel and to the 'wolf'.

We saw in Chapter VII that Sonnet 66 referred to the events which took place around 6th February, 1594. We have now seen that Sonnet 96 referes to the trial of Lopez on 28th February, and it is reasonable to suppose that it was written while the story was still very topical, perhaps no later than the end of March 1594. Between these two sonnets we have the whole tragedy of the split between Southampton and Shakespeare resulting from the appearance of Chapman's *Shadow of Night*, which was entered in the Stationers' Register on 31st December, 1593, and finally published between 25th March and 16th April, 1594, or thereabouts. On 6th February, the London theatres had again been closed because of the plague and Shakespeare was left with nothing to do. He therefore had plenty of time for writing poetry, and it appears that, in a desperate attempt to retain contact with Southampton, he must have written no fewer than 31 sonnets in a period of less than two months.

After Sonnet 96, as the tone of the following sonnets shows, there comes a gap in the relationship. Yet on 9th May, 1594, *The Rape of Lucrece* was entered in the Stationers' Register, and when this was published, perhaps two or three months later, it appeared with a warm dedication to the Earl of Southampton. Apparently the rift had been healed. What had happened in between?

CHAPTER XI

A Wintry Summer

MARCH 1594 was not a good time to be out of work. This is what the chronicler John Stow had to say about it:

> In this moneth of March, great stormes of wind overturned trees, steeples, barnes, houses, etc. namely, in Worcestershire, in Baudley forest many Oakes were overturned. In Horton wood more than 1500 Oakes were overthrowne in one day, namely on the thursday next before Palme Sunday. In Staffordshire, the steeple in Stafforde Towne, was rent in pieces along through the midst, and throwne upon the Church, wherewith the sayd roofe was broken. Houses and barnes were overthrowne in most places of those shires. In Canke wood more than 3000 trees were overthrowne, many steeples, above 50 in Staffordshire were perished, or blowne downe.[1]

The Thursday next before Palm Sunday, 1594, was 21st March. No wonder Shakespeare in Sonnet 90 implored Southampton:

> Give not a windy night a rainie morrow, . . .   90.7

As we have seen, it was just about this time Shakespeare was packing his bags after the collapse of the London theatre season and the withdrawal of Southampton's patronage. The two Sonnets, 97 and 98, tell us very plainly that he was away from Southampton for the spring and summer:

> And yet this time remov'd was sommers time,   97.5

and

> From you I have been absent in the spring,   98.1-3
> When proud pide Aprill (drest in all his trim)
> Hath put a spirit of youth in every thing: . . .

Here then is confirmation of our deduction from the mention in Sonnet 96 of Lopez's jewelled ring that the parting took place in March. In Sonnet 97 Shakespeare tells us where he went.

We saw in Chapter II that at the beginning of 1592, before the plague closed down the London theatres and compelled him to look for another source of livelihood, Shakespeare was probably with Lord Strange's players at the Rose theatre. Since that season ended, on 23rd June, 1592, this company had not been permitted to perform in London, except briefly at Hampton Court during the Christmas festivities at the end of that year. They had, however, been performing extensively in the provinces. On 6th May, 1593, the Privy Council issued a special warrant to Edward Alleyn, 'servant to the Lord High Admiral', and to Willian Kemp, Thomas Pope, John Heminges, Augustine Phillipes and George Brian, 'being al one companie, servauntes to our verie good Lord Strainge', which gave them authority 'in regard of the service by them don and to be done at the Court', to

> exercise their quallitie of playing comodies, tragedies and such like in anie other cities, townes and corporacions where the infection is not, so it be not within seaven miles of London or of the Coort, that they maie be in the better readiness hereafter for her Majesty's service Whensoever they shalbe thereunto called.[2]

The actors named in the licence include many who are recorded later as belonging to the Lord Chamberlain's company in which Shakespeare appears as a partner for the Christmas season of 1594, and from then onwards (though the company changed its name) until the end of his career.

The patron of this company, Ferdinando Stanley, Lord Strange, succeeded on 25th September, 1593, to the earldom of Derby, after which the company of players were known as Derby's men. Young and popular and a patron of literature, the Earl was one of the noblemen mentioned by Chapman, as we have already noted, in his dedication of the *Shadow of Night*, as a devotee of science. Shortly after succeeding to the title he was made the object of an absurd plot by the Jesuits on the Continent, who were misadvised by his cousin, Sir William Stanley, to put Ferdinando on the throne as a Catholic King of England. The Earl at once reported the plot to the authorities and arrested the Jesuit emissary. Not surprisingly, it was the Jesuits whom gossip blamed for the tragic fate which shortly overtook him. For this let us look again at Stow's *Annals*:

> The 16th of April, Ferdinando Earle of Darby deceased at Latham, whose strange sicknesse and death, gathered by those who were present with him at the time thereof, was such as followeth: his diseases apparant, were vomiting of sower or rusty matter with blood, the yealowe jaundice: melting of his fat, swelling, and hardnesse of his spleene, a vehement hickocke, and four days before he died stopping of his water. The manner of his death, was wondrous strange, whereof I have bene often required to set it down plainely, but I could never get the particulars Authentiquely.

There follows a very detailed account of the Earl's symptoms and treatment, rivalling the published accounts of the last days of Pope John XXIII; after this comes 'A true report of such reasons and conjectures, as caused many learned men to suppose him to be bewitched', including a story of the finding of a wax image with a hair similar to the Earl's own twisted through its belly. The suspicious circumstances were sufficient to persuade the Privy Council to order an enquiry into the whole matter, but no satisfactory conclusion was reached.

The heir to the earldom was Ferdinando's brother William, since Ferdinando had left only daughters. The new Earl was still a bachelor, so it seemed to the

G

indefatigable Lord Burghley a golden opportunity to make a match for his granddaughter, the Lady Elizabeth Vere, for whom her first betrothed, the Earl of Southampton, had shown such remarkably small enthusiasm. The new Lord Derby was agreeable, and Collins' *Peerage of England* gives the date of the wedding as 26th June, 1594. But this was not when it took place: from Stow's *Annals* we learn that: 'The 26 of January, William Earle of Darby, marryed the Earle of Oxfords daughter at the Court, then at Greenwich, which marriage feast was there most royally kept.' The wedding had thus been postponed to a date nine months and ten days after the late Earl of Derby's death. There is only one source of information as to the reason for this, and that is a letter sent on 19th November, 1594, by Father Garnet, Superior of the English Jesuits, to Father Parsons, whom we have met before as the writer of the pamphlet which accused Sir Walter Raleigh of running a school of atheism. One passage of the letter reads:

> The marriage of the Lady Vere to the new Earl of Derby is deferred by reason that he standeth in hazard to be unearled again, his brother's wife being with child, until it is seen whether it be a boy or no. The young Earl of Southampton, refusing the Lady Vere, payeth 5000[li]. of present payment.[3]

No more is heard of this posthumous child. The wife of Earl Ferdinando had three daughters, who became co-heirs to his baronies and were later engaged in protracted litigation over the estate with the new Earl. But Collins tells us that the youngest of these was already seven years and eight months old at the time of her father's death. The child mentioned by Garnet must therefore have died before or very soon after birth, if in fact the pregnancy was not a false alarm.[4]

Throughout the summer the dreadful weather persisted. Stow tells us:

> This yere in the moneth of May fell many great showres of raine: but in the moneth of June and July, much more; for it commonly rained every day or night, till Saint James day, and two dayes after together most extremely: all which, notwithstanding in the moneth of August, there followed a faire harvest, but in the moneth of September fel great raynes, wich raised high Waters, such as stayed the carriages, and bare downe Bridges at Cambridge, Ware, and elsewhere, in many places.

Meanwhile the late Earl of Derby's players appeared under his name at Ipswich on 8th May and at Southampton on 15th May. However, by the time they reached Winchester on 16th May, where they received six shillings and eightpence from the chamberlain of the city, they were calling themselves the Countess of Derby's players. By the beginning of June, when they appeared jointly with the Lord Admiral's men under Henslowe at the theatre of Newington Butts in London, they were already calling themselves the Lord Chamberlain's men. It was under this name that they appeared at the court at Greenwich the following Christmas season, when Shakespeare's name for the first time appears with those of Kempe and Burbage as one of the proprietors who received payment for the company's services.[5]

Now at last it is time to examine Sonnet 97:

> How like a Winter hath my absence beene 97.
> From thee, the pleasure of the fleeting yeare?
> What freezings have I felt, what darke daies seene?
> What old Decembers barenesse every where?
> And yet this time remov'd was sommers time,
> The teeming Autumne big with ritch increase,
> Bearing the wanton burthen of the prime,
> Like widdowed wombes after their Lords decease:
> Yet this aboundant issue seem'd to me,
> But hope of Orphans, and un-fathered fruite,
> For Sommer and his pleasures waite on thee,
> And thou away, the very birds are mute.
>   Or if they sing, tis with so dull a cheere,
>   That leaves look pale, dreading the Winters neere.

In the light of the events of 1594 can we not now paraphrase this as follows?—

I have been absent from you during the summer, but the weather has been so bad that it seemed just like winter, and I put this down to the effect of our separation. The autumn has in fact promised to be quite fruitful, and my own autumnal head is full of the poetry which you set teeming in it before we parted; but with you away these swelling harvests reminded me of posthumous children, like the one said to be in the Countess of Derby's womb. Like that child the Earl of Derby's players have lost their father, and working as the Countess's men we felt as insecure as orphans. There can be no real summer without help from you. As it is, your poet, like the birds, has had little heart for singing because he has been full of forebodings of a wintry future.

This sonnet is one of the most beautiful and most Shakespearian in the series, with its strong and unconventional images and its heartfelt appeal for renewal of friendship and support. The syntax and imagery seem strained, and have baffled many readers because, Shakespeare is using a poetic description of the unseasonable weather to convey an essential and factual message which it would be embarrassing to spell out in cold prose. There is none of the under-current of wounded feelings which runs through all the sonnets from 82 to 96. Hurt pride has been laid aside, but the new approach, though humble, is entirely dignified, the message of self-pity being gracefully disguised.

The participial absolute phrase 'The teeming Autumn . . . bearing the wanton burden . . .' has puzzled many editors, and many of them, including the usually meticulous Seymour-Smith, have arbitrarily changed the 'The' to 'And'. So the 'time remov'd' becomes summer and autumn at once. But this will not do, since in line 11 the poet returns to summer by itself. J. B. Leishman[6] has an amusing passage on the difficulties he sees in the concept of a pregnant Autumn being already in existence while the season is still summer; but really it is not so difficult, if one grasps that 'Autumn' is a symbol for Shakespeare himself:

> That time of yeere thou maist in me behold,   73.1–3
> When yellow leaves, or none, or few doe hange
> Upon those boughes which shake against the could, . . .

Similarly summer is frequently a symbol for Southampton, as in:

> For never resting time leads Summer on   5.5

and

> And Sommers greene all girded up in sheaves   12.7

and

> But thy eternall Sommer shall not fade,   18.9

and that is why Shakespeare says in this sonnet:

> For Sommer and his pleasures waite on thee, . . .   97.11

The 'ritch increase' which Autumn-Shakespeare is 'big with' in line six is *The Rape of Lucrece,* which was inspired by Southampon ('the onlie begetter' of such 'wanton burthens') in the prime of the year, just before Shakespeare left him. It was summertime (May 9th) when Shakespeare entered *The Rape of Lucrece* at the Stationers' Register, and would probably be autumn before it was finally published, complete with dedication to his patron. This sonnet is, amongst other things, a first delicate request for that patronage for the yet 'un-fathered fruite'.

The unusual metaphor:

> Like widdowed wombes after their Lords decease: 97.8

is for dating purposes perhaps the most important line in the whole of the Sonnets; or at any rate in Sonnets 1–106, the time-span of which is fixed by the three revolutions of the seasons described in Sonnet 104. Such a metaphor is not just dreamed up out of thin air, any more than was the picture in the previous sonnet of the base jewel on the Queen's finger. Without doubt it is suggested by the gossip of the posthumous pregancy of the Countess of Derby; but even so that would scarcely be a reason for dragging it into a sonnet unless Shakespeare had some special connection with the Countess and her deceased Lord. It becomes a highly relevant image if, as is in any case inherently probable, when the break with Southampton came Shakespeare went off to seek for better fortune under the aegis of the Earl of Derby. This sonnet is therefore valuable both as a topical landmark and also for this extra scrap of information which it gives about Shakespeare's career.

The next two sonnets, 98 and 99, appear to be connected in thought, but in style they are very different. Sonnet 98 is another treatment of the theme of

97; although part of the period during which Shakespeare has been absent from his patron was springtime, yet it seemed like winter. The language is largely conventional, as opposed to the deeply individual treatment of the theme in 97, but it is a very polished and satisfying example of this kind of style. Sonnet 99 continues the comparison between the young man's beauty and different types of flowers begun in 98, but in a wholly artificial and unpersuasive manner. The thought is not continuous between the two, as is shown by the fact that the lily and the rose, already dealt with in 98, appear again for further treatment in 99. Sonnet 99 is, in fact, no more than a pastiche of a well-known sonnet by Constable, which was published as one of his sequence addressed to *Diana* in 1592, and in a second edition in 1594.[7] The first 'quatrain' has five lines instead of four, as if Shakespeare had not decided on its final form but did not think it worthy of further attention. It is almost as if in these three sonnets Shakespeare was deliberately giving examples of his ability in three different styles: the first entirely his own, the second a good conventional style and the third that of the common hack. In the first his meaning is as deep as that of any passage of Chapman, yet the result is pleasing poetry instead of the strained and turgid obscurity of his rival. The second is good professional verse, with a personal message included; the third is sickly rubbish with no message other than blatant physical flattery. It would be interesting to know which Southampton liked best.

The main interest for us of Sonnet 98 is in the first quatrain:

> From you have I beene absent in the spring,
> When proud pide Aprill (drest in all his trim)
> Hath put a spirit of youth in every thing:
> That heavie *Saturne* laught and leapt with him.

It will be seen that *Saturne* is printed in italics. This need not necessarily mean anything in the Sonnets except that the word is a foreign one, but sometimes it seems to correspond to an underlining in the manuscript, and I think that is the case here. One of the astrological attributes of the planet Saturn was that it was said to influence poets and artists; it also represented age and melancholy. Here, then, Saturn has a reference to Shakespeare himself: 'this was the time when I should have been laughing and leaping under the influence of your spirit of youth'. April is of course one of the symbols for Southampton:

> Thou art thy mothers glasse and she in thee   3.9–10
> Calls backe the lovely Aprill of her prime, . . .

The word *Saturne* was underlined so that the reference to Shakespeare himself should not be missed. As we shall see, Sonnet 104 contains a similar underlining with the same intention.

George Wyndham in 1898 had the notion of finding out the years around the period of the Sonnets when the planet Saturn might be said to have 'laughed and leaped' in the night sky in the month of April. He satisfied himself (mistakenly) that there were only three occasions when Saturn was seen in opposition in the night sky in April between 1592 and 1609, namely on 4th April, 1600, 17th April, 1601 and 29th April, 1602. He favoured 1602.[8] Dover Wilson, on the same evidence favours 1600.[9] I thought it as well to look into this matter, and accordingly wrote to H.M. Nautical Almanac Office at Herstmonceux for information as to the visibility of Saturn from London in the night sky for each of the years 1591–1601. I received the following reply:

> The data regarding the visibility of Saturn from London is given herein. Because the planet is so slow moving it is not possible to give the dates to the nearest day, and thus only the month is given.
>
> The maximum altitudes, for each month the planet is visible, are given between the beginning and end dates for each period. It should be noted that these maximum altitudes occur in a dark sky for the middle 5–6 months only. At the beginning of each period the planet is visible in the eastern sky for a short while before dawn, rising earlier each night until it is visible all night at the middle of the period. At the end of each period the planet is only visible in the western sky for a short while after sunset.
>
> The Julian calendar, which was then in use in this country, is used in the following table.

Beginning of period of visibility	Maximum altitudes (in degrees) for each month in the range											End of period of visibility
							61	61	61	**61**	61	1591 May
1591 July	61	60	60	60	60	60	60	61	61	**61**	60	1592 May
1592 Aug.	59	58	57	57	57	58	58	59	**59**	59		1593 May
1593 Aug.	56	55	54	53	53	54	55	55	**56**	56	55	1594 June
1594 Aug.	53	51	50	49	49	50	50	51	**52**	52	52	1595 June
1595 Sept.	47	46	45	45	45	45	46	**47**	47	47	46	1596 July
1596 Sept.	43	42	41	40	40	40	41	**42**	42	42	42	1597 July
1597 Oct.	38	36	35	35	35	36	**37**	38	38	37	36	1598 Aug.
1598 Nov.	33	32	31	30	30	**31**	32	33	33	33	32	1599 Aug.
1599 Nov.	28	27	27	26	27	**27**	28	28	28	28	27	1600 Sept.
1600 Nov.	25	24	23	23	23	**23**	24	24	25	24	24	1601 Sept.
1601 Dec.	21											

What this table shows is that in the Aprils of 1600, 1601 and (as I have later confirmed) 1602, Saturn was visible all night when the sky was clear, but at rather a low altitude; never at more than the 27 degrees reached in April 1600. In April 1594, however, the planet was visible in the western sky for several hours after sunset, its maximum elevation being 56 degrees, from which it came down each night to the horizon. It seems to me, assuming that Shakespeare looked at the sky at all when writing this sonnet, that the behaviour of Saturn in April 1594 could at least as reasonably be described as 'laughing and leaping' as could that in the later years of the decade.

The mention of 'laughing and leaping' tells us what Shakespeare means by a 'summers story' in the next quatrain:

> Yet nor the laies of birds, nor the sweet smell   98.5–8
> Of different flowers in odor and in hew,
> Could make me any summers story tell:
> Or from their proud lap pluck them where they grew: . . .

It is one in which there is 'laughing and leaping', in other words, a gay comedy. Shakespeare was shortly to produce a flood of gay comedies, the *Comedy of Errors, Two Gentlemen of Verona* and A *Midsummer Night's Dream,* for instance, with which to start off the newly formed Chamberlain's company. This was a very different vein from that of *Henry VI and Titus Andronicus,* and one can imagine that the vicissitudes of 1594 would not be the ideal background for comic invention.

The most interesting line in Sonnet 99 is one which is not derived from the sonnet by Constable which I have already mentioned:

> And buds of marjerom had stolne thy haire, . . .   99.7

The following information about it has been kindly supplied by the Director of the Royal Botanic Gardens at Kew:

> It is thought that 'buds of marjoram' refers to sweet or knotted marjoram, 'knotted' in this instance being a form of 'knops', meaning buds or buttons. The 'buds' are actually the flowerheads with inconspicuous white or pinkish flowers in terminal clusters. Sweet marjoram, *Marjorana Hortensis,* was much used in the past as a strewing herb, and, according to Parkinson, was used for 'swete bages', 'swete powders' and 'swete washing water'. The flowering tops yield a dye which was formerly used in country districts to dye woollen cloth purple and linen a reddish brown, but the colour is neither brilliant nor durable.

Here, then, is a pretty clear indication that the hair of the person addressed was reddish brown, as was Southampton's. No doubt there is also a suggestion that the herb obtained its scent from the water in which he washed his hair, instead of the other way round; but this is of less interest to us than the question of the colour.

That the renewed approach to Southampton represented by Sonnets 97-99 was successful we can deduce from the dedication of *The Rape of Lucrece*:

> To the Right Honourable, Henry Wriothesley, Earle of Southampton, and Baron of Titchfield.
>
> The love I dedicate to your Lordship is without end: whereof this Pamphlet without beginning is but a superfluous Moity. The warrant I have of your Honourable disposition, not the worth of my untutored Lines makes it assured of acceptance. What I have done is yours, what I

have to doe is yours, being part in all I have, devoted yours. Were my worth greater, my duety would shew greater, meane time, as it is, it is bound to your Lordship; To whom I wish long life still lengthned with all happinesse.

Your Lordships in all duety.

William Shakespeare.

CHAPTER XII

'Oh Blame Me Not
If I No More Can Write!'

As Sonnets 36 to 39 referred to the publication of *Venus and Adonis,* so Sonnets 100 to 106 relate to that of *The Rape of Lucrece.* Sonnets 100, 103 and 105 are in fact little more than expansions of the theme of 38, as is shown by the closely similar language used.

> How can my Muse want subject to invent   38.1–8
> While thou dost breath that poor'st into my verse,
> Thine own sweet argument, to excellent,
> For every vulgar paper to rehearse:
> Oh give thyselfe the thankes if ought in me,
> Worthy perusal stand against thy sight,
> For who's so dumbe that cannot write to thee,
> When thou they selfe dost give invention light?

So the following year we have:

> Where art thou Muse that thou forgetst so long,   100.1–2
> To speake of that which gives thee all thy might?

and

> Sing to the eare that doth thy laies esteeme,   100.7–8
> And gives thy pen both skill and argument.

Also:

> The argument all bare is of more worth   103.3–4
> Than when it hath my added praise beside.

and

> Looke in your glasse and there appeares a face,   103.6–7
> That over-goes my blunt invention quite, . . .

Also

> Still constant in a wondrous excellence, . . .   105.6

> Faire, kinde, and true, is all my argument, . . .   105.9

> And in this change is my invention spent, . . .   105.11

Such a very close correspondence of thought and language argues that the occasions for them were very similar ones. But there is a difference in the other themes accompanying this common one in each of the two groups. In 1593 Shakespeare was at pains to stress that his patron and himself must not display too close an intimacy, although they felt themselves almost to be one person. Much has happened since. Southampton has changed from a bashful affectionate youth to an impatient young rake. Shakespeare is thus at pains to excuse himself for the long delay in the appearance of the 'graver labour' with which in the dedication of *Venus and Adonis* he had promised soon to 'honour' Southampton. No doubt it was partly sensitivity over the fact that he had nothing ready that caused him to feel so strongly about Southampton's showing interest in the *Shadow of Night*:

> I think good thoughts, whilst other write good wordes, . . .   85.5

He also wants to establish that Southampton's growing up and the gradual alteration in his boyish good looks make no difference to his devotion for him. Of course he does not really succeed in doing this, the flattery is too extreme. It is significant that he has again to turn for inspiration, as he did in Sonnet 99, to a much more conventional sonneteer, Henry Constable. Sonnet 106 apparently derives from the following quatrain of a sonnet which Constable had written by 1591:[1]

> Miracle of the world I never will denye   *Diana*
> That former poets prayse the beautie of theyre dayes   I.iii.4
> But all those beauties were but figures of thy prayse
> And all those poets did of thee but prophecye.

Shakespeare writes:

> I see their antique Pen would have exprest,   106.7–10
> Even such a beauty as you maister now.
> So all their praises are but prophesies
> Of this our time, all you prefiguring, . . .

Curiously, G. P. V. Akrigg imagines that Shakespeare borrowed the words 'prophesies' and 'prefiguring' from Chapman's dedication in 1598 of his *Seven Books of the Iliades of Homer* to the Earl of Essex. The dedication begins:

> Most true Achilles (whom by sacred prophecie Homere did but pre-figure in his admirable object). . . .

and, according to Akrigg, 'Shakespeare, it would seem, wrote Sonnet 106 as something of a compensatory piece for Southampton'.[2] In fact the borrowing if that is what it is, must be the other way round. However, Shakespeare may be making a reference to Chapman's criticisms of him in the first two lines of Sonnet 105:

> Let not my love be cal'd Idolatrie,   105.1–2
> Nor my beloved as an Idoll show, . . .

In his dedication of the *Shadow of Night* to Matthew Roydon, referring to those who think they can obtain the secrets of Skill without invocation, fasting and watching and giving up drops of their souls, Chapman says: 'Good Lord how serious and eternall are their Idolatrous platts for riches! no maruaile sure they here do so much good with them.'

The *Shadow of Night* was now printed and on sale, together with this vitriolic dedication. Shakespeare's lines were perhaps also influenced by the closing lines of that same sonnet of Constable's which inspired his own Sonnet 106:

> His [Petrarch's] songes were hymns of thee which only now before
> Thy image should be sunge for thow that goddesse art
> Which onlye we withoute idolatrye adore.

If Chapman recognized 105 as referring to his own remarks, it is not surprising that Shakespeare's following sonnet stuck in his mind until he came to write his dedication of the *Seven Books of the Iliades,* with its prefigured prophecy.

Sonnet 105 stresses that the virtues of Southampton are beauty, kindness and constancy,

> Faire, kinde, and true, is all my argument,   105.9–10
> Faire, kinde and true, varrying to other words, . . .

But the virtue of constancy is the whole theme of *The Rape of Lucrece.* It is necessary for Shakespeare to explain that *Lucrece* is nevertheless a poem of praise of Southampton's own virtues:

> Kinde is my love to day, to morrow kinde,   105.5–8
> Still constant in a wondrous excellence,
> Therefore my verse to constancie confin'de,
> One thing expressing, leaves out difference.

That is also why Sonnet 106 mentions the beauty of 'Ladies dead' as well as that of 'lovely Knights'. There is no 'lovely Knight' in *The Rape of Lucrece,* only the loathsome Tarquin. There is a real danger that Southampton might think that this character represents him, in view of his reputation with the ladies of the court and of the current fashion for satire. Shakespeare must make it clear that it is the heroine that derives from him; this was foreshadowed, before the story of the poem was decided, in Sonnet 53:

> On *Hellens* cheeke all art of beautie set,   53.7–8
> And you in *Grecian* tires are painted new: . . .

My mention of the word 'satire' recalls Sonnet 100:

> Rise resty Muse, my loves sweet face survay,   100.9–12
> If time have any wrincle graven there,
> If any, be a *Satire* to decay,
> And make times spoiles dispised every where.

This is exactly what Lucrece does try to do:

> 'Misshapen Time, copesmate of ugly Night,   *RL. 925–31*
> Swift subtle post, carrier of grisly care,
> Eater of youth, false slave to false delight,
> Base watch of woes, sin's pack-horse, virtue's snare;
> Thou nursest all and murd'rest all that are.
>   O, hear me then, injurious, shifting Time!
>   Be guilty of my death, since of my crime. . . .

> 'Time's glory is to calm contending kings,   *939–52*
> To unmask falsehood and bring truth to light,
> To stamp the seal of time in aged things,
> To wake the morn and sentinel the night,
> To wrong the wronger till he render right,
>   To ruinate proud buildings with thy hours
>   And smear with dust their glitt'ring golden towers;

> To fill with worm-holes stately monuments,
> To feed oblivion with decay of things,
> To blot old books and alter their contents,
> To pluck the quills from ancient ravens' wings,
> To dry the old oak's sap and cherish springs,
>   To spoil antiquities of hammered steel
>   And turn the giddy round of Fortune's wheel; . . .

It is not only a satire of time and decay that is contained in *The Rape of Lucrece*. There is also a satire of Chapman's beloved Night:

> 'O comfort-killing Night, image of hell!   *RL. 764–71*
> Dim register and notary of shame!
> Black stage for tragedies and murders fell!
> Vast sin-concealing chaos! nurse to blame!
> Blind muffled bawd! dark harbour for defame!
> Grim cave of death! whisp'ring conspirator
> With close-tongued treason and the ravisher!

> O hateful, vaporous and foggy Night! . . .

and so on for several more stanzas. Could anyone in 1594, and particularly Southampton, fail to grasp the contrast with Chapman's 'Hymnus in Noctem'?—

> Come to this house of mourning, serve the night,   *HN. 328–37*
> To whom pale day (with whoredome soked quite)
> Is but a drudge, selling her beauties use
> To rapes, adultries, and to all abuse.
> Her labours feast imperiall Night with sports,
> Where Loves are Christmast, with all pleasures sorts:

And whom her fugitive, and far-shot rayes
Disjoyne, and drive into ten thousand wayes,
Nights glorious mantle wraps in safe abodes,
And frees their neckes from servile labors lodes: . . .

Lucrece fights back on behalf of Day:

'O Night, thou furnace of foul-reeking smoke,   RL. 799–805
Let not the jealous Day behold that face
Which underneath thy black all-hiding cloak
Immodestly lies martyred with disgrace!
Keep still possession of thy gloomy place,
   That all the faults which in thy reign are made
   May likewise be sepulchred in thy shade!

Shakespeare won the day. It was left to Chapman in the dedication to his
next work, *Ovid's Banquet of Sense*, to compare him with Euippe's daughters,
that 'throng of stolid sisters' who, according to Book V of Ovid's *Metamorphoses,*
challenged the Muses to a contest of song and after being soundly defeated were
turned into chattering magpies.

It remains to notice that what made Shakespeare feel he must ward off the
charge of idolatory in the first two lines of Sonnet 105 was that all his praises
were

To one, of one, still such, and ever so.   105.4

This is exactly what he says in the dedication of *The Rape of Lucrece*:

What I have done is yours; what I have to do is yours; being part in all I
have, devoted yours.

In the same dedication the sentence:

The warrant I have of your Honourable disposition, not the worth of my
untutored lines, makes it assured of acceptance . . .

is reflected in the following lines from Sonnets 100 and 103:

Sing to the eare that doth thy laies esteeme,   100.7

and

Alack what povertie my Muse brings forth, . . .   103.1

It seems that between writing Sonnets 97 to 99, whose purpose was to test the
ground for a renewal of his friendship with Southampton, and Sonnets 100 to
106, which deal with *The Rape of Lucrece* and the gracious and rewarding
reception it received, Shakespeare did get a positive indication of his patron's
esteem, a warrant of his disposition. Sonnet 97 was written at the end of summer
or beginning of autumn, perhaps in September, when the printer was nearly
ready to deliver his as yet unfathered fruit and asking whether there was a
dedication to be set up in type. October 6th was Southampton's twenty-first

birthday and the best time to expect a large present from him. It has often been pointed out that Sonnet 104 seems to suggest, particularly in its first and last lines, that it was written in connection with a birthday:

> To me fair friend you never can be old,   104.1

and

> Ere you were borne was beauties summer dead.   104.14

The birthday is now plainly that of 6th October, 1594, when Southampton came of age and for the first time was legally entitled to control of his own fortune. Shakespeare certainly must have experienced a change in his fortunes at this time, for we find him that Christmas one of the partners in the Lord Chamberlain's company, which was now free of Henslowe's financial management. Sir William Davenant, Shakespeare's godson, is said by Nicholas Rowe to have handed down the story that Lord Southampton at one time gave Shakespeare £1000 'to enable him to go through with a purchase which he heard he had a mind to'.[3] There is probably one nought too many, but it seems most likely, as Dover Wilson has suggested, that the gift was used to finance the Lord Chamberlain's company.[4] On 8th October Lord Hunsdon (the Lord Chamberlain) was negotiating with the Lord Mayor of London for the use 'by my nowe companie' of the Cross Keys Inn for the winter season. When Southampton was blithely handing over £5000 to Lord Burghley for refusing to accept Lady Elizabeth Vere, the odd £100 for Shakespeare in recognition of *The Rape of Lucrece* would have seemed a trifle.

It is time now to look closely at Sonnet 104, which I have left until last among the '*Rape of Lucrece* group' because of its importance in dating all the sonnets between early 1592 and late 1594.

Dover Wilson thinks that this sonnet is misplaced, and that it should fall with the 97–99 group. He finds this proved by the repetition in 104 of some of the rhymes found in 97 and 99.[5] I do not think this means anything at all: 104 also echoes rhymes from 103. What is more important is that there is a natural sense-link: the exhortation in 103 to the young man to look at his beauty in his glass, in order to see why no poetry can match it, leads naturally to the chill thought that perhaps his beauty is after all imperceptibly fading, as a dial hand moves without seeming to do so. Perhaps the glass and dial are the same ones as were mentioned in Sonnet 77;

> Thy glasse will shew thee how thy beauties were   77.1–2
> Thy dyall how thy pretious mynuits waste, . . .

But in 77 the purpose of the glass was to show up wrinkles which

> Of mouthed graves will give thee memorie, . . .   77.6

Naturally this unpleasant thought on a birthday occasion leads on to the assurance of Sonnet 104:

To me faire friend you never can be old,
For as you were when first your eye I eyde,
Such seemes your beautie still: Three Winters colde,
Have from the forrests shooke three summers pride,
Three beautious springs to yellow *Autumne* turn'd,
In processe of the seasons have I seene,
Three Aprill perfumes in three hot Junes burn'd,
Since first I saw you fresh which yet are greene.
Ah yet doth beauty like a Dyall hand,
Steale from his figure, and no pace perceiv'd,
So your sweet hew, which me thinkes still doth stand
Hath motion, and mine eye may be deceaved.
    For feare of which, heare this thou age unbred,
    Ere you were borne was beauties summer dead.

The next Sonnet, 105, returns, as we have seen, directly to the subject of the group, the presentation of *The Rape of Lucrece,* and the last of this series, 106, continues the thought that poetry about any beautiful person is really praise of Southampton's beauty, the 'master-hue'. The sonnet ends with the complement to the thought expressed in 104; for whereas the latter instructs future ages to realize that, with the fading of Southampton's beauty, the epitome of beauty died, Sonnet 106 says that past ages also had no beauty to celebrate except by way of prefiguring him. Master H^e W. is thus the pattern for both past and future.

But Sonnet 104 has another function which is of more direct interest for us, namely to look back over the period since the Sonnets began and thus confirm their timespan:

For as you were when first your eye I eyde,
Such seemes your beautie still: Three Winters colde,
Have from the forrests shooke three summers pride,
Three beautious springs to yellow *Autumne* turn'd,
In processe of the seasons have I seene,
Three Aprill perfumes in three hot Junes burn'd,
Since first I saw you fresh which yet are greene.

Three winters have replaced three summers, three springs have turned to autumn, three Aprils to June. Notice that Shakespeare does not say that three winters have turned to spring. The inference is that it is winter now (that is also why winter is the first season to be mentioned), and that the first meeting occurred in the spring; so only two winters can have turned to spring. We have confirmation that the relationship started in the spring; two sonnets earlier Shakespeare says:

Our love was new, and then but in the spring,   102.5–6
When I was wont to greet it with my laies,

and in the first sonnet of all he had said:

> Thou that art now the worlds fresh ornament,   1.9–10
> And only herauld to the gaudy spring, . . .

Winter in England may be said to start any time after about the middle of October, and the Julian calendar of the fifteen-nineties was in any case ten days behind the present Gregorian reckoning. The sonnet need not therefore have been written many days after Southampton's twenty-first birthday. We can imagine that the young Earl would not have had much time to think of such matters, for between 5th and 17th October he was busily engaged in arranging the escape of his friends Sir Henry and Sir Charles Danvers, who foolishly murdered one Henry Long in Wiltshire on 4th October. They were concealed at Southampton's home at Titchfield until they could be smuggled to France.[6] It is unlikely that Shakespeare received his gift until after this distracting episode, which is thought by some to have provided him with material for his play *Romeo and Juliet*.

> Oh blame me not if I no more can write!   103.5

There was real meaning in this line, for Shakespeare was indeed about to take a rest from sonnet writing. With Southampton's coming of age he had plenty to do and think about, and no doubt less interest in poems flattering his adolescent charms. We shall look briefly in succeeding chapters at the activities and events that occupied his time in the long period which intervened before Shakespeare addressed him again in sonnets. For Shakespeare also several very busy years were to follow. When he wrote of Southampton's appearance again he was to find it necessary to say:

> So that eternall love in loves fresh case,   108.9
> Waighes not the dust and injury of age,
> Nor gives to necessary wrinckles place,
> But makes antiquitie for aye his page,
>   Finding the first conceit of love there bred,
>   Where time and outward forme would shew it dead.

What a change from the last sonnet of 1594! —

> I see their antique Pen would have exprest,   106.7–8
> Even such a beauty as you maister now.

CHAPTER XIII

'Darkning Thy Powre To Lend
Base Subjects Light'

ALTHOUGH the Dark Lady Sonnets are printed after 126, which clearly ends the series addressed to the young man, that is certainly not their chronological place. It is easy enough, however, to tell where they fit in, since among the sonnets addressed to the young man there are sonnets referring to the lady, and conversely, in some of the sonnets which are primarily about the lady there is reference to the man.

I mentioned in Chapter V that it would be convenient to take Sonnets 33-35 and 40-42 together with 127-154, although they were written, as we saw in that chapter, somewhere around the time of the publication of *Venus and Adonis*, and not long after the death of Marlowe. If there was the usual gap between registration and publication we might expect the latter event to have taken place about June or July 1593, since the registration was on 18th April. Marlowe was killed, it will be remembered, on 30th May. June or July fits in well with the picture of a summer morning in England which Shakespeare gives us in Sonnet 33:

> Full many a glorious morning have I seene,   33.1-8
> Flatter the mountaine tops with soveraine eie,
> Kissing with golden face the meddowes greene;
> Guilding pale streames with heavenly alcumy:
> Anon permit the basest cloudes to ride,
> With ougly rack on his celestiall face,
> And from the for-lorne world his visage hide
> Stealing unseene to west with this disgrace: ...

Now let us see how this little group of sonnets, which deals with the theft of Shakespeare's mistress by the young man, fits into the main Dark Lady series.

The first six sonnets in this series, 127-132, contain no criticism of the mistress. Sonnets 127, 130, 131 and 132 are variations on the paradox that a woman of dark complexion may yet be fair:

> Thy blacke is fairest in my judgements place.   131.12

Sonnet 128 envies the keys of the virginal which are able to kiss the beloved's hand as she plays on it; while 129 is a soliloquy on the madness and the inevita-

H

bility of lust. There is nothing in any of these sonnets to indicate any strain in the relationship. It is true that in Sonnet 131 Shakespeare says:

> In nothing art thou blacke save in thy deedes,   131.13

but here the black deeds referred to are only the conventional tyranny of the loved one who enslaves and torments her lover by her beauty:

> Thou art as tiranous, so as thou art,   131.1–2
> As those whose beauties proudly make them cruell; . . .

This is confirmed in 132, where the lady's eyes are said to have put on black in pity because they know that her heart torments the poet with disdain. There is thus no reason to doubt that these sonnets were written before the affair was treacherously turned into a triangular one.

The next two sonnets are concerned with the seduction of the friend, and the blame is put entirely on the lady:

> I'st not ynough to torture me alone,   133.4
> But slave to slavery my sweet'st friend must be.

Also,

> My selfe Ile forfeit, so that other mine,   134.3–6
> Thou wilt restore to be my comfort still:
> But thou wilt not, nor he will not be free,
> For thou art covetous, and he is kinde, . . .

It seems likely, then, that these two sonnets are later than 33 and 34, in which Shakespeare blames his friend rather than his mistress for what has happened. After the tearful reconciliation,

> Ah but those teares are pearle which thy love sheeds,   34.13–14
> And they are ritch, and ransome all ill deeds.

Shakespeare is concerned to excuse his friend:

> Such civill war is in my love and hate,   35.12–14
> That I an accessary needs must be,
> To that sweet theefe which sourely robs from me.

and more explicitly,

> I doe forgive thy robb'rie gentle theefe   40.9–14
> Although thou steale thee all my poverty:
> And yet love knowes it is a greater griefe
> To bear loves wrong, then hates knowne injury.
>   Lascivious grace in whom all il wel showes,
>   Kill me with spights yet we must not be foes.

By the time we reach 41 it appears that Southampton was wooed as Venus wooed Adonis:

> Gentle thou art, and therefore to be wonne,   41.5–8
> Beautious thou art, therefore to be assailed.
> And when a woman woes, what womans sonne,
> Will sourely leave her till he have prevailed.

Southampton is not wholly forgiven:

> Aye me, but yet thou mighst my seat forbeare,   41.9–11
> And chide thy beauty, and thy straying youth,
> Who lead thee in their ryot even there.

but in the following sonnet Shakespeare explains the matter away by saying that he and Southampton are really one person:

> Sweete flattery, then she loves but me alone.   42.12

Nothing more is said about the lady in the series of sonnets to the young man, but the story is continued in the Dark Lady series with 133 and 134, as I have already mentioned. The impression one gains is that these latter sonnets are just as much written for Southampton as the 'young man' series, even though ostensibly addressed to the lady.

From here onward all the sonnets to the Dark Lady mention her promiscuity and grow more and more disillusioned:

> Thou blinde foole love, what doost thou to mine eyes,   137.1–2
> That they behold and see not what they see: . . .

At first the tone is light, with the punning *Will* Sonnets (135 and 136). Some have thought that these sonnets indicate that the name of the other member of the triangle, as well as Shakespeare's, was Will; there is nothing, however, to require this. The pun is simply on the cant meaning of 'will' as sexual desire and, more concretely, sexual parts:[1]

> So thou beeing rich in *Will* adde to thy *Will*,   135.11–12
> One will of mine to make thy large *Will* more.

The sonnets become more and more ribald, no doubt reflecting the growing rakishness of Southampton's tastes and behaviour. There is nothing like them in the sonnets addressed directly to the young man:

> My soule doth tell my body that he may,   151.7–14
> Triumph in love, flesh staies no farther reason,
> But rysing at thy name doth point out thee,
> As his triumphant prize, proud of this pride,

> He is contented thy poore drudge to be
> To stand in thy affaires, fall by thy side.
> No want of conscience hold it that I call,
> Her love, for whose dear love I rise and fall.

This is reminiscent of Thomas Nashe's poem, *The Choise of Valentines*, though a good deal less crudely erotic in its language. Nashe's work is not, as Rowse has called it, 'a bunch of lascivious valentines'[2] but a narrative poem about a young man going out to find himself a woman on St Valentine's Day. What befalls bears a marked similarity to certain of those parts of Petronius's *Satyricon* which used in old translations to be left in the original Latin. The poem is addressed 'To the right Honorable the lord S.' and is prefaced by a sonnet:

> Pardon sweete flower of matchless Poetrie,
>> And fairest bud the red rose ever bare;
>> Although my Muse devor'st from deeper care
>> Presents thee with a wanton Elegie.
> Ne blame my verse of loose unchastitie
>> For painting forth the things that hidden are,
>> Since all men acte what I in speache declare,
>> Onelie induced by varietie.
> Complaints and praises everie one can write,
>> And passion-out their pangu's in statelie rimes,
>> But of loves pleasure's none did ever write
>> That hath succeeded in theis latter times.
> Accept of it Dear Lord in gentle gree,
>> And better lynes ere long shall honor thee.[3]

There is little doubt that this was written to Southampton. E. K. Chambers says that 'Southampton had no claim to be addressed as the "fairest bud the red rose ever bare"', but this is only true if one insists on regarding the 'red rose' as the rose of Lancaster. Shakespeare constantly addresses him as or compares him with the rose in the Sonnets. Indeed, in the very first sonnet the words 'rose' and 'bud' are both used in relation to the young man. I find it very difficult to believe that in the first line of Nashe's sonnet he is not addressing Southampton as the sweet flower of *Shakespeare's* matchless poetry, just as he referred to Shakespeare in the dedication of *The Unfortunate Traveller*.* The lines:

> Complaints and praises euerie one can write,
> And passion-out their pangu's in statelie rimes,

probably also refer primarily to Shakespeare, in view of the fact that Nashe's last line so strongly resembles Shakespeare's dedication of *Venus and Adonis*:

> . . . till I have honoured you with some graver labour.

At the end of the poem there is an epilogue:

* See pp. 78-9.

> Thus hath my penne presum'd to please my friend;
>   Oh mightst thow lykewise please Apollo's eye.
> No: Honor brooke's no such impietie;
>   Yett Ovids wanton Muse did not offend.
> He is the fountaine whence my streames doe flowe.
>   Forgive me if I speake as I was taught,
>   A lyke to women, utter all I knowe,
>   As longing to unlade so bad a fraught.
> My mynde once purg'd of such lascivious witt,
>   With purifide word's, and hallowed verse
>   Thy praises in large volumes shall rehearce,
>   That better maie thy graver view befitt.
> Meanewhile yett rests, yow smile at what I write,
>   Or for attempting, banish me your sight.

On the other hand, some have suggested that 'Ovid's wanton Muse' in the fourth line is a reference to Shakespeare's *Venus and Adonis*. But surely this is made most unlikely by what Nashe says in his first sonnet:

> But of loves pleasure's none did ever write
> That hath succeeded in theis latter times.

If that is so, how could he claim a modern poet as his teacher? There is in fact no comparison between the gentle lasciviousness of *Venus and Adonis* and the unashamed pornography of *The Choise of Valentines*. It is far more likely that Nashe was in fact referring to Ovid, translations of whose *Art of Love* used until quite recently to be kept on special shelves in certain Soho bookstalls.

The Choise of Valentines was never printed, and we can only surmise when it was written. I think it very probable that it was presented to Southampton in February 1594, and that his 'lascivious grace' was sufficiently amused by it for Shakespeare to decide to be rather more Rabelaisian than usual in some of the Dark Lady sonnets.

There is only a little more in the rest of the Dark Lady series that helps with their dating. There are no references to characters or events which may be identified. Some of these sonnets, to wit 145–146 and 153–154, appear to have no connection with the main sequence, though that does not necessarily mean that they were not written in the order in which they appear in the 1609 Quarto.

We are given a *terminus ad quem* in respect of Sonnets 138 and 144 by the fact that versions of both of these appear in *The Passionate Pilgrim*, published in 1599. There is also a resemblance between 146 and a sonnet by Bartholomew Griffin, published in 1596, which may indicate that Shakespeare's sonnet had been written by that date.[4] Here are the first two quatrains of Griffin's twenty-eighth Sonnet to *Fidessa*:

> Well may my soule immortall and divine,
>   That is imprison'd in a lump of clay

> Breath out laments, untill this bodie pine,
>   That from her takes her pleasures all away.
> Pine then thou loathed prison of my life;
>   Untoward subject of the least aggrievance,
> O let me dye: mortalitie is rife,
>   Death comes by wounds, by sicknes, care & chance.

And here is Shakespeare's sonnet as it appears in the 1609 Quarto:

> Poore soule the center of my sinfull earth,   146
> My sinfull earth these rebbell powres that thee array,
> Why dost thou pine within and suffer dearth
> Painting thy outward walls so costlie gay?
> Why so large cost having so short a lease,
> Dost thou upon thy fading mansion spend?
> Shall wormes inheritors of this excesse
> Eate up they charge? is this thy bodies end?
> Then soule live thou upon they servants losse,
> And let that pine to aggravat thy store;
> Buy tearmes divine in selling houres of drosse:
> Within be fed, without be rich no more,
>   So shalt thou feed on death, that feeds on men,
>   And death once dead, ther's no more dying then.

Griffin was a notorious plagiarist (for instance of Daniel), and it is thus unlikely that Shakespeare was the borrower here.

In passing we may note that a great many attempts have been made to amend the second line of this sonnet, where the words 'My sinfull earth' have fairly obviously been repeated by the printer from line one. To my mind far the best suggestion is that of Palgrave, of *Golden Treasury* fame:

> Foil'd by these rebbell powres that thee array, . . .

The double sense of 'frustration' and 'a setting for a jewel' contained in the word 'foil' fits in well. Ingram and Redpath have recently suggested that there may also be another pun on 'foil'd' and 'fil'd' (meaning defiled), which were probably pronounced almost alike.[5]

It should be mentioned that 'earth' in the first line of the sonnet has, as well as that of body, the sense of 'domain', as in *King John*,

> and by this hand I swear   KJ. II.i.344
> That sways the earth this climate overlooks,

and *Romeo and Juliet*,

> She is the hopeful lady of my earth: RJ. I.ii.15

So the transition to 'mansion' is not as abrupt as it first appears.

It is interesting to read together with this sonnet the speech of King Richard II on arriving at Barkloughly Castle:

> I weep for joy   *RII*.III.
> To stand upon my kingdom once again.   ii.4–7 & 12–13
> Dear earth, I do salute thee with my hand,
> Though rebels wound thee with their horses' hoofs: . . .
> Feed not thy sovereign's foe, my gentle earth,
> Nor with thy sweets comfort his ravenous sense; . . .

Here the rebel is Henry Bolingbroke, Duke of Hereford. E. K. Chambers places *Richard II* in 1595, so it might be that Shakespeare had started thinking about it when he wrote Sonnet 146.

Sonnets 147, 148, 149, 150 and 152 all repeat, with variations of language, the contents of the following couplet:

> For I have sworne thee faire, and thought thee bright,   147.13–14
> Who art as black as hell, as darke as night.

And indeed, the poet had certainly done just that:

> Then will I sweare beauty her selfe is blacke,   132.13–14
> And all they foule that thy complexion lacke.

This immediately recalls the first quatrain of Sonnet 100:

> Where art thou Muse that thou forgetst so long,   100.1–4
> To speake of that which gives thee all thy might?
> Spendst thou thy furie on some worthlesse songe,
> Darkning thy powre to lend base subjects light.

The implication seems to me to be that since Shakespeare left Southampton he had sent him nothing except sonnets about the Dark Lady. He had said at the parting:

> But doe thy worst to steale thy selfe away,   92.1–2
> For tearme of life thou art assured mine,

and, although he addressed no poetry directly to his patron between 96 in March and 97 in about September, Sonnet 100 suggests that he had gone on sending him sonnets which were not addressed directly to him. Indeed, Shakespeare may have felt consciously or unconsciously that the sonnets abusing the Dark Lady were a good way of letting off steam against Southampton himself without appearing to do so, since the lady's neglect of Shakespeare stemmed from her infatuation with the young Earl. However that may be, Shakespeare's 'femall evill' certainly fits the description of a 'base subject', who caused him to darken his power to lend her light, much better than does his play-writing, which has usually been suggested as the explanation of this passage. After all, Southampton was notoriously fond of play-going, and in any case it would be absurd to describe a play as a 'songe'. Furthermore, 'base' in sixteenth-century usage could mean 'of dark colour';[6] it is used in that sense in Sonnets 33.5 and 34.3. The lady was thus doubly a 'base subject'. Indeed, she was herself the 'base clouds' of 33 and 34 which disgraced the 'sun'.

We now have, therefore, a final date for the Dark Lady series; as we have seen, they began around the time of the publication of *Venus and Adonis*, in the summer of 1593, and it now appears from Sonnet 100 that they ended before the publication of *The Rape of Lucrece*, in the autumn of 1594. Apart from this, there is little more information that can be gained about the story of the Dark Lady. By the nature of things it is not to be expected that she would make a great mark on history, and speculations as to her identity are thus profitless.

G. B. Harrison, followed by Leslie Hotson, has suggested that she was Lucy Morgan, a notorious brothel-keeper of the time, sometimes referred to as Black Luce. Hotson proffers several supposed punning references to her name from the text of the Dark Lady sonnets.[7] But as good a case could be made out for her name being Susan Barnes, quoting the repeated use of words such as 'sue' or 'suit' and 'store' both in the sonnets and in the play *Love's Labour's Lost* where references to a dark and flighty lady occur![8]

Mention should perhaps be made of the intriguing satirical poem, *Willobie His Avisa*, which appears to contain references to Southampton and Shakespeare. Although these identifications have been doubted, there has been no other theory which so convincingly fits the following prose passage introducing a section of the poem:

> H. W. being sodenly infected with the contagion of a fantasticall fit, at the first sight of A, pyneth a while in secret griefe, at length not able any longer to indure the burning heate of so fervent a humour, bewrayeth the secresy of his disease unto his familiar friend W. S. who not long before had tryed the curtesy of the like passion, and was now newly recovered of the like infection; yet finding his frend let bloud in the same vaine, he took pleasure for a tyme to see him bleed, & in steed of stopping the issue, he inlargeth the wound, with the sharpe rasor of a willing conceit, perswading him that he thought it a matter very easy to be compassed, & no doubt with payne, diligence & some cost in time to be obtayned. Thus this miserable comforter comforting his frend with an impossibilitie, eyther for that he now would secretly laugh at his frends folly, that had given occasion not long before unto others to laugh at his owne, or because he would see whether an other could play his part better then himselfe, & in vewing a far off the course of this loving Comedy, he determined to see whether it would sort to a happier end for this new actor, then it did for the old player. But at length this Comedy was like to have growen to a Tragedy, by the weake & feeble estate that H. W. was brought unto, by a desperate vewe of an impossibility of obtaining his purpose . . .

Professor G. P. V. Akrigg has recently suggested that the 'Avisa' of the poem, who drives so many suitors to despair by her chastity, is intended to represent

Queen Elizabeth, and that the various disappointed lovers are either actual suitors, such as the Earl of Leicester and the Duke of Anjou, or courtiers who sought to ingratiate themselves with her. If this is so, the case for the identification of H. W. with Southampton is strengthened. To quote Akrigg:

> A glance at Elizabeth's court in mid-1594 supplies us with the answer. Southampton was among the foremost of the contenders for royal favour. The previous year he had reportedly been nominated for the Order of the Garter. Not until 1595, when his attentions to Elizabeth Vernon became obvious, did he forfeit the Queen's affection. The 'H. W.' who was seeking Avisa's favour in 1594 can only have been Henry Wriothesley, Earl of Southampton.[9]

If this interpretation is correct, we are brought back immediately to Sonnet 70:

> Thou hast past by the ambush of young daies,   70.9-14
> Either not assayld, or victor beeing charg'd,
> Yet this thy praise cannot be soe thy praise,
> To tye up envy, evermore inlarged,
>   If some suspect of ill maskt not thy show,
>   Then thou alone kingdomes of hearts shouldst owe.

It will be recalled that in Chapter VIII I interpreted the last line as relating to Southampton's chances of obtaining the favour of Queen Elizabeth. Although 'Willobie' puts Shakespeare's advice into rather less respectful language:

> She is no Saynt, She is no Nonne,
> I think in tyme she may be wonne . . .

it nevertheless seems possible that this sonnet and the gossip surrounding it may have been the basis for this part of 'Willobie's' satire.

Akrigg suggests that the words: ' . . . his familiar frend W. S. who not long before had tried the curtesy of the like passion . . .' may indicate that Shakespeare himself had suffered some rebuff from the Queen, such as refusal of an office. But there is really no reason to suppose that the passion referred to is anything other than Shakespeare's infatuation for the Dark Lady, now turned to disillusionment. If 'Willobie' had access to Sonnet 70 he may well have seen some of the Dark Lady sonnets too.

Willobie His Avisa was entered in the Stationers' Register on 3rd September, 1594, and published some time in the same year. It contains a reference to *The Rape of Lucrece*, but only in the commendatory verses at the beginning, which would probably have been added during the final printing. In 1599 an attempt was made by the authorities to suppress it, so it must have been considered to contain some objectionable libels. Nevertheless, it was popular enough to run through five editions in fifteen years. Although it has little enough to tell us about the Dark Lady, it does add something to our knowledge of Shakespeare and Southampton.

CHAPTER XIV

An Interval

ALTHOUGH the sonnets, as will appear in Chapter XVIII, make a leap from 1594 to 1603, we cannot, if we are to understand their background, make the same leap without pausing to take note of some of the things which took place during the eventful years which lay between. But this is in no sense a history book, and I shall glance only at events which affected characters who have been referred to in the preceding sonnets or who will be encountered in the twenty which are still to come.[1]

Besides Shakespeare and Southampton we have already been introduced by direct or indirect allusion to the following historical personages:

Mary, Countess of Southampton	(3.9–10)
Barnabe Barnes	(21)
Sir Walter Raleigh	(25.5–12 and 66.12)
Lady Bridget Manners	(39.1)
Francis Bacon	(66.2)
Edward Coke	(66.3)
Sir Robert Cecil	(66.5)
Queen Elizabeth	(66.6 and 96.5–6)
Earl of Essex	(66.7)
Lord Burghley	(66.8)
George Chapman	(66.10–11 and 78–86)
Alice, Countess of Derby	(97.8)

This list includes only those who were still alive at the end of 1594. Those already dead were:

Anthony Browne (Southampton's uncle)	(12.8)
Christopher Marlowe	(30)
Dr Roderigo Lopez	(96.9–10)
Ferdinando, Earl of Derby	(97.8)

In the Jacobean sonnets, Nos. 107–126, we shall meet with several more, most of whom also played a part in the events of the final years of Queen Elizabeth's reign. It will be convenient also to list these here:

The late Queen Elizabeth	(107.5 and 14)
George Chapman	(107.6)
King James I	(107.7, 114.2 and 10, 115.6)
Sir Philip Herbert	(110, 113.9–12, 125.1–2)

Lord Cecil of Essendon   (113.9–12, 114.5)
Stephen Harrison and collaborators   (123, 125.3–4)
Sir Robert Dudley   (124.1–4)
Lord Grey of Wilton and his friends   (124.7–8 and 13–14)
Earl of Essex (and others)   (125.5–8)
Lord Wriothesley   (126)

Let us now pick up the threads from the year 1594.

Southampton's mother, the beautiful Mary, daughter of Viscount Montague, had now been a widow for thirteen years. With her son due to enter into his inheritance in October 1594, she was anxious not to be in the position of the dowager described in the opening lines of *A Midsummer Night's Dream*:

> Now, fair Hyppolyta, our nuptial hour
> Draws on apace; four happy days bring in
> Another moon; but, O, methinks, how slow
> This old moon wanes! She lingers my desires,
> Like to a step-dame or a dowager,
> Long withering out a young man's revenue.

Her father, who (as we saw in Chapter III) died towards the end of 1592, had appointed as overseer of his will the Vice-Chamberlain of Queen Elizabeth's household, Sir Thomas Heneage, an elegant and capable courtier. Heneage's wife died in November 1593, and he lost little time in choosing Lady Southampton to succeed her. The wedding was duly solemnized on 2nd May, 1594.

Queen Elizabeth was not pleased to hear of the marriage; her reaction was the same whenever any of those close to her announced marriage plans or, worse still, got married without consulting her. Soon afterwards she had another marriage to fume over, that of one of her favourite ladies-in-waiting, Lady Bridget Manners.

In Chapter V we found Lady Bridget being addressed, together with Southampton and other members of the nobility, by Barnabe Barnes in a flattering dedicatory sonnet to accompany his *Parthenophil and Parthenophe*. The previous year, in November 1592, the Queen had instructed Sir Thomas Heneage to write to Lady Bridget's mother, the Countess of Rutland, commending highly 'the exceeding good modest and honorable behaviour and carriage of my lady Bridget your daughter with her careful and diligent attendance of her Majestie'.

Either Southampton or the Earl of Bedford, both of whom, together with Lady Bridget's brother, the Earl of Rutland, were wards of the Crown under the guardianship of Lord Burghley, might have been thought an ideal match for her; but Bridget had other ideas, and, so, it seems, did her mother. Bridget's uncle, Roger Manners, wrote to the Countess on 19th June, 1594, that he was 'very glad of the conclusion you have made with the executors of Mr Tyrwhitt, for the wardship and marriage of the young gentleman'. On 5th July Mary

Harding, a gentlewoman attendant on Lady Bridget, wrote to the Countess of Rutland:

> If your Ladyship ask Mr. Manners his advice, he will speake stryghte of my Lord of Bedford, or my Lord Southampton. If they were in her choice, she saith, she would choose my Lord Wharton before them, for they be so young, and fantasticall, and would be so caryed awaye, that yf anything should come to your Ladiship but good, being her only stay, she doubteth their carridge of themselves, seynge some expearyance of the lyke in this place.[2]

It is fortunate that Mistress Harding did not know that Mr Manners had already expressed approval of a match with young Tyrwhitt, or we might have been denied this beautiful character sketch of the two Earls, so reminiscent of the *Two Gentlemen of Verona*, or of the young bloods in *Romeo and Juliet*. The Lord Wharton whom she mentions was a middle-aged widower with several children, the greatest possible contrast to these two gay sparks.

The Countess of Rutland on 18th July applied for her daughter to be given leave to come home after her five years absence on duty at court. This was granted, but shortly afterwards the Queen was enraged to learn that Lady Bridget had got herself married to young Robert Tyrwhitt. She ordered that Tyrwhitt be committed to prison and Bridget to the custody of the Countess of Bedford. After some obstruction from Bridget's mother this was duly done. The Queen did not relent until November, when both were released. Lady Bridget had loyally taken all the blame on herself, but the Queen rightly surmized that her mother was a party to the transaction and made it clear that she held the Countess chiefly responsible. Every mother must have been on the Countess's side!

Lady Bridget Manners has no further part to play in our story, but apart from her brief appearance in Sonnet 39 she is important in filling out the background to the sonnets of early 1594 and to *A Lover's Complaint* and the early comedies, as well as to Chapman's description of Cynthia's virgin chamber. She lived to enjoy no more than ten years of married life, and was buried in Bigby Church by the time Shakespeare finally closed his sonnet sequence.

We have already glanced in Chapter XI at yet another wedding which was in the news about this time, that of the new Earl of Derby to the Lady Elizabeth Vere, whom Southampton had originally been expected to marry. This was celebrated on 26th January, 1595, and was clearly much more agreeable to the Queen than either of the other two I have mentioned, since it took place at her own palace of Greenwich where the court had been spending the Christmas season, entertained from time to time by the Lord Chamberlain's new company of players.

It has often been suggested that Shakespeare's *A Midsummer Night's Dream*, the ending of which indicates that it was first performed at some great wedding, formed part of the celebrations by which the Derby marriage feast was 'most royally kept'. Others, however, have thought that the occasion was the Heneage-Southampton wedding of May 1594,[3] but we can now see that this is so unlikely as to be virtually impossible. For there can be no doubt that Southampton attended his own mother's wedding; for him to have stayed away would have occasioned great gossip and scandal of which some record would certainly remain. There is no reason to suppose that he disapproved of the match, as we know he did of her later marriage to Sir William Harvey. It was entirely in his own interest that his mother should be securely provided for. It is equally difficult to believe that if *A Midsummer Night's Dream* had been presented on that occasion Shakespeare would not have been there.

From Sonnets 97 and 98 we now know very well that Shakespeare could not have been present, since we have deduced that he was separated from the young Earl throughout the spring and summer of 1594. The suggestion that the *Dream* was presented at the Heneage-Southampton wedding can thus be safely dismissed. It is interesting to find, however, that in the *Dream* Shakespeare uses the same conceit that we noticed in Sonnet 97 of unseasonable bad weather being due to an estrangement:

> These are the forgeries of jealousy; *MND* II.i.81–92
> And never, since the middle summer's spring,
> Met we on hill, in dale, forest, or mead,
> By paved fountain, or by rushy brook,
> Or in the beached margent of the sea,
> To dance our ringlets to the whistling wind,
> But with thy brawls thou hast disturb'd our sport.
> Therefore the winds, piping to us in vain,
> As in revenge, have suck'd up from the sea
> Contagious fogs; which, falling in the land,
> Hath every pelting river made so proud
> That they have overborne their continents.

> . . . .

> And thorough this distemperature we see 106–17
> The seasons alter; hoary-headed frosts
> Fall in the fresh lap of the crimson rose;
> And on old Hiems' thin and icy crown
> An odorous chaplet of sweet summer buds
> Is, as in mockery, set. The spring, the summer,
> The childing autumn, angry winter, change
> Their wonted liveries; and the mazed world,
> By their increase, now knows not which is which.
> And this same progeny of evils comes
> From our debate, from our dissension;
> We are their parents and original.

In the one case the estrangement was between Shakespeare and Southampton; now it is between Oberon and Titania. The bad weather, as has often (so far as the *Dream* is concerned) been suggested before, is that of the summer of 1594 both in the sonnet and the play, and there can be little doubt that they were both written about the same time, the autumn of 1594. In the case of the play we have another dating point; it is in Bottom's warning against frightening the ladies with a stage lion:

MND. III.i.31–35

Masters, you ought to consider with yourselves: to bring in—God shield us!—a lion among ladies, is a most dreadful thing; for there is not a more fearful wild-fowl than your lion living; and we ought to look to it.

On 30th August, 1594, Prince Henry of Scotland had been christened at Stirling with great ceremony:

That night was held a very magnificent banquet, at which, after the guests had refreshed themselves at the first service, there entered a blackamoor, very richly attired, drawing as it seemed, a triumphal chariot wherein stood Ceres, Fecundity, Faith, Concord, Liberality, and Perseverance, set round a table richly set out. This chariot should indeed have been drawn by a lion, but because his presence might have brought some fear to the nearest, or the sight of the lights and torches might have moved his tameness, it was thought best to supply the blackamoor in his place.

A pamphlet giving the full account of the celebrations, including this intriguing detail, was registered on 24th October and, apparently, read with interest by Shakespeare. All in all, there is little room for doubt that it was the Derby wedding in the following January for which the Chamberlain's Men presented *A Midsummer Night's Dream*. Was the play given that title because it was originally commissioned to be performed at a June wedding? If so, the postponement was an added reason why Shakespeare should say in Sonnet 98:

Yet nor the laies of birds, nor the sweet smell   98.5–7
Of different flowers in odor and in hew,
Could make me any summers story tell: . . .

For Shakespeare the Christmas season of 1594–5 was the first of a long series given by his company at the court, first of the Queen and then of King James, which continued up to and after his own death. Southampton's gift at the end of 1594 was all he required to set his career in motion, and so to ensure his immortality 'even in the eyes of all posterity'.

For Southampton the road was to be far more devious and full of pitfalls, mostly of his own digging. He was still a favourite to succeed Essex as darling of the Queen, but he did nothing to help his own prospects. No doubt she was well aware of how he had helped the Danvers brothers to escape to France in

October 1594, and of his closeness to the unruly Essex. On 23rd September, 1595, Rowland Whyte wrote to Sir Robert Sidney:

> I was told that Sir William Cornwallis doth often trouble her majesties eares with tales of my Lord of Essex, who is thought to be an observer of all his doings and to examine Mudriff, which brings unquietnes in the Queene and occasions the like in my Lord. My Lord of Southampton doth with too much familiarity courte the faire Mrs Vernon, while his frends, observing the Queene's humours towards my Lord of Essex, doe what they can to bring her to favour him, but it is yet in vain.

At the beginning of October came another report:

> My Lord of Essex kept his Bed all Yesterday; his Favour continues . . . Yet my Lord of Southampton is a carefull Waiter here, and *sede vacante* doth receve Favors at Her Majestyes Handes; all this without Breach of Amity between them.[4]

But not long afterwards Southampton was rebuffed when he offered to help the Queen to her horse. There were several reasons why he found it so difficult to gain her favour; his father had been involved in the Ridolfi plot to oust Elizabeth and put Mary Queen of Scots on her throne, so great circumspection would in any case have been required of his son. Instead of this he chose to risk the royal displeasure by philandering with the Maids of Honour; furthermore, if one may judge from the Sonnets, he was much more disposed to receive flattery himself than to pay the absurdly extravagant compliments which the ageing Queen expected from her courtiers. He was too impatient to be a 'careful Waiter' on her pleasure for very long without result, and the contrast with his indefatigable loyalty to the Earl of Essex must have been all too apparent to the Queen.

Meanwhile the ex-favourite Raleigh had managed to get permission to take a small fleet out against the Spaniards and to retain any booty collected, after payment of duties, as recompense for those who helped to finance the expedition. Among these investors were both Lord Burghley and his son Sir Robert Cecil; so clearly Raleigh's rehabilitation had made considerable progress, though it was still far from complete. The fleet set sail in February 1595, but three of the five ships were lost as they tried to cross the Atlantic. Raleigh visited Trinidad, where he left his two remaining ships and went on in boats to Guiana. They reached the Orinoco river, but had to turn back because of storms and floods. The expedition arrived back in England in September bringing very little in the way of reward for the promoters, but a great deal of information about these strange parts.

Another explorer to pay a visit to Guiana was Robert Dudley, the bastard son of the Earl of Leicester, who set sail with four ships in November 1594 and returned in May 1595. We shall hear more of him in Chapter XX when he tries to establish that his mother, Lady Sheffield, was the lawful wife of the

Earl and that he himself is thus entitled to the earldoms of Leicester and Warwick.

The same autumn another book was circulated in England by Father Parsons, the Jesuit whose previous pamphlet had contained the allegations of Raleigh's atheism. The new book, issued this time under the pseudonym of Doleman, was called *A Conference about the next Succession to the Crown of England*, and it was shrewdly dedicated, without permission, to the Earl of Essex. Nothing could have been calculated to infuriate Queen Elizabeth more, as she refused to hear any mention of the subject of the succession until she was on her death-bed. In this case, however, the publication came at a convenient moment, since it gave her the excuse to move decisively against Essex's candidate for the still vacant post of Solicitor-General, Francis Bacon. The Queen most charmingly accepted Essex's protestations that he was in no way responsible for the book being dedicated to him, even visiting him in his chamber on 4th November while he lay ill from the shock. The following day she appointed Serjeant Fleming as Solicitor.

The exchange which then took place between Essex and Bacon is very revealing as regards the characters of both of them. Essex paid a special visit to the Bacon household at Twickenham Park to say to his disappointed aide:

> Master Bacon, the Queen hath denied me yon place for you and hath placed another. I know you are the least part of your own matter, but you fare ill because you have chosen me for your mean and dependence. You have spent your time and your thoughts in my matters; I die if I do not somewhat towards your fortune; you shall not deny to accept a piece of land which I will bestow upon you.

Bacon's immediate reaction was that by accepting the gift he might be incurring too great an obligation to Essex which could prove an embarrassment in the future. However, since Essex was so pressing he replied:

> My Lord, I see I must be your homager and hold land of your gift: but do you know the manner of doing homage in law? Always it is with a saving of his faith to the King and his other Lords. And therefore, my Lord, I can be no more yours than I was, and it must be with the ancient savings, and if I grow to be a rich man, you will give me leave to give it back to some of your unrewarded followers.[5]

Essex must have thought of these words a few years later when he found Bacon getting up in court to prosecute him for his life.

CHAPTER XV

Southampton and Essex

THE story of the years from 1596 to 1601 is largely that of the Earl of Essex and his ill-fated determination to make himself at once the Queen's chief political adviser and controller of patronage and her supreme military commander. Although the Queen tried where possible to avoid refusing him directly, she had little confidence in his judgment and no intention whatever of succumbing to his domination. Yet his personal attraction remained very powerful, both for Elizabeth and for his own band of devoted young followers, most of whom remained loyal to the disastrous and inevitable end.

At the beginning of April, 1596, Essex was appointed to take charge of a rescue force to save Calais from being taken by the Spaniards. He lay fuming at Calais impatient to be performing splendid feats of military heroism, while the Queen waited for Henri IV of France to agree to her terms for providing the assistance. She was not interested in the glory of war; her charge to Essex was 'Do in no wise peril so fair an army for another Prince's town'. As it turned out, Henri did not agree in time to the Queen's terms and Calais fell. Essex's force never left Dover harbour. But the Queen was right to be hesitant: Stow tells us that the French were more willing that the Spaniards should take Calais than that the English should relieve it; they felt they could hope to get it back quicker from the Spaniards than from the English, once they were in possession. Had not Queen Mary died with 'Calais' engraved on her heart? Essex might thus have found that both besiegers and defenders were ranged against him and his 'fair army'.

Elizabeth was particular about the young gallants that Essex might be permitted to take with him as officers on such expeditions. One of those expressly forbidden to join the Calais force was Essex's most loyal admirer, the Earl of Southampton. He was also refused permission to join a more promising enterprise which set sail the following June. This was the famous expedition to 'singe the King of Spain's beard'.

The previous July four hundred Spanish soldiers had landed in Cornwall and sacked Penzance and two other villages. In October a captured Spanish pilot had reported that an invasion of Ireland was in preparation. There was thus good reason to teach the King of Spain a lesson, and the Queen had a 'Declaration' to that effect published in several languages and circulated round Europe. The two commanders for the expedition were the Lord Admiral (in charge of the fleet) and Essex (in charge of the army). With them were Sir Walter Raleigh (as Rear-Admiral), Sir Francis Vere and Sir Conyers Clifford. Essex's dislike of Raleigh never remained far below the surface, and it was not long before Raleigh found reason to complain that he was being ignored in favour of Vere. Essex smoothed this over by saying that Raleigh would take precedence by sea and Vere by land.

In the event, it was Raleigh's wisdom and skill that enabled the Spanish fleet to be smashed in front of Cadiz, so that the English troops were able to make a successful landing and sack the town. Since both the naval and the military commanders could thus both claim equal success, relations between Essex and Raleigh were for the time being very cordial. The Earl was able to return to England in triumph, and Raleigh was able to come a little nearer to regaining the favour of the Queen. But there was one fly in the ointment: what had happened to the vast booty taken from Cadiz? The Queen was disgusted to find that less than £13,000 value had been brought back for the exchequer, whereas he had disbursed £50,000 beforehand for the cost of the expedition. In spite of the lesson that should have been learned from the capture of the grand carrack in 1592, the rest of the booty had all been pilfered by her loyal subjects, and Essex was to blame.

In March 1597 we find that 'Sir Walter Raleigh hath been very often private with the Earl of Essex and is said to be a mediator of peace between him and Sir Robert Cecil, who likewise hath been private with him'. Relations with the Queen remained bad, and Essex was prepared to listen to any suggestions for improving them. Nevertheless, he insisted on pressing that his friend Sir Robert Sidney should be made Warden of the Cinque Ports, and thus as usual made it certain that the Queen would choose someone else. She chose one of his enemies, the new Lord Cobham, whose lately deceased father had previously held the post. Essex announced that he was going to leave the court and spend some time in Wales; just as he was setting off the next day the Queen called him back and offered him the appointment of Master of the Ordnance, an important office of state.

So all seemed peaceful again; but a week later the patent for the appointment had still not been signed, and even when Essex took it in himself to the Queen she still did not sign it. She was determined to keep him in suspense as to whether the appointment of the hated Cobham would be signed before his own, and she took her own time.

On 18th April Essex, Cecil and Raleigh patched up their quarrels (or rather, Essex's quarrels with the other two) and celebrated the occasion with a dinner. They decided that another successful sea expedition was what was required to restore both Essex and Raleigh to favour, as well as to protect England from further molestation by the King of Spain. In June a fleet and an army to travel in it were duly got together, and this time Essex was made commander both by sea and by land, with Lord Thomas Howard as Vice-Admiral and Sir Walter Raleigh as Rear-Admiral.

In the meantime the Queen had only been persuaded with great difficulty to approve the expedition, and at one stage had sent Lord Thomas Howard strict instructions not to put to sea. However, the rarity of finding the Cecils,

Essex and Raleigh all agreeing with one another must have been enough to do the trick. She not only agreed to the expedition but on 1st June restored Raleigh to favour and to his place at court as Captain of the Guard. The Earl of Southampton was at last permitted to prove his prowess, and was given command of a good-sized ship called the *Garland*, with 190 mariners, 30 gunners and 80 soldiers.

Alas, the venture was ill-starred from the beginning. There was a severe storm in the Channel and many of the ships were badly damaged. Essex was driven into Falmouth and Raleigh into Plymouth. The whole fleet which sailed out so boldly from Plymouth on 10th July all had to be recalled there, and it was 17th August before they were able to set out again. They limited their objective to the Azores. In October they returned with, sad to say, almost nothing achieved, except a final end to any further chances of restoring friendly relations between Essex and Raleigh. The one to come best out of the whole enterprise was the Earl of Southampton, who did at least capture and sink a Spanish frigate.

Before Essex returned to Plymouth the Queen decided to promote the Lord Admiral, Lord Howard of Effingham, who had been with him on the Cadiz voyage, to be Earl of Nottingham. When Essex eventually arrived he sulked for several weeks and kept away from court, until the Queen finally relented by creating him Earl Marshal, which gave him precedence again over the Lord Admiral. For a time honour was satisfied.

Following a visit by a special ambassador from the King of France, the Queen decided early in 1598 to return the compliment by sending Sir Robert Cecil on a mission to Paris, and he obtained permission for the Earl of Southampton to accompany him. In spite of his recent success as a naval commander, Southampton's way of life was still giving cause for concern. Since his coming of age he had lived so extravagantly that he had found it necessary to hand over the administration of his whole estate to three attorneys, so that they could endeavour to sort out his affairs and pay off his debts, if necessary by the sale of land. Meanwhile, instead of getting married to some wealthy heiress who would restore his fortunes, he was still carrying on an affair with Essex's cousin, the penniless Elizabeth Vernon.

Mistress Vernon was heartbroken at the prospect of being left behind in England while Southampton toured the Continent; and well she might be, since it turned out that he had left her pregnant. To make matters worse, Southampton had offended the Queen by having a fight in the precincts of the court with Mr Ambrose Willoughby, who, in his capacity as Esquire of the Body, had told him to pack up his game of primero late one night in the Presence Chamber. The Queen banished him from court for a short while, but he was permitted back again in good time to accompany Sir Robert Cecil to France on 10th February.

When Cecil returned to England in April, Southampton stayed on in Paris with his friends the two Danvers brothers, who had escaped to France in 1594 with his help. They were pardoned and permitted to return to England in August, and Southampton secretly returned with them, though he had no permission to do so. However, his reason was an honourable one, for he came to marry Elizabeth Vernon. As soon as this was done he hastened back to Paris.

In a day or two the Queen had found out the whole story and exploded with wrath. The new Countess was summarily committed to the Fleet prison (though to the 'sweetest and best apointed lodging' there). Instructions were sent for Southampton to return to London immediately, but he lingered on in Paris for a while, gambling heavily, on the pretext that he must wait for money to be sent him from England. By November he also was in the Fleet prison in London, and his wife was delivered of a daughter the same month.

Besides having infuriated the Queen, Southampton was now at loggerheads with his own mother. His father-in-law, Sir Thomas Heneage, had not long survived his second marriage; by now he had been dead for three years. Lady Southampton decided to marry again, and this time she accepted the proposal of a suitor with a much longer expectation of life, Sir William Harvey, who was still in his thirties. Unfortunately, though he had a fine record of service in the defeat of the Armada and on the Cadiz voyage, he was not well endowed with material goods. As executor under the will of Sir Thomas Heneage, Lady Southampton had had to find a good deal of cash to settle his accounts as Vice-Chamberlain of the Household, and her son had already wasted too much of his patrimony to have anything to spare for her. It was exasperating to find his mother being as improvident as himself in her choice of a marriage partner.

The Countess's marriage was rumoured to have taken place in May 1598, while Southampton was away in Paris. The Earl of Essex worked very hard, with the assistance of Lord Henry Howard, to get the couple not to go through with it without Southampton's blessing, and in fact they did not do so until January 1599. But the Countess felt strongly that her son's behaviour with Elizabeth Vernon gave him no right to criticize her own plans. Lord Henry Howard reported to Essex:

> My Lady told me that her son could take no just exception to the party who had been more plain with her in his defence than any man alive. To your Lordship she would ever give all honourable satisfaction in this, or any matter, so far as she might with regard of her own estate and liberty, that she could possible devise, but hoped that her son would look for no account of her proceedings in the course of marriage that made her so great a stranger to his own; and therefore as she would give no cause of unkindness by her fault, so she would not imagine that unkindness could arise without a just occasion.[1]

Finally Southampton was reconciled to the marriage, and fortunately he was released from prison in time for its celebration.

Meanwhile Essex had made little progress in improving his own relations with the Queen. He courted trouble by philandering with her ladies-in-waiting in a shameless manner. In the Privy Council he was constantly advocating forays against Spain, yet his voyage to the Islands had been disastrous. The most serious danger at the time was the rebellion in Ireland, which was being constantly fomented by Spain. Essex considered that the only way to settle the Irish question was to smash Spain, while Lord Burghley and his son were for achieving the same end by making peace with King Philip. In the meantime someone had to be sent to fill the post of Lord Deputy of Ireland which had recently become vacant, and as usual Essex and the Cecils had different candidates.

The matter had come to a head while Southampton was still away in France, at the end of June 1598. The task of pacifying Ireland was by no means eagerly sought after, since the risks of failure were so great. The Cecils, therefore, suggested an Essex man for it; his uncle, Sir William Knollys, Controller of the Household, and, as a fellow Privy Councillor, a useful ally whose support would be lost if he was removed to Ireland. Essex countered by proposing Sir George Carew, a Cecil man whom he disliked. Eventually the Queen tried to settle the question by announcing that she had decided upon Sir William Knollys. Essex gave her a scornful look and turned his back on her. She stepped forward and gave him a box on the ear and told him to go and be hanged.

The Earl laid his hand on his sword, whereupon the Lord Admiral stepped in front of him; but he swore a great oath that he neither would nor could put up with such an indignity, nor would he have taken it from her father, Henry VIII, and withdrew in a passion from the court.

What amazed everyone was that the Queen did not immediately have Essex arrested, strip him of his honours, and chop off his head. Like the wise old lady she was, she gave him no opportunities for flamboyant martyrdom; she left him to his sulks, like a spoilt little boy. That was how to deal with the tantrums of the Earl Marshal of England.

The days dragged by, and still Essex made no attempt to obtain a reconciliation. The Queen thought of sending an intermediary to make soundings as if of his own accord, but then decided that this would be too risky. On 20th July the Lord Keeper, Sir Thomas Egerton, wrote to Essex warning him of the dangers of his present behaviour and saying that it was not too late to put matters right. Essex remained stubborn; 'As for me,' he replied, 'I have received wrong and feel it. My cause is good, I know it.'

On 4th August the Queen's grand old workhorse, Lord Burghley, after all the strains and burdens of his long life, 'went away so mildly as in a sleep, that it could scarce be perceived when the breath went out of his body'. This was the worst of all times for Essex to remain away from court, when the balance of power was bound to be redistributed, yet he still made no move. As Earl Marshal, however, he could not avoid attending Burghley's state funeral, which took place on 29th August, and it was noted he went straight back to his house at Wanstead. This was the time that Southampton came back to England to marry Essex's cousin, and this was a further point of strain with the Queen. Nevertheless, by 10th September Essex somehow brought himself to come back to the Council and make his peace with her.

The news from Ireland continued to grow worse, and still no Lord Deputy had been appointed. Another supporter of Essex was suggested, Lord Mountjoy, the paramour of Essex's sister, Lady Rich. As before, Essex strongly objected. He then, as Camden tells us, insisted that 'into Ireland must be sent some prime man of the nobility which was strong in power, honour, and wealth, in favour with military men, and which had before been general of an army; so as he seemed with the finger to point to himself'. Nothing could have suited Sir Robert Cecil better than that Essex should put his head in the lion's jaws, but he carefully refrained from setting a name to the description which Essex had sketched. Knollys' name was put forward again, and Essex was goaded into personally offering himself for the post, without anyone else having voiced the suggestion. The Queen announced her decision: if Essex was so anxious for the office he should have it. He was convinced, for a time, that he had won a great victory.

It was now November, but it would require until March for Essex's army and entourage to be ready to leave for Ireland. There was much to be done in preparing men, horses and supplies, and also much time-wasting negotiation and intrigue as to who should have the various commands and staff appointments. As usual, the Queen was afraid that Essex would appoint his young friends regardless of their abilities, and she gave strict instructions that certain young nobles, including the Earl of Southampton, should not be given important posts.

One ambitious young peer who went with the expedition was Lord Grey of Wilton, son of a former Lord Deputy of Ireland. In 1598 he was still only twenty-three, but he had already seen service on the Islands voyage, having joined Essex's expedition without the Queen's permission. In July, while Essex was sulking after having his ears boxed, he expressed surprise that Grey should be in such high favour at court, especially with the Queen, and asked him to declare whether he had joined the Cecil camp. Grey replied with some spirit that he was not prepared to be a base dependent of Essex, and that since Cecil had shown him favour he would not show ingratitude in return. Essex flared up and told him that he need never expect any advancement from him. From then on the breach between Grey on the one hand and Essex and Southampton on the other was never healed, as we shall later see.

The Lord Chamberlain's company of players continued to prosper; on Boxing Day and New Year's Day it was performing at Whitehall and on 20th February at Richmond Palace. One of these occasions may well have been the first performance of Shakespeare's *Henry V*, with its complimentary reference to Essex's mission in Ireland in the prologue to Act V. Only the previous September Shakespeare had received notice in a book by Francis Meres as the best English dramatist, both for comedy and tragedy, comparable with Plautus and Seneca among the Latins. He was also numbered among the best lyric and love poets. What price Barnabe Barnes now!

That indefatigable sonneteer had in 1595 published *A Divine Century of Spiritual Sonnets,* dedicated to Dr Toby Matthew, Bishop of Durham. Barnes was himself the son of a former Bishop of Durham. In spite of these impeccable ecclesiastical connections we find him in May 1598 summoned before the Privy Council on a charge of having attempted to poison the Recorder of Berwick. Having been committed to the Marshalsea to await trial, he broke out of prison in July and managed to escape up north, and out of our story.

The lawyers whom the Council had appointed to examine Barnes's case included the Attorney-General, Edward Coke, and Her Majesty's Counsel at large, Francis Bacon. After he had been finally passed over for the post of Solicitor-General the Queen had relented just enough to give Bacon this nominal 'unsworn' appointment (as Coke scornfully described it) of Queen's Counsel. The fees from it were not enough to prevent him being arrested for debt in the autumn of 1598 by an importunate goldsmith to whom he owed £300. Bacon had made another attempt to mend his fortunes after losing the Solicitorship: he had sought the hand of Lady Hatton, the daughter of Sir Robert Cecil's elder brother and widow of Sir William Hatton. Again Essex had been asked to assist, which he did with a vehement letter to Sir Thomas Cecil. Again all was in vain; Lady Hatton duly remarried in November 1598, but to Edward Coke! Did anyone recall Shakespeare's lines from February 1594:

> As to behold desert a begger borne,   66.2–3
> And needie Nothing trimd in jollitie, . . . ?

CHAPTER XVI

Rage and Rebellion

How London doth pour out her citizens!   *HV.* V.pr.24–34
The mayor and all his bretheren in best sort —
Like to the senators of th' antique Rome,
With the plebeians swarming at their heels —
Go forth and fetch their conqu'ring Caesar in;
As, by a lower but loving likelihood,
Were now the General of our gracious Empress —
As in good time he may — from Ireland coming,
Bringing rebellion broached on his sword,
How many would the peaceful city quit
To welcome him!

ON 27th March, 1599, 'the General of our gracious Empress' duly set out for
Ireland, accompanied by the Earls of Southampton and Rutland and the
Lords Grey, Audley and Cromwell and a force which (it was hoped) amounted
to 16,000 foot and 1,400 horse. Essex's commission gave him the full powers
of a commander-in-chief to appoint staff, with no mention of the verbal
stipulations which the Queen had made to him. The only reservation was over
the right to come back to London when he thought fit; this was included in a
separate document so that it could be revoked more easily if the Queen desired.

Essex arrived in Dublin on 14th April, and the very next day he signed a
warrant appointing the Earl of Southampton Lord General of the Horse in
Ireland. Southampton's friend Sir Henry Danvers was appointed Lieutenant of
the Horse, and the Earl of Rutland, whom the Queen had also forbidden to
join the campaign, Lieutenant-General of the Infantry.

The leader of the Irish rebels was Hugh O'Neill, whom Elizabeth had
created Earl of Tyrone. He had trained and armed both his local peasant army
and his Scottish mercenaries into a respectable fighting force, which had
established its reputation at the Battle of the Yellow Ford on 14th August, 1598,
when it soundly defeated an English relief force sent to raise the siege of a fort on
the banks of the Blackwater river. Tyrone was a formidable adversary for the
splendid but largely amateur group of commanders led by Essex.

Southampton's first clash with the enemy, though otherwise unremarkable,
proved to have very serious consequences. One of his subordinate officers was
the mettlesome Lord Grey of Wilton, who took it upon himself to lead a
charge in pursuit of the rebels into the bogs and woods, after Southampton had
prudently ordered him to turn back. For this act of indiscipline Southampton committed Grey to the custody of the Marshal for one night. Grey

was furious; he saw to it that the news got quickly back to London, and on 10th June the Privy Council sent Essex a very peremptorily worded message pointing out that he had appointed Southampton General of the Horse against Her Majesty's specific instructions and ordering him to be removed from that office forthwith.

Before this letter reached Essex, Southampton continued to acquit himself very well, particularly in a skirmish outside Arklow where he showed great courage and resource. Southampton was in fact a very fine horseman himself, as Shakespeare has described for us in *A Lover's Complaint*:

> 'Well could he ride, and often men would say, LC. 106–12
> "That horse his mettle from his rider takes:
> Proud of subjection, noble by the sway,
> What rounds, what bounds, what course, what stop he makes!"
> And controversy hence a question takes,
> Whether the horse by him became his deed,
> Or he his manage by th'well-doing steed . . .'

He was also proving himself an able cavalry commander. It was all the more difficult, therefore, for Essex to admit his fault and remove Southampton from his post. He decided first to appeal against the order, but the letter he sent back to London merely added fuel to the flames of the Queen's wrath. Southampton had to give up his appointment, and Essex thereupon abolished the post. Southampton remained with him as a personal staff officer, demoted from general to captain.

Meanwhile the campaign made no progress, and the Queen became more and more impatient at Essex's reluctance to attack Tyrone in Ulster. Instead he had set out on a tour of Leinster and Munster. To goad him into the northern campaign the Queen revoked his licence to return to England at his own discretion for personal consultation, so that his enemies in London were free to slander him behind his back. They had now been joined by Lord Grey, who decided he had had enough of Ireland and the Essex-Southampton partnership. Rumour had it that two of these enemies, Sir Walter Raleigh and Sir John Stanhope, were likely to be made Privy Councillors. Though this did not take place, Sir Walter Raleigh was given the appointment of Warden of the Stanneries. (Stanhope did join the Council two years later in the post of Vice-Chamberlain.) Essex now began to consider plans of action, not against the Irish rebels but against his own government.

First of all Essex took Southampton to see Sir Christopher Blount, the Marshal into whose custody Lord Grey had been committed the previous May. Blount was Essex's stepfather, having married his mother in 1589, though she continued to use the title of Countess of Leicester which she had gained from her second husband. At this time he was lying in bed at Dublin Castle recovering from a wound, when Essex announced to him that he had decided to sail for Wales with two to three thousand of his best troops and then march on London.

He then withdrew to give Blount time to think over the proposal, and returned the next day to receive his answer.

Fortunately both Blount and Southampton were against the plan. Blount said that it would involve far too much bloodshed, and advised Essex if he must return to England against the Queen's instructions to take only enough friends to protect him against his private enemies. For the time being Essex gave up the idea and even prepared to mount the attack on Tyrone, although eighteen of his officers had put their names to a declaration in support of his opinion that the army was not fit for the purpose.

But such were the security arrangements of Essex's headquarters that even Tyrone soon learned of the way his mind was moving. Essex had set out from Dublin on 28th August; a few days later Tyrone sent word that 'if the Earl would be guided by him, he would make him the greatest man in England'. The same day he sent an officer to Essex to try and arrange a parley. Essex replied with spirit that if Tyrone wanted to meet him he would find him in the field of battle at the head of his army.

The next day, 6th September, Tyrone's emissary appeared again with the message that his commander desired to submit himself to the Queen's mercy and begged Essex to meet him at Bellaclynthe ford. This time Essex agreed. Leaving his escort some way away, with the Earl of Southampton to see that they did not come within earshot, he met Tyrone alone in the middle of the stream, where they talked for the best part of an hour while their horses stood patiently in the water. Tyrone, who was expecting assistance to arrive from Spain, incited Essex to abandon his allegiance to the Queen, whereupon he would join forces with him. Essex rejected this outright; but three concealed spies had heard the shocking proposal.

Tyrone asked for another parley, with other principal officers present on both sides. This was agreed, Essex taking with him Southampton, Sir Henry Danvers and four others. It was decided that a truce should be arranged, terminable at fourteen days' notice. Essex wrote a report of the matter to the Queen, which arrived at court on 16th September. The result was an explosion and a command not to enter into any terms with Tyrone until he had obtained detailed approval in writing. Essex's response was to leave at once for England, taking with him Southampton and a number of other reliable friends, as Sir Christopher Blount had suggested the previous month. They made for the Queen's house of Nonsuch, where the court was in residence.

On his journey southward to Nonsuch, Essex had to pass through London. Southampton left the party to visit his wife, who was staying with Essex's sister, Lady Rich, probably at Lees in Essex. Essex and his remaining followers crossed the Thames at Lambeth and commandeered some horses to ride to Nonsuch, but by now Lord Grey of Wilton had heard of their intention and he galloped off ahead of them to warn Cecil of Essex's arrival. Essex was determined that no one should be able to speak to the Queen before he did, and he went straight to her personal apartments and burst into the royal bedchamber, like Hamlet bursting in upon Queen Gertrude, to find Elizabeth at her toilet.

The surprising thing was that the Queen appeared to deal very kindly with him, excited and travel-stained as he was. Perhaps she had in mind the remark Francis Bacon had made to her a few days previously:

> If you had my Lord of Essex here with a white staff in his hand, as my Lord of Leicester had, and continued him still about for society to yourself, and for an honour and ornament to your attendance and Court in the eyes of your people, and in the eyes of foreign ambassadors, then were he in his right element, for to discontent him as you do and yet put arms and power into his hands, may be a kind of temptation to make him prove cumbersome and unruly.[1]

Certainly he must have looked 'cumbersome and unruly' enough as he knelt before her and kissed her hands with his face covered in mud. She was wise to treat him gently, at this point. But the next day he was summoned before the Privy Council, and the day following, 1st October, committed to the custody of Lord Keeper Egerton in York House.

The factions for Cecil and for Essex marked themselves off clearly at dinner at Nonsuch just before the Privy Council hearing. Those who sat with Cecil and away from Essex were the Earl of Shrewsbury, the Lord Admiral, Lord Thomas Howard, Lord Cobham, Lord Grey, Sir Walter Raleigh, and Sir George Carew. These were the leaders of the group who Essex convinced himself were anxious to ensure a Spanish succession to the throne, and against whom he conceived it his duty to protect the kingdom, as well as himself.

While Essex was imprisoned at York House, Southampton took up residence at Essex House. He passed his time going to plays every day with his friend the Earl of Rutland; one of particular interest would have been Shakespeare's *Julius Caesar,* which was produced about this time.

Lord Mountjoy was appointed to succeed Essex in Ireland, though he was still an Essex man rather than a member of the Cecil faction. In November he discussed seriously with Southampton whether they should raise a rebellion on Essex's behalf, or attempt a sudden coup at court. They decided that it would be better for Essex to flee to France, accompanied by Southampton and Sir Henry Danvers. But Essex was not prepared to be an ignominious fugitive. He turned the proposal down and began to drift into a decline of health and spirit, but by January 1600 he had recovered health again to such an extent that Mountjoy was constrained to agree to bring troops over from Ireland to stage a rebellion. He stipulated that nothing should be done against the Queen's person or sovereignty, and that James King of Scots as her rightful successor should agree to the scheme. The King, probably intentionally, delayed giving any reply to Mountjoy's enquiry on this point before the new Lord Deputy had to set out for Ireland on 7th February.

The Queen dropped her original intention to bring charges against Essex in the Star Chamber, and in March she allowed him to return to his own house. But he was still a prisoner there, his relatives and friends being compelled to move out and leave him in the custody of two gentleman keepers. Southampton now at last made every attempt to regain the Queen's favour, but with little success. He was given permission to return to Ireland under Lord Mountjoy, but was unable to secure any audience. His enemy Lord Grey had also hoped to obtain a substantial command under the new Lord Deputy, but Mountjoy understandably had no time for him. Grey now issued a challenge to Southampton to a duel in satisfaction for the insult he had suffered in being committed to the Marshal's custody in Ireland. This was a piece of gross impertinence, since Southampton was acting well within his authority at the time as Grey's superior officer. However, he agreed to meet Grey in Ireland at any port he might choose. Alternatively, he would meet him at a French port, should he himself not go to Ireland. Grey refused Ireland, because the Lord Deputy and most of his officers were partial to Southampton. The arrangements dragged on as inconclusively as those for a modern peace conference, until Grey threatened to publish the correspondence. Southampton challenged him to do so.

On Monday 21st April Southampton eventually left for Ireland in command of a batch of reinforcements. He left a message for Grey saying he would meet him in any 'post town', but Grey had decided to go off to the Low Countries to serve with the Dutch army. Arrived in Ireland, Southampton once again acquitted himself well, so much so that he persuaded Mountjoy to recommend him for the post of Governor of Connaught. Needless to say, the Queen refused him the appointment, and in July he decided, like Grey, to see if he could win fame in the Low Countries. At once the Privy Council sent letters both to him and to Grey forbidding them to indulge in their duel. It is not certain whether the duel finally took place, but there is some reason to suppose that it did and that Southampton was wounded in it. At any rate, he returned home to England in September, and it was then reported that 'he hath bene extreme sicke, but is now recovered'.

Meanwhile Essex's case had, on 5th June, at last been brought before the Privy Council. Edward Coke, Serjeant Yelverton, Serjeant Fleming and Francis Bacon were all there to take part in the prosecution, which was held, not as usual in Star Chamber, but privately at York House. It was the first time that Bacon, Essex's erstwhile protégé, had come out openly against him, after having been so long his counsellor and friend. The four lawyers raked over Essex's misdemeanours for eleven hours, Coke as usual overstating his case and so building up sympathy for the accused. Essex behaved with abject humility, kneeling on the floor until Archbishop Whitgift 'desired he might stand, and then that he might lean; and lastly that he might sit'. He was stripped of his appointments and honours, but eventually on 26th August he was released from his house arrest, on condition that he did not come to court without permission. A few days previously Sir Walter Raleigh strongly urged Cecil not to relent,

on the grounds that Essex would ascribe the alteration to the Queen's pusil-
lanimity and not to Sir Robert's good nature; 'if he have his liberty then we
have seen the last of her good days and all ours'. But Essex was given another
chance.

Essex's chief worry was that he was now left with very little money. He
began to write pitiful letters to the Queen, with the object of obtaining a
renewal of his farm of sweet wines, for which he had been collecting the
customs duties in return for an annual compounded rental which he paid to the
exchequer. It was her final refusal in October to let him continue the farm that
changed his attitude back from sorrow and repentance to rage and rebellion.
In December it was much noted how he entertained all kinds of out of work
soldiers and disaffected persons at his house in London.

On Christmas Day Essex wrote at length to King James accusing the Cecil
faction of conspiring with the Spanish Infanta and declaring that he himself
would endeavour to relieve the country of the malice, wickedness and madness
of these men. On 9th January the ineffable Lord Grey attacked Southampton
in the street, and a page of Southampton's had his hand cut off in the mêlée.
Essex took this as an indication that the Cecil party was out to murder him and
all his friends, particularly when Grey, who had at first been committed to the
Fleet prison, was released as early as 2nd February.

A revolutionary committee was formed, which held meetings at Drury
House, the residence of Sir Charles Danvers, under the chairmanship of
Southampton. First they were for capturing the Tower, then for concentrating
on the palace of Whitehall. Nothing was agreed, so Essex himself decided on
the capture of Whitehall. As usual with his plots, security precautions were
almost non-existent, and on 7th February, 1601 he received a summons to
present himself before the Privy Council at the house of Lord Buckhurst, the
Lord Treasurer. He refused to attend on the pretext of ill health. The next
morning three hundred armed men were assembled in the courtyard of Essex
House, on the grounds that Lord Cobham and Sir Walter Raleigh had designs
on his life.

Two evenings before, some of Essex's friends had paid the Lord Chamberlain's company of players forty shillings to put on a performance of Shakespeare's
Richard II, which portrayed the deposition of a sovereign of England. The same
theme had been used two years previously by Dr John Hayward in a book
which he dedicated to the Earl of Essex. Hayward was later committed to the
Tower for this offence, and the implications of the story of Richard II were well
known to the public. It would have been difficult for the Council not to notice
that something was afoot.

At about ten o'clock on 8th February the mountain decided to come to
Mahomet: the Lord Keeper, the Comptroller of the Household, the Lord
Chief Justice and the Earl of Worcester called at Essex House to find out what
was happening. He locked them up in a back room, and, instead of taking his
armed men straight away to capture Whitehall, set out to obtain the support of

the Lord Mayor of London, through the agency of Sheriff Smith. While Essex and his party waited in Smith's house, Cecil's brother, Lord Burghley, and the Garter King of Arms arrived with a proclamation from the Queen declaring Essex a traitor. He and Southampton went on through the City, their following dwindling as they went, and then made for the river, where they took a boat back to Essex House and barricaded themselves in. The four prisoners had already been rescued and taken back to Whitehall. Eventually Essex and Southampton and their followers surrendered to the Lord Admiral and were taken first to Lambeth Palace and then to the Tower, where they arrived at three o'clock in the morning of the 9th. So ended the Essex Rebellion.

CHAPTER XVII

'Death Is Now The Phoenix' Nest'

THERE was no delay in bringing Essex and Southampton to trial. On 19th February 1601 they were arraigned in Westminster Hall before Lord Buckhurst, as Lord High Steward, assisted by eight judges, to rule on matters of law, and a jury of nine earls and sixteen barons. Once more Coke, Fleming, Yelverton and Bacon appeared for the prosecution, accompanied this time by John Croke, Recorder of London, and Serjeants Heale and Harris. One of the noblemen of the jury was Lord Grey, and when his name was called Essex nudged Southampton with a scornful laugh and asked the court whether the accused had the ordinary right of commoners to challenge jurymen for prejudice. It was ruled that the integrity of a peer could not be impugned.

The evidence consisted largely of the reading of depositions, supported by lengthy speeches by Yelverton and Coke. There was little dispute as to the facts alleged, which were well enough known and easy to establish. The main argument was as to motive, with Coke imputing dastardly intentions against the person and throne of the Queen and Essex trying to establish that all his actions had been motivated by self-preservation and by the desire to rid the Queen of evil advisers, particularly Lord Cobham, Cecil and Sir Walter Raleigh. Southampton declared that he had acted only out of loyalty and gratitude to his friend Essex, and not from any motives of political dissatisfaction. He also said that, although various plans had been discussed at Drury House, there had not been any actual attempt to put them into practice; he had only tried with a few attendants to protect Essex from the attacks of private enemies.

The Attorney-General asked Southampton whether he did not think the plan to confine the Queen and set her palace under guard was not treason. Southampton played into Coke's hands by asking him to say what he thought they intended to do to the Queen when they had taken possession of her court. Coke referred to the play which Shakespeare's company had been paid to put on shortly before the incident: 'How long, my lord, lived King Richard the Second after he was surprised in the same manner?' It was a shrewd thrust.

Reference was made to the judges as to whether the facts established could constitute rebellion. They ruled both that the facts alleged against Essex and Southampton did indeed constitute rebellion against the sovereign, and also that all who adhered to them were traitors except such as joined briefly and dispersed upon the reading of the proclamation.

Francis Bacon, anxious to throw off any possible stigma from his many years of close association with and dependence on the Earl, got up and slashed Essex's defence to ribbons, comparing him with the Greek Pisistratus, who cut his body and ran bleeding through the streets of Athens calling on the citizens to defend him against his enemies. Essex's appeal to the City of London for assistance had been no spur-of-the-moment action but a plot of three months' devising. 'I confess I loved my Lord of Essex as long as he continued a dutiful subject,' said Bacon, 'and I have spent more hours to make him a good subject of her Majesty than ever I did about my own business.' He did not mention the many hours Essex had spent about Bacon's business.

Essex then accused Cecil of having sold England to the Spaniard, and said that he had declared the Infanta's claim to the crown to be as good as any other's. Cecil had not been visible in court, but he now stepped out from behind the arras and prayed leave to address the prisoner. He demanded the source of the slander, and Southampton, after some hesitation, named Essex's uncle, Sir William Knollys. When he appeared, Knollys said that Cecil had merely quoted the words from the book published in the autumn of 1595 by the Jesuit Father Parsons, *A Conference about the next Succession to the Crown of England*, and had not expressed any approval of them. It was widely thought, however, that the Cecil family had at least been keeping all options open on the succession question, and Cecil's excitement over this slander was scarcely calculated to remove that impression. However, the point had no real relevance to the trial, which continued its course until it was time for the inevitable verdict.

After the two Earls had been pronounced guilty Essex stated that he was willing to die, but he entreated their Lordships to recommend her Majesty to pardon the Earl of Southampton. When his turn came to speak, Southampton made a moving appeal for clemency. The Lord High Steward then pronounced that they should both be hanged, drawn and quartered.

Essex asked for his chaplain, Ashton, who came to him in the Tower the next day and found him 'cheerful and prepared with great content for his end'. But Ashton soon changed all that. Instead of comforting him he upbraided him for his wickedness until Essex broke down and made an abject confession of his treasonable intentions, casting blame on many of his friends and even on his sister, Lady Rich, for urging him on. After some hesitation by the Queen, Essex's execution was fixed for 25th February.

During all this time we have heard little of Shakespeare, except for the part played in the events by his play *Richard II*. The last of his sonnets to Southampton, 100–106, had been written towards the end of 1594*, after which Southampton's marital affairs and his devotion to Essex can have left him little time for the kind of close relationship with Shakespeare which was possible in the three years up to his twenty-first birthday; nor could that intensity of emotion which Shakespeare's first 106 sonnets evidence be expected to last into Southampton's maturity, even if a cooler type of friendship survived. Shakespeare had given himself ample warning of this; for instance:

* See Chapter XII.

> Against that time when thou shalt strangely passe,   49.5–6
> And scarcely greete me with that sunne thine eye,

and in *The Merchant of Venice* and *Henry IV Part II* the partings of Antonio and Bassanio and of Falstaff and Prince Hal respectively reflect in different ways the same thought. Nevertheless, it would be quite past belief to imagine that Shakespeare was not very deeply shocked and grieved by the fiasco of the Irish campaign and the inexorable descent of Southampton and Essex into disaster. And indeed, as soon as the two death sentences were announced he distilled the essence of his grief into one of the most remarkable poems in the English language.

The Phoenix and Turtle was first published later in 1601 in an undistinguished collection of verses on Phoenix and Turtle themes. These included a long and bad poem entitled *Love's Martyr: Or Rosalin's Complaint*, which was followed by *Divers Poeticall Essaies on the former Subject; viz.: the Turtle and Phoenix*. Among the latter were poems by Chapman, Marston and Jonson as well as that of William Shakespeare. Shakespeare's poem has no obvious connection with the rest of the book except the general subject, and can therefore be considered alone.

The poem consists of thirteen four-line verses followed by a 'Threnos' of five verses of three lines. It is thus quite different in form from any of Shakespeare's other poetry; but the language of the 'Threnos' links up immediately with that of his last-written group of sonnets; in particular with 104 and 105:

> For feare of which, heare this thou age unbred,   104.13–14
> Ere you were borne was beauties summer dead.

and

> Faire, kinde, and true, is all my argument,   105.9–14
> Faire, kind and true, varrying to other words,
> And in this change is my invention spent,
> Three theams in one, which wondrous scope affords.
>   Faire, kinde, and true, have often liv'd alone.
>   Which three till now, never kept seate in one.

Compare the Threnos:

> Beauty, truth and rarity,
> Grace in all simplicity,
> Here enclosed, in cinders lie.
>
> Death is now the phoenix' nest;
> And the turtle's loyal breast
> To eternity doth rest.
>
> Leaving no posterity,
> 'Twas not their infirmity,
> It was married chastity.

K

> Truth may seem, but cannot be;
> Beauty brag, but 'tis not she;
> Truth and beauty buried be.
>
> To this urn let those repair
> That are either true or fair;
> For these dead birds sigh a prayer.

There is clearly a close connection of thought here. Perhaps it is conceivable that Shakespeare might have plagiarized himself in order to use these ideas in totally different contexts; but it must not be overlooked that the same Sonnet 105 contains the lines:

> Since all alike my songs and praises be   105.3–4
> To one, of one, still such, and ever so.

Surely he would not have used these same themes in a poem of such deep seriousness as *The Phoenix and Turtle* obviously is without intending a reference to the same 'one', still such and ever so.

Once we have got as far as this it is difficult to escape the conclusion that the two 'dead birds' must be Essex and Southampton, and that the whole poem is an elegy written in the belief that both were as good as dead. In fact, of course, Southampton was reprieved; but as late as 25th March, more than a month after the trial, spectators flocked to Tower Hill in the expectation that he was to be executed that day. In the first shock after the verdict was pronounced there can have been no reason for Shakespeare to suppose that the sentences on both the Earls would not be carried out, as that on Essex very soon was. Let us therefore look more closely at the poem in this light.

The first five verses describe a funeral of birds which is obviously based on Matthew Roydon's elegy[1] on the death of Sir Philip Sidney in the anthology entitled *The Phoenix' Nest*, published in 1593. In that poem the Phoenix is one of the mourners, whereas for Shakespeare it is one of the deceased. However, there are several similarities in the descriptions of the other mourners, as the following stanzas, the first group from Roydon and the second from Shakespeare, will show:

(1)   Upon the branches of these trees
> The airy winged people sat,
> Distinguished in od degrees,
> One sort is this, another that,
> > Here Philomell, that knows full well
> > What force and wit in love doth dwell.
>
> The skiebred Egle, roiall bird,
> Percht there upon an oke above;
> The Turtle by him never stird,
> Example of immortal love.
> > The swan that sings about to dy,
> > Leaving Menander, stood thereby.

And that which was of woonder most,
The Phoenix left sweet Arabie,
And, on a Caedar in this coast,
Built up her tombe of spicerie,
 As I conjecture, by the same
 Preparde to take her dying flame.

  . . .

The Turtle dove with tunes of ruthe
Shewd feeling passion of his death;
Me thought she said, I tell thee truthe,
Was never he that drew in breath,
 Unto his love more trustie found,
 Than he for whom our griefs abound.

The swan, that was in presence heere,
Began his funerall dirge to sing;
Good things (quoth he) may scarce appeere,
But passe away with speedie wing:
 This mortall life is death as tride,
 And death gives life; and so he di'de.

(2)

  Let the bird of loudest lay,
  On the sole Arabian tree,
  Herald sad and trumpet be,
  To whose sound chaste wings obey.

  But thou shrieking harbinger,
  Foul precurrer of the fiend,
  Augur of the fever's end,
  To this troop come thou not near!

  From this session interdict
  Every fowl of tyrant wing,
  Save the eagle, feath'red king:
  Keep the obsequy so strict.

  Let the priest in surplice white,
  That defunctive music can,
  Be the death-divining swan,
  Lest the requiem lack his right.

  And thou treble-dated crow,
  That thy sable gender mak'st
  With the breath thou giv'st and tak'st,
  'Mongst our mourners shalt thou go.

This description of the funeral is followed by an 'anthem' which contains a eulogy of the two dead birds. This portion contains the only elucidation of the respective sexes of the birds:

> Hearts remote, yet not asunder;
> Distance, and no space was seen
> 'Twixt this turtle and his queen:
> But in them it were a wonder.
>
> So between them love did shine,
> That the turtle saw his right
> Flaming in the phoenix' sight;
> Either was the other's mine.

The odd thing is that it is the phoenix which is female and the turtle dove which is male, although one might have expected the reverse to be the case. But the phoenix is a 'queen', and in the Threnos we heard of the 'turtle's loyal breast'. The turtle is thus clearly not a king, but a subject.

The rest of the anthem describes the intense mutual love of the two birds, in terms reminiscent of the earlier sonnets:

> Oh how thy worth with manners may I singe,   39.1–4
> When thou art all the better part of me?
> What can mine owne praise to mine owne selfe bring;
> And what is't but mine owne when I praise thee, . . .

Incidentally, these lines put beyond doubt the correct interpretation of

> Either was the other's mine.

Some editors have absurdly suggested that 'mine' here means a place from which minerals are dug, in the sense of a source of figurative wealth.[2] The real meaning is, of course, that each was the other's own. Clearly Shakespeare is giving to the Phoenix and the Turtle the same sentiments which he used to ascribe to himself and Southampton in the year 1593. There is only one person who could conceivably be linked with Southampton in this way in 1601, and that of course is Essex.

Why then is the Phoenix 'his queen'? Surely because it is a matter of historical fact that Southampton had given to Essex the loyalty which properly belonged to the Queen. Some people thought it went further than that; in the Star Chamber on 13th February Sir Robert Cecil declared that for six years Essex had designed to become King of England.[3] No attempt was made to prove this at the trial, but it was mentioned in the proclamation and also by Coke in one of his prosecution speeches. In fact, according to a letter written by the Venetian ambassador on 15th May, 1603, the aims of the rebellion, as set out in a document signed by six conspirators were (a) to create a rising in which Cecil and Raleigh would be killed, and (b) to cry 'Long live the Queen and after her long live King James of Scotland, the sole and rightful heir to the English Crown'. But Sir Christopher Blount said before his execution on 18th March that 'if they had failed of their ends they would (rather than have been disappointed) have drawn blood even from the Queen herself'.[4]

The third stanza of the poem bears this interpretation out:

> From this session interdict
> Every fowl of tyrant wing,
> Save the eagle, feath'red king:
> Keep the obsequy so strict.

It has often been suggested that it is Queen Elizabeth who is meant here as the fowl to be interdicted, while James VI of Scotland is the eagle who is to be admitted. I think this is correct. Later we shall see that the phrase 'tyrants crests' in Sonnet 107 also refers to Queen Elizabeth, who had behaved so tyrannically towards Southampton over his marriage, and over the posts of General of the Horse and Governor of Connaught.

The Phoenix and the Turtle must be of different sexes for the purposes of the poem because the conventions of the fable demanded it. Given that convention, Shakespeare has nevertheless been able in a remarkable way to fit these symbols to the personalities of Essex and Southampton, the last representatives of mediaeval chivalry and magnificence who, in that sense, left no posterity. Traditionally a new phoenix had always been born from the funeral pyre of the old, but not any more.

Strangely enough, in view of the explicit statement in the Threnos that there was no posterity, the 'bird of loudest lay' in the first stanza of all has been taken by some to be a new phoenix. It is true that the 'sole Arabian tree' is the traditional throne of the phoenix, but the 'bird of loudest lay' here surely represents the poet himself. His reputation had by now grown to such an extent that he might well claim this title.

The 'shrieking harbinger' in the second stanza is the screech-owl which, as Puck says in *A Midsummer Night's Dream*.

> Puts the wretch that lies in woe   *MND* V.i.366–7
> In remembrance of a shroud.

He sits outside the house waiting for the end of the fever which will mean death. It is tempting to equate this bird with Francis Bacon, ghoulishly waiting to put in his screech when his former friend Essex was sufficiently helpless; whether this is right or not, it is likely that the stanza conceals some specific allusion.

The reference to the 'priest in surplice white' in the fourth stanza recalls the preoccupation with religion which affected Essex from the time of his Irish debacle until his death. While he was imprisoned in York House he wrote to Southampton imploring him to remember that he was accountable to God and praying that he might 'feel the comfort I now enjoy in my unfeigned conversion'. This suggests that Southampton was far from being a religious man at the time, and ties up with the indication in Sonnet 67 that he may well have flirted with atheism.

It is true that Essex's chaplain Ashton, for whom he asked in the Tower during his last days, may not have worn a surplice, since he was a Puritan; nevertheless the phrase is appropriate for the white plumage of a swan. In any case, it may well be that Southampton's mother arranged for a Catholic priest to see him; or merely that Shakespeare thought that this would be suitable.

The Countess of Chambrun has suggested that the 'treble-dated crow' of the fifth stanza is a reference to the aged Archbishop Whitgift.[5] He showed kindness to Essex in the Privy Council hearing of 5th June, 1600,* and, much earlier, had been the bishop who granted Shakespeare's special marriage licence. In 1593 he had passed *Venus and Adonis* for publication. In the service of ordination in the Elizabethan prayer book reference was made to the transmission of the Holy Spirit through the breath, so one could regard the celibate archbishop as engendering his sable-cassocked curates in this manner.

In considering what Shakespeare would have thought it worth while to symbolize in the poem one must remember that the audience he would have had in mind must have been the surviving relatives and friends of Essex and Southampton, perhaps especially the younger Earl's mother and wife. The references would therefore be such as might appeal to them. We should not expect to find, therefore, any disparagement of Cecil, with whom both Countesses had remained on good terms and to whom both at once wrote appealing for clemency to Southampton. He clearly still retained a great affection for his father's erstwhile ward, in spite of all the trouble he had caused. On 2nd March he wrote to Mountjoy, 'The man that grieveth me to think what may become of him is the poor young Earl of Southampton'. The Queen must have been persuaded that she had punished him enough, for she agreed to commute his sentence to imprisonment in the Tower. Perhaps it was Mountjoy himself who was luckiest of all, for in spite of his known complicity in the planning he remained as Lord Deputy in Ireland, successfully carrying on the campaign against Tyrone.

Essex's execution on 25th February did not extinguish his phoenix-image with the public at large, who had found him a more attractive figure than the cold hunchback Cecil, the arrogant and atheistical Raleigh or the rest of their party, who were still more than half-believed to be in league with Spain behind the Queen's back. There were many ballads and lampoons full of praise of Essex and slanders of Cecil and his party. As an act of clemency beheading had been substituted for hanging, disembowelling and quartering, but the headsman's blade fell first on Essex's back and then on his head before the third blow severed the neck. For his clumsiness the headsman narrowly escaped lynching at the hands of the angry crowd. Cecil saw the signals, and carefully disengaged himself from Raleigh, Cobham and Grey during the two years which were left before James of Scotland succeeded to the throne.

* See p. 140.

CHAPTER XVIII

The End of a Reign

THE month of February, 1601, which saw the downfall of Essex and South-ampton, also brought trouble for another young Earl. William Herbert had only the previous month succeeded to the title of Earl of Pembroke and the ancestral estates at Wilton, near Salisbury, where his mother, the sister of Sir Philip Sidney, had for long presided over a cultured salon. In the midst of all her preoccupations the old Queen found time to commit the young Earl to the Fleet prison for that most heinous of offences, philandering with one of her ladies-in-waiting, the brown-haired Mistress Fitton. (He was released again in April.) Mary Fitton was now pregnant, but the Earl, although freely admitting his offence, did not follow the example of Southampton in similar circum-stances; he refused point blank to marry the girl.[1]

At this time the Earl was not yet twenty-one, and his younger brother, Philip Herbert, little more than sixteen. They had been educated by the poet Samuel Daniel, whom Lady Pembroke had engaged as tutor to young William when the boy was ten years old and had kept at Wilton ever since. Both of them were generous patrons of literature and of the stage all their lives, and they share the distinction of having had the First Folio edition of Shakespeare's plays dedicated to them on its publication in 1623. We shall be meeting them again a little later in our story.

At the end of October, 1601, the Queen called what was to be her last Parliament, and King James thought it a suitable moment to send an emissary, the Duke of Lennox, to her to try to settle the question of the succession. Needless to say, he was unable to raise the matter. But Cecil, whose power, since the suppression of the Essex rebellion, was now unchallenged, was in constant correspondence with James; so also were Raleigh, Cobham and the Earl of Northumberland. Cecil took care that James should not place any trust in this little group; in one of his letters he said of Raleigh and Cobham that 'hell did never spew such a couple when it cast up Cerberus and Phlegethon'. And yet Cecil was a financial partner in Raleigh's enterprises of exploration and their respective families had often played together at Raleigh's house at Sherborne.

The Earl of Northumberland, the 'Wizard Earl', was one of the members of Raleigh's scientific and free-thinking circle, and he, Cobham and Raleigh were sometimes known as the 'Diabolical Triplicity'. During December this trio were noticed to be meeting every day at Durham House, Raleigh's London residence, and it seemed that Northumberland, at any rate, was speaking against the claims of the King of Scots. But by May 1602 it appeared that all three were now come round to the party of King James. Indeed, although the Queen refused to admit that there was anything wrong with her health, attending gay dancing parties and going out riding as usual, all her leading courtiers were busy ensuring that their names were favourably known to King James, and Cecil was secretly passing judgment on them all.

Meanwhile the Lord Chamberlain's players continued to go from strength to strength, despite their performance of *Richard II* at the time of the Essex troubles. Shakespeare's *Julius Caesar*, *Twelfth Night* and *Hamlet*, all of which far outstripped the work of any other English playwright, living or dead, were first produced about this time. More important for our purposes, though far less successful as plays, are *Troilus and Cressida* and *All's Well that Ends Well*, both of which throw a little light on Shakespeare's state of mind in the period between the Essex affair and the accession of James I.

Troilus and Cressida was entered for printing in the Stationers' Register on 7th February, 1603, with the note, 'as yt is acted by my lord Chamberlens Men'. It was not in fact printed, however, until 1609. Then the first issue describes it as having been 'acted by the Kings Maiesties seruants at the Globe', but a second issue the same year carried a declaration that it had never been 'stal'd with the Stage'. Presumably any performance that it had been given was a private one.

The resemblances between the Achilles of *Troilus and Cressida* and the Essex of 1599-1600 have often been pointed out; they are the more striking in that Chapman's translation of seven of the books of Homer's *Iliad*, published in 1598, had been accompanied by an epistle explicitly comparing Essex with Achilles in a favourable sense. Ulysses in the play might be Cecil speaking of Essex in the Star Chamber of 13th February, 1601:

> The seeded pride   *T&C.* I.iii.316-20
> That hath to this maturity blown up
> In rank Achilles must or now be cropp'd
> Or, shedding, breed a nursery of like evil
> To overbulk us all.

In the end Achilles, who has been taking more interest in his affairs with the girls than in the war with Troy, is spurred to action by the slaughter of his bosom-friend, Patroclus. But he kills his adversary, Hector, in a most cowardly manner by coming upon him alone and unarmed and setting his Myrmidons upon him. The whole tone of the play is anti-heroic, an expression of deep disillusion and disgust. Somehow the phoenix has turned into a carrion-crow.

If *Troilus and Cressida* appears to deal cruelly with Essex, *All's Well that Ends Well* is far from complimentary to Southampton, now languishing in the Tower. The resemblances between Bertram, Count of Rousillon, and Henry, Earl of Southampton, have been described too many times before to need elaborating here.[2] Bertram is made a fool of, and tricked into returning to the wife whom he has run away abroad to avoid. But at least he does learn his lesson and is forgiven for his lascivious and selfish behaviour. He is just 'a foolish idle boy', even though the Duke of Florence has seen fit to make him General of the Horse, the very same title that the Earl of Essex gave to Southampton. The character of Shakespeare's sublime turtle-dove has become that of South-ampton as Cecil saw him, a foolish boy with no real harm in him, whom the Queen could safely be advised to reprieve. It is scarcely a dignified picture.

That Shakespeare was fully conscious of the disloyalty involved in these portrayals may be deduced from the great third scene of Act III of *Troilus and Cressida*, which might almost be considered a part, like *The Phoenix and Turtle*, of the Sonnet story. 'And not a man', says Achilles.

> for being simply man   *T&C*. III.
> Hath any honour, but honour for those honours   iii.80–87
> That are without him, as place, riches, and favour,
> Prizes of accident, as oft as merit;
> Which when they fall, as being slippery too,
> Doth one pluck down another, and together
> Die in the fall.

And Ulysses speaks of the chief villain of the Sonnets, that old wretch, Time:

> Time hath, my lord, a wallet at his back,   145–7
> Wherein he puts alms for oblivion,
> A great siz'd monster of ingratitudes . . .
> For Time is like a fashionable host,   165–9
> That slightly shakes his parting guest by the hand;
> And with his arms out-stretch'd, as he would fly,
> Grasps in the comer. The welcome ever smiles,
> And farewell goes out sighing.

How far did Shakespeare feel a sincere urge to point out the faults of Essex and Southampton, and how far was he merely bound to play up to the pre-judices of their opponents, since they were now the only patrons left? He will give his own answer, in the course of the twenty sonnets that remain for us to consider. Meanwhile, there is an enigmatic passage in *All's Well that Ends Well* which seems as if it must express something deep in Shakespeare's mind; it occurs in the first scene, when Helena is bandying words with Parolles about the dangers which beset a girl's virginity. Parolles jests coarsely about the uselessness of virginity, and asks if Helena intends to do anything with hers. She is deeply in love with the rakish young Count of Rousillon, who is just going off to follow the court, and she replies to Parolles,

> Not my virginity yet.   *AWTEW*.
> There shall your master have a thousand loves,   I.i.181–202
> A mother, and a mistress, and a friend,
> A phoenix, captain, and an enemy,

A guide, a goddess and a sovereign,
A counsellor, a traitress, and a dear;
His humble ambition, proud humility,
His jarring concord, and his discord dulcet,
His faith, his sweet disaster; with a world
Of pretty fond adoptious christendoms
That blinking Cupid gossips. Now shall he—
I know not what he shall. God send him well!
The court's a learning place, and he is one—

PAR. What one, i' faith?

HEL. That I wish well. 'Tis pity—

PAR. What's pity?

HEL. That wishing well had not a body in't
Which might be felt; that we the poorer born,
Whose baser stars do shut us up in wishes,
Might with effects of them follow our friends
And show what we alone must think, which never
Returns us thanks.

It is difficult to find a justification for Helena's prophetic catalogue of loves in the play alone; who can the phoenix be? But if we imagine that it is not Helena but Shakespeare speaking the passage links up both with the associations which caused Southampton's downfall and also with Sonnets 66–70; in particular with the lines:

If some suspect of ill maskt not thy show,   70.13–14
Then thou alone kingdomes of hearts shouldst owe.

If Southampton had listened to his friend's counsel in early 1594, how differently his life might have turned out. But Shakespeare was of

the poorer born,
Whose baser stars do shut us up in wishes,

and his wishes could not save Southampton from himself. Meanwhile, life had to go on.

But not the old Queen's life; that came at last to its end in the early hours of 24th March, 1603, and Sir Robert Carey, brother of the Lord Chamberlain, patron of Shakespeare's company of players, sped off to Edinburgh to bring the news to James.

Because of the Queen's unwillingness to hear any talk of the succession while she lived, there was great trepidation as to what might happen when the moment actually arrived. The King of Spain and the Pope were determined to restore England to the Catholic fold and had been energetically building up a base from which this might be achieved. Apart from this, there were many who did not fancy handing England over to the mercy of a Scottish king when several English noblemen with some royal blood flowing in their veins were available instead. There is little doubt, for instance, that if Essex had succeeded in his bid to take over the government he would have been under strong pressure to accept the succession himself rather than pursue his avowed intentions of paving the way for James. There were also the Seymours, descendants of the Lord Protector Somerset, who never completely lost sight of their claim. It had long been feared that something akin to the Wars of the Roses might break out again if Elizabeth died without establishing her heir. So Chapman, in his 'Hymnus in Cynthiam', had compared the likely aftermath of the Queen's death to the horrors of the Battle of Cannae:

> So (gracious Cynthia) in that sable day,   *HC.* 58–75
> When interposed earth takes thee away,
> (Our sacred chiefe and soveraigne generall,)
> As chrimsine a retrait, and steepe a fall
> We feare to suffer from this peace, and height,
> Whose thancklesse sweet now cloies us with receipt.
>   The Romanes set sweet Musicke to her charmes,
> To raise thy stoopings, with her ayrie armes:
> Usde loud resoundings with auspicious brasse:
> Held torches up to heaven, and flaming glasse,
> Made a whole forrest but a burning eye,
> T'admire thy mournefull partings with the skye.
> The Macedonians were so stricken dead,
> With skillesse horrour of thy changes dread:
> They wanted harts, to lift up sounds, or fires,
> Or eyes to heaven; but usd their funerall tyres,
> Trembld, and wept; assur'd some mischiefs furie
> Would follow that afflicting Augurie.

Chapman affects to be speaking of an eclipse of the moon, but he makes it quite clear that he is referring to the permanent loss of the Queen (Our sacred chiefe and soveraigne generall), and not to any temporary danger which would later pass, as the earth's shadow passes from the moon.

That James was able to succeed peacefully to the throne was very largely due to the preparations made by Cecil. On 17th March he had taken the precaution of calling Lord Thomas Howard, Lord Cobham and the Earl of Northumberland for consultation with the Privy Council about the succession, since they had been thought to be against the claims of King James. There were stories that Lady Arabella Stuart, a cousin of James, had proposed to the old Earl of Hertford, head of the Seymour family, that he should arrange a marriage for her with one of his sons, thus combining her own and the Seymour claims to the succession. The Earl wisely reported the matter to the Council, who saw that she was kept under close guard at the home of her grandmother, the

Countess of Shrewsbury. Another rumour was that there were forty thousand Catholics pledged to keep James out of England.

At last, on 22nd March, the Lord Admiral, the Lord Keeper and Cecil finally prevailed upon the Queen, as she lay ill in bed, to confirm that she wanted her cousin of Scotland to succeed her, and this she repeated the following afternoon by means of gestures. The next morning the death of the Queen and the accession of James were duly proclaimed throughout London in an atmosphere of quiet relief, without any tumult or attempt at contradiction. From all over the country reports came in of similar reactions, wholly confuting the prophets of violence and disaster.

The King lost no time in setting out for London to enter upon his inheritance. He left Edinburgh on 5th April, after signing a letter to the 'nobilitie and peeres of the Realme of England, and to our right trustie, and welbeloved our Councillors of State now assembled at White Hall', commanding the release from the Tower of the Earl of Southampton. By 10th April Southampton was a free man once more. He went up to Huntingdon to meet the King, who gave him the Sword of State to carry before him. Here the King was sumptuously entertained from 27th to 29th April by Master Oliver Cromwell, uncle of the future Lord Protector, and during this time the funeral of Queen Elizabeth was celebrated with great pomp and magnificence in London, the Coat of Arms, the Sword, Target, Helm and Crest being carried in front of the catafalque by the Officers of Arms, and a lifelike image of the Queen in her Parliament robes being set above the coffin.[3]

After the funeral most of the nobility and of the Councillors went up to meet the King at Cecil's great house, Theobalds, in Hertfordshire, twelve miles from London, on 3rd May. He finally arrived at the Tower of London on 11th May, but before this the Council was instructed to remove Sir Walter Raleigh from his post as Captain of the Guard and to replace him by Sir Thomas Erskine.

On 13th May the King created several new barons, one being Sir Robert Cecil, who became Lord Cecil of Essendon. Since entering England he had continually been conferring knighthoods, and by this date the number of these was close to 240.

As early as 17th May James found time to instruct that the Lord Chamberlain's company of players should henceforward be the King's players, and a patent was accordingly drawn up on 19th containing the names of William Shakespeare, Richard Burbage and the rest, headed by Laurence Fletcher, who had previously arranged performances by English actors for the King in Scotland. Lord Hunsdon, who had had a stroke in 1600 and was now partially paralysed, was relieved of the office of Lord Chamberlain on 4th May at Theobalds, and died a few months later. The change of patronage thus came at a very opportune moment for Shakespeare's company.

As King of Scotland, James had been at peace with Spain, but now that he was also King of England a state of war still existed which he was determined to wind up as early as possible. The invitation of foreign ambassadors to the coronation ceremony afforded a good opportunity to put peace negotiations in hand; meanwhile a proclamation was issued ordering the cessation of acts of piracy against what had been legitimate enemies of the realm. A thoughtful proviso allowed booty captured before 24th April not to be handed back, as otherwise many great personages might have been severely out of pocket over their investments in freebooting ventures.

The date of the coronation was appropriately fixed for St James's Day, 25th July, 1603, and earlier in the month several new Knights of the Garter were installed, including Prince Henry and the Earl of Southampton. On 21st Southampton was restored formally to his full titles and precedence, after two years as plain Master Henry Wriothesley following his attainder for treason. Lord Mountjoy, who had now successfully ended the campaign in Ireland, was created Earl of Devonshire, and another Essexite, Sir Henry Danvers, was created Lord Danvers of Dauntsey. In the general rash of knighthoods Francis Bacon was not overlooked. The stern accuser of the days of the trial of 1601 had hurried in with a letter to Southampton assuring that 'it is as true a thing that God knoweth, that this great change hath wrought in me noe other change towards your Lordship than this, that I, may safely bee nowe that which I was truly before.'[4] Southampton's stepfather, Sir William Harvey, was granted the office of Remembrancer of the First Fruits and Tithes in reversion after the death of the present holder. Southampton and all about him seemed to be on the crest of the wave. Samuel Daniel and John Davies of Hereford hailed his rehabilitation in verse, and Shakespeare sought to bridge the gap of nearly nine years with two new sonnets:

> Not mine owne feares, nor the prophetick soule,   107
> Of the wide world, dreaming on things to come,
> Can yet the lease of my true love controule,
> Supposde as forfeit to a confin'd doome.
> The mortall Moone hath her eclipse indur'de,
> And the sad Augurs mock their owne presage,
> Incertenties now crowne them-selves assur'de
> And peace proclaimes Olives of endlesse age.
> Now with the drops of this most balmie time,
> My love lookes fresh, and death to me subscribes,
> Since spight of him Ile live in this poore rime,
> While he insults ore dull and speachlesse tribes.
>   And thou in this shalt finde thy monument,
>   When tyrants crests and tombs of brasse are spent.

> What's in the braine that Inck may character,   108
> Which hath not figur'd to thee my true spirit,
> What's new to speake, what now to register,
> That may expresse my love, or thy deare merit?

Nothing sweet boy, but yet like prayers divine,
I must each day say ore the very same,
Counting no old thing old, thou mine, I thine,
Even as when first I hallowed thy faire name.
So that eternall love in loves fresh case,
Waighes not the dust and injury of age,
Nor gives to necessary wrinckles place,
But makes antiquitie for aye his page,
    Finding the first conceit of love there bred,
    Where time and outward forme would shew it dead.

We need have no doubt that these two sonnets were written together, because in 115 Shakespeare tells us so by referring to both of them at once. I will say more about this when we reach that sonnet; meanwhile the most striking things are, how closely and concisely 107 describes the events of April to July 1603, and how both 107 and 108 look backward over the years to the period of the earlier sonnets.

With regard to the topical references in the first sonnet of the pair, I do not think one can do better than quote Professor Akrigg's accurate paraphrase:

> I myself in my fears had thought, like everybody else, that the future held nothing for you beyond continued confinement in the Tower. But now Queen Elizabeth, so often likened to Cynthia, the virgin goddess of the moon, has finally been eclipsed by death. Since she had no acknowledged heir, pessimists had feared that her passing would bring a disastrous civil war, but now even they mock their earlier dismal prophecy. With the peaceful accession of King James, feelings of uncertainty give way to feelings of security. Our new King, dedicated to peace, brings us an unending era of peace and prosperity. The refreshing showers of this pleasant spring give new vigour to my love for you. Poor though my verse may be, it forces death to submit to me. I shall attain a literary immortality denied to the inarticulate masses. And this poetry of mine will provide you with a monument which will keep you remembered when elaborate tombs, like that to be raised for our late tyrannic Queen, have disappeared.[5]

There is really nothing more to be said about the dating of these two sonnets; most of those who have chosen to link 107 with different events, such as the Queen's climacteric in 1596 or the Lopez affair of 1593-4, have been motivated by an inability to accept that there is a long gap between it and the preceding sonnets. And yet Shakespeare could hardly put things more plainly than he does in 108, with its talk of the 'dust and injury of age' and of 'necessary wrinckles'.

In re-opening the sonnet sequence, which Shakespeare had once thought closed for ever, his mind naturally travels back to the year 1594, when the last sonnets had been written. That was when Chapman's *Shadow of Night* fell

between him and young Southampton: how strange to recollect that now! And
how wrong Chapman had been in his obscure and turgid 'Hymnus in Cynthiam' when he made his sad auguries about what would happen when that
old termagant, Queen Elizabeth, eventually passed away.* Now he was lining
up with the rest to cheer the new King. Southampton would appreciate a hit at
that, since the death of the old tyrant was a godsend to him:

> The mortall Moone hath her eclipse indur'de   107.5–6
> And the sad Augurs mock their owne presage, . . .

No harm in putting in a touch of the old neoplatonic nonsense which Chapman
was so keen on, and which Southampton seemed to be taken with when he was
flirting with the Raleigh circle:

> . . . the prophetick soule,   107.1–2
> Of the wide world, dreaming on things to come, . . .

But to recapture the mood of adulation of 1592–4 is not too easy. Surely
everything possible has already been said:

> What's new to speake, what now to register,   108.4–5
> That may expresse my love, or thy deare merit?

The point to make must be that true love remains as strong as ever, and Southampton still, in the mind's eye, a sweet young boy of twenty-one, though,
heaven knows, those disastrous years took a heavy toll of his wonderful looks.
Surely that is flattery enough, and still sincere too.

Akrigg, speaking of Sonnet 107, comments, 'We have no way of knowing
how Southampton responded to Shakespeare when he presented him with the
sonnet'. If that is so, we have little excuse for not guessing correctly, because
Shakespeare spends the next seventeen sonnets replying to Southampton's
response, and he tells us pretty clearly at the outset what it was:

> O never say that I was false of heart, . . .   109.1

* See p. 155.

CHAPTER XIX

The New Era

As soon as Queen Elizabeth's funeral was over various lords and ladies of the court went up to Berwick to meet the new Queen and escort her down to London.[1]

The court returned to Windsor on 30th June, 1603, and the very next day a quarrel broke out between the Earl of Southampton and Lord Grey. Queen Anne was talking to Southampton about the Essex rebellion and expressing surprise that so many great men were able to achieve so little. Southampton replied that they were forced to yield because they were proclaimed traitors to Queen Elizabeth; if it had not been for that, none of their private enemies, who were the only people against whom they had any quarrel, would have been able to oppose them. Lord Grey overheard the conversation and said that he and his friends could have done the job much better, whereupon he was given the lie direct. The Queen told them to remember where they were and sent them back to their lodgings, where they were put under guard. The following day the Council condemned them to be sent to the Tower; but the King intervened and forgave them their offence on condition that they made up their quarrel, which they undertook to do.

Lord Grey did not remain at liberty for long. On 14th July he, Sir Walter Raleigh, Lord Cobham and Cobham's brother, George Brooke, were suddenly arrested on suspicion of treason. Shortly afterwards warrants were issued for the arrest of two priests, William Watson and William Clarke, and of Sir Griffin Markham, a cousin of Sir John Harington.

Sir Walter Raleigh reacted even more emotionally than when Queen Elizabeth had sent him to jail in 1592. On 20th July he tried to commit suicide by stabbing himself in the chest, but bungled the attempt.

It appeared that Sir Griffin Markham and George Brooke, who had been in touch with the King before his accession, had found that their hopes of any benefit from him had come to nothing. They thus developed grudges against the King and most of the Councillors, whom they thought had stood in their way. Observing that Lord Grey was also discontented because of the favour which was now being bestowed on the remnants of the Essex faction, they joined with him in planning to capture the King and rid him of his advisers. Incredibly enough, they appeared to think they could successfully accomplish exactly the same kind of coup which Essex had so miserably failed to bring off. The two priests, Watson and Clarke, had been expecting the King to announce a policy of toleration for the Catholic religion, which he showed no signs of doing. They got together with a notorious religious controversalist, Anthony Copley, and arranged to join forces with George Brooke's group, in spite of the fact that the latter were not Catholics but Puritans. They intended that, after the present Councillors had been got rid of, Lord Grey should be made Earl Marshal, Griffin Markham, Secretary (the post held by Cecil), Brooke, Lord Treasurer, and Watson the priest, Lord Chancellor. What a Philippi would have followed then!

Lord Cobham was not involved in this particular plan; his intention was, first, to go abroad to enlist the support of Archduke Albert of Austria and the King of Spain; then, on his return, to meet Sir Walter Raleigh in Jersey to decide how to make the next move, which would be to oust King James. He discussed all this with his brother, George Brooke, who informed the rest of his group.

Sir Walter Raleigh seems not to have indicated any particular intentions, but he had been visibly discontented ever since the King came to the throne, even though he had received some financial compensation for the offices which had been removed from him. He had long been known to be friendly with Lord Cobham, and it was therefore generally thought likely that he was fully implicated in the latter's plans. Immediately on his arrest, Lord Cobham confessed his plot and alleged that Sir Walter not only knew all about it, but in fact had been the prime instigator.

Of these two conspiracies, that of George Brooke and the priests became known as the Bye Plot, while that alleged against Cobham and Raleigh was known as the Main. The only real link between them was the relationship of the brothers Brooke and Cobham.

Because of a fresh outbreak of plague in London, the celebration of the coronation on 25th July was on a reduced scale, and the great procession through London, for which arches of triumph were already in building, was postponed until March 1604.

It had already become apparent that the King's eye had lighted upon the handsome young Philip Herbert, brother of the Earl of Pembroke, and he was soon established as James's first English favourite. Together with Lord Cecil of Essendon, he rapidly became one of the main channels of access for those seeking the favour of the King, for James could never be without a good-looking young confidant. Philip Herbert was to hold this position until 1607, when the young page Robert Carr had the great good fortune to be thrown from his horse in front of James at a jousting tournament, just as he was about to present his master's shield to the King. But at least Herbert, by then Earl of Montgomery, was able to relinquish his position gradually and without harm to himself. Carr, on the other hand, ended up in the Tower for complicity in a murder, and his successor Villiers, who lasted into Charles I's reign, fell to an assassin's knife.

Philip Herbert at James's arrival in England was eighteen and a half, and a very personable young man. But whereas his brother the Earl was noted for his culture and charm, Philip was boorish and foul-mouthed, with

L

few interests beyond dogs and horses, the gaming table, the tiltyard and the bowling alley. Nevertheless, it was he that attracted the royal favours; in May 1603 he was made a Gentleman of the Privy Chamber and in July a Knight of the Bath. The King and Queen paid a brief visit to the Herbert estate at Wilton on 29th and 30th August, before going to Woodstock, and then returned again with the whole court in September or October. The court was based on Wilton until the King returned to Hampton Court in December, though he also made visits to Salisbury and Winchester during this time.

During the Essex rebellion the sympathies of the Herbert family had lain firmly on the opposite side; the Earl of Pembroke had written of 'bringing those (men, I cannot call them) to their ruin for their wicked action'.[2] This attitude was, no doubt, sharply modified with the accession of James and the release of Southampton, but the Earl's mother felt very strongly about the arrest of Raleigh, which she attributed to the machinations of Cecil. This was, probably, a major motive for inviting the King and Queen and their vast retinue to spend so long at Wilton; and with Sir Philip Herbert providing so strong an attraction acceptance was assured.

Because of the plague the Privy Council decided that the law term should be held in Winchester instead of London, and the conspirators in the Bye and Main plots were all brought down in early November and lodged in the Castle. The Brooke party, with the exception of Lord Grey, were tried on 15th November, and all were found guilty of treason except one, Sir Edward Parham, against whom the evidence was weak. It was shown that the conspirators had intended to surprise the King and Prince Henry at Greenwich and convey them to the Tower. They would then have demanded a general pardon and toleration of religion, and the removal of the Lord Chancellor, the Lord Treasurer and the Lord Chief Justice.

On 17th November Sir Walter Raleigh was brought to trial, and on this occasion Edward Coke, the Attorney-General, had a much harder task, since there was no evidence at all except the statements made by Lord Cobham, himself a prisoner awaiting trial. On the grounds that an accused person could not be sworn to give evidence which would help to convict himself, Raleigh's request to have Cobham brought before the court was refused. The only witness produced was a seaman named Dyer, a paid informer, who testified that once when he was in Portugal he had heard a Portuguese gentleman say that James would never be crowned King of England 'for Don Raleigh and Don Cobham will cut his throat ere that day come'. Coke tried to make up in bluster and vituperation what he lacked in evidence. 'Thou art the most vile and execrable Traitor that ever lived,' he shouted. 'The King's safety and your clearing cannot agree; I protest before God I never knew a clearer treason.' On such asseverations Raleigh was found guilty. But although he had been shouted and jeered at on his way down to Winchester from the Tower of London, Raleigh's performance at the trial gained him great sympathy and respect. As the prolific letter-writer, Dudley Carleton, reported,

He answered with that temper, wit, learning, courage and judgment, that, save it went with the hazard of his life, it was the happiest day he ever spent. And so well he shifted all advantages that were taken against him, that were not *fama malum gravius quam res,* and an ill name, half hanged, in the opinion of all men he had been acquitted.[3]

On 18th November Lord Cobham was tried and condemned, and the next day so also was Lord Grey. In each trial Southampton was a member of the jury, as they had been in his. The priests, Watson and Clarke, were hanged, drawn and quartered on 29th November, and on 5th December George Brooke suffered the less savage penalty of beheading.

Lest the King and Queen become too disturbed by these grisly events, Shakespeare's company of players was summoned down from Mortlake, where they had probably been rehearsing for the Christmas season, to give a performance on 2nd December at Wilton. The play is believed to have been *As You Like it*. Shakespeare was thus in a good position to hear all the news of the events at Winchester, and perhaps to attend in person.

On 9th December Sir Griffin Markham, Lord Grey and Lord Cobham were taken out to the Castle yard at Winchester for execution, and there began the solemn farce which provided Shakespeare with the inspiration for the ending of his play *Measure for Measure*, which was first performed just over twelve months later.

Markham was brought first to the scaffold, and he behaved bravely enough, though at first he complained that he was not ready, 'having been deluded with hopes and brought to that place unprepared'. After he had made his devotions and begun to make himself ready for the block, the Sheriff who was in charge of the proceedings was called away to receive a letter which had just been brought by a messenger from the King. When the Sheriff returned, he told Markham that since he was so ill prepared he should have two hours' respite. He was accordingly taken away and locked up in the Great Hall of King Arthur inside the Castle.

Next came the turn of the gallant and hot-headed young Lord Grey, who was escorted by a troop of young courtiers. He had such gaiety and cheer in his countenance, according to a contemporary letter in Howell's *State Trials*,[4] 'that he seemed a dapper young bridegroom'. He fell on his knees on the scaffold, and his preacher and he both made long prayers, which he followed with a long prayer for the King 'which held the standers-by a good half-hour in the rain'. When he was ready for the block the Sheriff told him that he had received orders to change the order of execution, and he was also led into Arthur's Hall.

Next came Lord Cobham, whose bold and confident demeanour was very different from his craven attitude at his arrest and during his trial. He 'did so outpray the company that helped to pray with him that a stander-by said, he had a good mouth in a cry but was nothing single'. Whereas his brother George Brooke had said before his death that Cobham and he had attempted to obtain support from Raleigh but had received none, Cobham declared upon the hope of his soul's resurrection that what he had said of Sir Walter Raleigh was true. He was then told that he was to be confronted with some of the other prisoners and must wait.

Grey and Markham were then brought back to the scaffold, and the Sheriff delivered a homily about the justness of their trials and the lawfulness of their execution, to which they assented. He then proclaimed that the King in his mercy had reprieved all three. The streets of Winchester were filled with shouts of applause and cries of 'God save the King'.

Raleigh had made a request that Cobham should be executed before him, in the hope that the imminence of death would cause him to withdraw the accusations which had been the only basis for Raleigh's own convictions. Instead of this, it seems likely that Cobham was given the hint that provided he maintained his story he himself might be reprieved.[5] Perhaps it was the resulting change in his demeanour that Shakespeare was thinking of when he made the Duke say near the end of *Measure for Measure*:

> By this Lord Angelo perceives he's safe;   MFM. 492–4
> Methinks I see a quick'ning in his eye.
> Well, Angelo, your evil quits you well.

Prior to this Angelo had fully admitted the justice of the Duke's sentence of death:

> I am sorry that such sorrow I procure;   MFM. 472–5
> And so deep sticks it in my penitent heart
> That I crave death more willingly than mercy;
> 'Tis my deserving, and I do entreat it.

Like so may of those convicted of treason in Elizabethan and Stuart times, the Lord Angelo was one of those 'fools of time' who wished to:

> . . . die for goodnes, who have liv'd for crime.   124.14

In the letter James had sent to the Sheriff (which, with its strange Scots spelling, must have taken that Hampshire worthy some time to read), the King made it clear that he was really only interested in the fate of the two nobles, Cobham and Grey:

as likewise in regaird that Iustice hath in some sort gottin course already by the execution of the two Priests, and *George Brooke*, that vaire the principall plotteris and intisaris of all the rest, to the embracing of the saidis treasonabill Machinations, Ve thair fore (bing resoluid to mixe Clemency with Iustice) aire contented, and by these presentis command you, our present Sheriffe of Hampshire, to supereseide the execution of the saidis two Noblemen, and take thaim backe to thair prison againe quwhile our further pleasure bee knowin. And since ve vill not haue our Lawis to haue respect to personis, in sparing the great, and strikking the meaner sort, It is our pleasure, that the like course be also taken with *Markeham*....[6]

After naming Brooke and the two priests as the principal plotters, the King could scarcely proceed with the execution of Raleigh, in spite of Coke's assertions at the trial that he was behind the whole affair. It was sufficient that Cobham had been induced, apparently in imminent expectation of death, to maintain his accusations against him. Raleigh and the other prisoners were reprieved without further histrionics and returned on 15th December for indefinite imprisonment in the Tower of London.

The court made its way back from Wilton to Hampton Court, arriving there on 23rd December. His Majesty's players were kept very busy; between Boxing Day and New Year's Day no less than six plays were presented. Financially, they must have been more than satisfied; but there is some reason to think that certain of their members were already feeling some disappointment over their social status as His Majesty's players.

In 1603 John Davies of Hereford published a poem called *Microcosmos*, which contained many interesting observations on the public scene. One section ran as follows:

> Players, I love yee, and your *Qualitie*,
> As ye are Men, that pass time not abus'd:
(W. S., R. B.) And some I love for *painting, poesie*,
> And say fell *Fortune* cannot be excus'd,
> That hath for better *uses* you refus'd:
> *Wit, courage, good shape, good partes,* and all *good,*
> As long as all these *goods* are now *worse* us'd,
> And though the *stage* doth staine pure gentle *bloud,*
> Yet generous yee are in *minde* and *moode*.[7]

There is little doubt that the initials in the margin against the third line apply to William Shakespeare and Richard Burbage, since Burbage, as well as being chief actor of the King's Players, was well-known for his skill as a painter, while Shakespeare was of course by now celebrated for 'poesie' as well as for drama.

In October 1596 Shakespeare had secured for his father a grant of arms from the College of Heralds, and was thus indisputably ranked as a gentleman. In May 1597 he completed the purchase of New Place, one of the finest properties in Stratford, and established himself as a person of substance. He had excelled the university-educated poets in creating both lyrical and dramatic poetry of intellectual content as well as artistic beauty; yet as a member of His Majesty's Company of players he was no more than an honorary Groom of the Chamber, ranking with the young messenger whom James had sent to deliver his letter to the Sheriff at Winchester. Samuel Daniel, Michael Drayton and John Marston, all of whom Shakespeare easily excelled, were to be ranked as Esquires.

On 17th July, 1603, James issued a proclamation that anyone with land having an annual value of £40 should come and be knighted, on payment of a fee of £30, or else suffer a penalty. Yet Shakespeare, Burbage and the rest were no more than humble Grooms. The old stigma which classed members of the theatrical profession with itinerant vagabonds, only to be tolerated if accepted as being servants to some grand personage, could still not be erased, however many *Julius Caesars, Hamlets* or *Othellos* such vagabonds might produce.

Although the Christmas season at court was a very busy one for the players, they were still forbidden on account of the plague to perform in public. For this they were compensated on 8th February, 1604, with a grant of £30 from the King. Probably because they had been so busily engaged in entertaining Their Majesties at court, the King's Players and their playwright were given no part in the preparation of the pageants and masques which were devised by Ben Jonson, Drayton, Webster, Dekker, Daniel and others in connection with the coronation procession through London. This had been postponed until 15th March, 1604, when it was hoped that the danger from the plague would have sufficiently abated.

The City authorities had prepared seven very elaborate arches of triumph, which were designed and erected under the supervision of an architect named Stephen Harrison, whose illustrated booklet describing them all is still available today in the Bodleian and British Museum libraries. Almost at the eleventh hour the City of Westminster decided to join with the Duchy of Lancaster in building an eighth arch in the Strand, which was 'thought on, begun, and perfected in twelve days'. Ben Jonson's description of this arch is to be found in Nichols' *Progresses*:

> The invention was a Rainbow, the Moon, Sun and those Seven Stars which antiquity hath styled the Pleiades of Vergiliae, advanced between two magnificent pyramids of 70 foot in height, on which were drawn his Majestie's several pedigrees, England and Scotland.[8]

One of the Pleiades, Electra, was represented by a speaker suspended in the air, who delivered a speech about ancient Troy which was supposed to call to mind London ruined with sickness by the plague. The themes of this and the pageants at the other seven arches were all severely classical, and many of the speeches written for them were too impossibly long and boring to be delivered to the King as he made his six-hour progress along the triumphal route. The indefatigable authors, however, made sure that such gems of learning were not wasted by publishing them all in pamphlets shortly afterwards, whether they had actually been delivered or not.

In the accounts of the Lord Chamberlain for the expenses of the procession are included four and a half yards of red cloth for each of the players for their liveries as Grooms of the Chamber. Shakespeare's name comes first in the list. The players are not mentioned in the official schedule of those who took part in the procession, but there is little doubt that anyone to whom the livery was issued would have taken some part; probably it was among the humble Messengers of the Chamber who are listed first.

The Barons of the Cinque Ports had the right to support the rich canopy over the King as he rode on his white jennet; but the journey was far too long and arduous for these eminent personages to be permitted actually to carry out this duty. Their place was taken by eight Gentlemen of the Privy Chamber, of whom one would naturally have been Sir Philip Herbert, the King's young and stalwart favourite. Southampton walked in his due place with the other Earls.

No sooner was the procession out of the way than it was time for the King to open his first English parliament, which he did on 19th March with a speech from the throne. It was typical of the slipshod organization which was to dog his reign that, although everything was arranged on a lavish and magnificent scale, the little matter of summoning the faithful Commons to the Bar of the Lords to hear the gracious speech was forgotten until it was halfway through. Those responsible had mistaken the swarms of followers who had accompanied the King, and were now crowded outside the Bar, for the members of the House of Commons!

One of the matters which the Commons examined during the session was the vexed question of purveyance; that is to say, of the abuses of the agents who were authorized to requisition supplies and transport for the use of the court. The prices to be paid were fixed by the purchasing agents to their own great profit, under powers conferred by statute. Much more was requisitioned than the court properly required; the palace servants had their own servants who took away wood, coal, butter, fruit, spices and the like to their hearts' content. Half the foodstuffs coming into the kitchens were sold for the profit of the staff. Because the prices paid were too low, or because payment was long delayed, the quality of goods supplied was frequently well below standard. The accumulating debts made it harder and harder to pay the King's servants, so that they resorted more and more to graft.[9]

Although many of these abuses had merely continued from the previous reign, there was no doubt that under the new regime things were getting rapidly worse. The King had been led to believe by the lavish hospitality which had been extended to him by local magnates on his way down from Scotland to London that England was overflowing with riches; his own level of expenditure accordingly rose to prodigious heights. Gifts of thousands of pounds were handed out to favourites in exchange for a few words of flattery, and fabulous entertainments devised to please the Queen or royal guests from overseas. It was small wonder that those employed about the court thought it only reasonable that they should seize a good share for themselves, since so much was in any case going to waste.

His regal duties the King took as lightly as possible, spending most of his time at his hunting lodges at Royston and Newmarket or at the country seats of any of his nobles who could be made to entertain him. The effect of these visitations on the surrounding inhabitants, who had to meet the requisitions of the purveyors and suffer vast hordes of huntsmen to tread down their crops, was ruinous. It was not surprising that the first enthusiasm for the new monarch very rapidly waned. Time-serving flattery, frivolity and corruption seemed likely to be the only passports to success in the opening years of the new reign.

CHAPTER XX

The Jacobean Sonnets

THE seventeen Sonnets 109–125, like the slightly shorter series at 86–96, express the deeply-felt emotions of a wounded heart; but in this case the reasons behind Shakespeare's grief are quite different. At the beginning of 1594 he was accusing Southampton of callousness in spurning his sincere offerings (and also his kindly-meant advice) in favour of the pretentious verse and laboured flattery of a rival: now he is on the defensive, answering the accusation of Southampton that he is no more than a fair-weather friend. So much is apparent to any casual reader, but by setting these sonnets in their proper place against the background of the time we can go rather further than that.

The first two sonnets in this group tell us exactly how Southampton reacted to the presentation of 107 and 108, and what it was he accused Shakespeare of:

O never say that I was false of heart,   109
Though absence seem'd my flame to quallifie,
As easie might I from my selfe depart,
As from my soule which in thy brest doth lye:
That is my home of love, if I have rang'd,
Like him that travels I returne againe,
Just to the time, not with the time exchang'd,
So that my selfe bring water for my staine,
Never beleeve though in my nature raign'd,
All frailties that besiege all kindes of blood,
That it could so preposterouslie be stain'd,
To leave for nothing all thy summe of good:
   For nothing this wide Universe I call,
   Save thou my Rose, in it thou art my all.

Alas, 'tis true, I have gone here and there,   110
And made my selfe a motley to the view,
Gor'd mine own thoughts, sold cheap what is most deare,
Made old offences of affections new.
Most true it is, that I have lookt on truth
Asconce and strangely: But by all above,
These blenches gave my heart an other youth,
And worse essaies prov'd thee my best of love,
Now all is done, have what shall have no end,

> Mine appetite I never more will grin'de
> On newer proofe, to trie an older friend,
> A God in love, to whom I am confin'd.
>> Then give me welcome, next my heaven the best,
>> Even to thy pure and most most loving brest.

Shakespeare admits in the first of these sonnets that he has deserted Southampton and sought other company, but denies vehemently that he had forgotten his friend's past benevolence and just callously written him off. His soul still lies in Southampton's breast, just as it did in 1592:

> For all that beauty that doth cover thee,   22.5–8
> Is but the seemely rayment of my heart,
> Which in thy brest doth live, as thine in me,
> How can I then be elder then thou art?

Though he may have ranged far away when Southampton was out of circulation, now he is back again on the dot, unchanged by the passing of time. The rest of the world is nothing, for the cipher on Southampton's title is as true as ever it was:

> *Thy worth and truth, Rose, are my life's onlie hope.*

In the second he admits that the evidence looks black against him. He has made a fool of himself, and contracted new associations that are hurtful to his old friend. The line:

> Gor'd mine own thoughts, sold cheap what is most deare,   110.3

is explained later on in 122, when Shakespeare admits that he has given away a notebook, the gift of Southampton, which contained a record of his love:

> Thy guift, thy tables are within my braine   122.1–2
> Full characterd with lasting memory, . . .   & 11–14
> Therefore to give them from me I was bold,
> To trust those tables that receave thee more,
>> To keepe an adjunckt to remember thee,
>> Were to import forgetfulnesse in mee.

The second and third quatrains of 110 admit that Shakespeare has been inconstant (the word 'truth' in line 5 is used, as so often in the earlier sonnets, in the sense of 'constancy'), and in such a way that 'these blenches gave my heart an other youth'. This can surely only mean that he had fastened his love on an object similar to the Southampton of years ago, in other words, upon another handsome young patron. Now this is all finished, and the experience has merely reinforced his abiding love for Southampton.

Now we can see what must have been written in those tables which Shakespeare gave away; surely they were some of the earlier sonnets, which he was faithless enough to address to his new young friend. No wonder Southampton's attitude had turned so icy. This above all would provide justification for the charge of being 'false of heart'.

The last couplet of Sonnet 110 has caused difficulties for some. It has been oddly suggested that 'my heaven' in line 13 refers to the poet's mistress, but this would be contrary to the whole thesis of the Sonnets, which contrasts his pure love for his patron with his lust for women,

> Two loves I have of comfort and dispaire, . . .   144.1

The meaning is simpler than that; 'heaven' just means heaven, as in Sonnet 29:

> Haplye I thinke on thee, and then my state,   29.10–12
> (Like to the Larke at breake of daye arising)
> From sullen earth sings himns at Heavens gate,. . .

For Shakespeare's soul to lie in Southampton's breast is the next thing to being in heaven. It should be noted, incidentally, that line 14 carries no picture of a physical embrace; we are still in the context of the conceit by which the heart or soul of each loving friend is said to be held in the other's breast.

To return for a moment to line 3 of 110, the phrase 'Gor'd mine own thoughts' means 'pierced 'or 'savaged' mine own thoughts, but it is possible that it also carries another meaning. A 'gore' is a triangular piece of cloth, and a clown's 'motley' contained triangular or diamond-shaped pieces of different coloured cloth. 'To gore' can mean to cut up into gores. So the motley of line 2 could be considered as made of Shakespeare's old thoughts cut up and used a second time to decorate his clownish garb, when he selected some of the old sonnets to please a new patron.[1]

In the next sonnet Shakespeare asks to be excused for his behaviour on the grounds that he has no alternative but to try to earn a living as best he may:

> O for my sake doe you wish fortune chide,   111.1–8
> The guiltie goddesse of my harmfull deeds,
> That did not better for my life provide,
> Then publick meanes which publick manners breeds.
> Thence comes it that my name receives a brand,
> And almost thence my nature is subdu'd
> To what it workes in, like the Dyers hand,
> Pitty me then, and wish I were renu'de, . . .

His nature is almost subdued to mercenary ends, as the dyer's hand carries the stains of his trade. But Dyer is spelled with a capital letter, and we should not forget that the mercenary informer who was the sole witness against Sir Walter Raleigh was called Dyer.* Doubtless the nature of informers is subdued to what they work in, that is to say, to money, as may be that of public players.

From Sonnet 112 it is clear enough that Shakespeare's pursuit of a new patron

* See p. 162.

has been the subject of public gossip, but he will not mind that if Southampton is sympathetic:

> For what care I who calles me well or ill,   112.3–4
> So you ore-greene my bad, my good alow?

It has been suggested that 'ore-greene' is a reference to Southampton's help in 1592 in causing Chettle to apologize for publishing Robert Greene's slanders of Shakespeare as an ignorant plagiarist.[2] Since all these 'Jacobean' Sonnets continually look backward to the halcyon days of 1592–4, I think this is correct; without that the metaphor of 'grassing over' a bad patch of ground seems rather strained, Shakespeare's reputation needs the same kind of support now as Southampton gave it then.★

In passing we may note that the word *Abisme* in line 9 of this Sonnet:

> In so profound *Abisme* I throw all care   112.9

is printed in italics because it is a foreign word, to be pronounced with silent s, *abîme*. This was the usual pronunciation at the time.[3]

The last couplet has been often misunderstood because of the inadequate punctuation:

> You are so strongly in my purpose bred,   112.13–14
> That all the world besides me thinkes y'are dead.

To understand it one must look at line 5,

> You are my All the world, and I must strive,
> To know my shames and praises from your tounge,

where the capital A tells us that All-the-world is a single phrase. If Southampton is Shakespeare's All-the-world, then obviously it is logical to say that All-the-world-besides can be considered to be dead. The phrase is in the vocative case:

> That, All-the-world-besides, methinks you're dead!

is how it should be represented in modern spelling and punctuation. Tyler gives the correct sense,[4] but nearly all other editors mangle the line by arbitrarily dropping the 'y'', although it is most unlikely that a printer would have inserted this 'y'' by accident.

The next two sonnets are very important, because they tell us about the 'worse essaies' which proved Southampton to be Shakespeare's 'best of love'

> Since I left you, mine eye is in my minde,   113.
> And that which governes me to goe about,
> Doth part his function, and is partly blind,
> Seemes seeing, but effectually is out:

★ Cf. pp. 19 and 38.

For it no forme delivers to the heart
Of bird, of flowre, or shape which it doth lack,
Of his quick objects hath the minde no part,
Nor his owne vision houlds what it doth catch:
For if it see the rud'st or gentlest sight,
The most sweet-favor or deformedst creature,
The mountaine, or the sea, the day, or night:
The Croe, or Dove, it shapes them to your feature.
   Incapable of more,* repleat with you,
   My most true minde thus maketh mine untrue.

Or whether doth my minde being crown'd with you   114
Drinke up the monarks plague this flattery?
Or whether shall I say mine eie saith true,
And that your love taught it this *Alcumie*?
To make of monsters, and things indigest,
Such cherubines as your sweet selfe resemble,
Creating every bad a perfect best,
As fast as objects to his beames assemble:
Oh tis the first, tis flatry in my seeing,
And my great minde most kingly drinkes it up,
Mine eie well knowes what with his gust is greeing,
And to his pallat doth prepare the cup.
   If it be poison'd, tis the lesser sinne,
   That mine eye loves it and doth first beginne.

In 113 the conceit is artificial enough; because Shakespeare's mind has been obsessed with Southampton since they parted, it converts anything his eye sees to a vision of Southampton. Therefore it is the constancy of his mind that has caused his affections to be inconstant. But the importance of the sonnet is in the third quatrain, where five pairs are contrasted:

Rudest sight	or	gentlest sight
deformedst creature	or	most sweet-favour
mountain	or	sea
night	or	day
Crow	or	Dove

It is easy enough to see which side to classify each item with the possible exception of the mountain and the sea; however, there are two reasons for classifying mountain as 'rude' and sea as 'gentle'; first, because the pairs seem to be placed alternately one way round and then the other (rude-gentle, gentle-rude, rude-gentle, gentle-rude, rude-gentle), and secondly, because mountainous country was usually thought of as rude and wild. As regards night and day, Chapman

* In Q Willen and Reed: more repleat,

might have put them the other way round, but Shakespeare is always anti-night and pro-day, as we saw in *The Rape of Lucrece*.

Now Shakespeare is still excusing himself here for his inconstancy to Southampton, so these descriptions of 'rude' and 'gentle' can only apply to two persons to whom he had offered his devotion and from whom he had expectations as patrons. Two obvious candidates at once spring to mind, the hunchback Lord Cecil, the most important figure in the government, and the handsome young Sir Philip Herbert, the King's chief favourite, the patronage of either of whom would be of great value to the King's Players in general and to Shakespeare's personal aspirations in particular; greater than would be the patronage of Southampton.

In Sonnet 114 only the 'rudest sight' is mentioned:

> To make of monsters, and things indigest,   114.5–6
> Such cherubines as your sweet selfe resemble, . . .

and it is flattery, the 'monarks plague', that has really been responsible for Shakespeare's cleaving to the 'indigest monster' and abandoning Southampton; he cannot any longer maintain the pretence that it is his mind's obsession with Southampton that has misled his eye. Just as Cecil, the deformed and indigest creature with (like Richard III) a mountain on his back, has this sonnet to himself, so Philip Herbert had Sonnet 110; for affection for Cecil could scarcely have been described as giving Shakespeare's 'heart another youth', whereas an infatuation for Herbert might well have seemed to do so, until experience of his unpleasant character overcame it.

In the first line Shakespeare describes himself as elevated to the rank of a king in his profession through the love of Southampton, and he goes on to present himself as behaving like a monarch, or rather, like one particular monarch, the King whom he has lately been able to observe at Wilton and Hampton Court, drinking-in flattery, and regarding the flatterers as cherubins instead of monsters.

Sonnet 115 is very important for two reasons, one of which I have already mentioned in Chapter XVIII, namely that it tells us that Sonnets 107 and 108 were written together; the other reason is that it shows that some time has passed since Shakespeare presented 'Those lines that I before have writ'. At the time Shakespeare wrote Sonnet 108, he says, he thought it sufficient to affirm that his love was as strong as ever it had been, and that there was nothing new to say about it except what he had already said many times in the old days. Outward appearances might give one to think that this was impossible, but for him at the time of the King's coronation the mental picture of his friend remained just as it was in 1592-4. That was the time

> When I was certain ore in-certainty,   115.11–12
> Crowning the present, doubting of the rest:

or, as he had said in 107, when

> Incertenties now crowne them-selves assur'de,   107.7

but these were only the uncertainties of the past that he had in mind; he dared not then think of the future, because of the tyranny of reckoning Time, which he had already described so graphically in a similar way through the mouth of Ulysses in *Troilus and Cressida*. Time erodes vows between the firmest friends; reverses the decrees of kings, such as those which had restored Southampton to his titles and established the King's Players; tans the sacred beauty of the 'master-hue' and diverts the firmest intentions. Now Shakespeare realizes that he was wrong: true love does not reach a peak and then remain static; it is always growing, and that is why Cupid is represented as a baby.

Perhaps this is a suitable moment to pause and consider Shakespeare's references to the sacredness of the young Southampton's beauty, and of his name.

> but yet like prayers divine,   108.5–6 & 8
> I must each day say ore the very same, . . .
> Even as when first I hallowed thy faire name.

'Hallowed be thy name': C. C. Stopes pointed out that Southampton's name was Henry, probably shortened to Hal as well as Harry, like Falstaff's Prince Hal.[5] 'To hallow' also meant to call out, like halloo and holler today.[6] So 'hallow' means both to shout our 'Hal' and to bless. This might be empty coincidence, were it not for the following passages:

> . . . and in my tongue,   89.9–11
> Thy sweet beloved name no more shall dwell,
> Least I (too much prophane) should do it wronge:

and

> That tongue that tells the story of thy daies, . . .   95.5 & 7–8
> Cannot dispraise, but in a kinde of praise,
> Naming thy name, blesses an ill report.

Hal W. could be vocalized to 'hallow', just as H. W. could be vocalized to 'hew'. Whether that occurred to Shakespeare or not, there was clearly at the height of his love a sacred quality for him in Southampton's name, as well as in his godlike beauty.

The next sonnet is the tremendous 'Let me not to the marriage of true mindes', one of the best known poems in English literature. Although the first couplet makes a reference to the wording of the marriage service, the sonnet has nothing specifically to do with the marriage of man and woman; it is, of course, primarily about the harmony of the minds of Shakespeare and his friend.

Shakespeare continues his rejection of Ulysses' cynical view of the power of Time over love, which he has only just found to be wrong:

> Lov's not Times foole, though rosie lips and cheeks   116.9–14
> Within his bending sickles compasse come,
> Love alters not with his breefe houres and weekes,
> But beares it out even to the edge of doome:
>   If this be error and upon me proved,
>   I never writ, nor no man ever loved.

In the last line it is likely that 'no man' is the object, not the subject, of 'loved'; what the couplet says is 'if I am wrong in this, then I never wrote love-sonnets nor ever loved a man, because that which I have felt is unaltering; therefore if love does alter with time what I feel must be something else.'

Sonnets 117 and 118 frankly admit that Shakespeare had turned aside from Southampton:

> Accuse me thus, that I have scanted all,   117.1–8
> Wherein I should your great deserts repay,
> Forgot upon your dearest love to call,
> Whereto al bonds do tie me day by day,
> That I have frequent binne with unknown mindes,
> And given to time your owne deare purchas'd right,
> That I have hoysted saile to al the windes
> Which should transport me farthest from your sight.

But Shakespeare tries to laugh the matter off by bringing in a singularly unconvincing conceit that he was just testing Southampton's constancy to him. Too much sweetness has made him turn to bitter sauces for contrast, as unpleasant purgatives are taken sometimes by healthy people to ward off possible future ills. The result has been disastrous. In 119 and 120 he writes with much more sincerity:

> What potions have I drunke of *Syren* tears   119.
> Distil'd from Lymbecks foule as hell within,
> Applying feares to hopes, and hopes to feares,
> Still loosing when I saw my selfe to win?
> What wretched errors hath my heart committed,
> Whilst it hath thought it selfe so blessed never?
> How have mine eies out of their Spheares bene fitted
> In the distraction of this madding fever?
> O benefit of ill, now I find true
> That better is, by evil still made better.
> And ruin'd love when it is built anew
> Growes fairer then at first, more strong, far greater.
>   So I returne rebukt to my content,
>   And gaine by ills thrise more then I have spent.

That you were once unkind be-friends mee now, 120
And for that sorrow, which I then didde feele,
Needes must I under my transgression bow,
Unlesse my Nerves were brasse or hammered steele.
For if you were by my unkindnesse shaken
As I by yours, y'have past a hell of Time,
And I a tyrant have no leasure taken
To waigh how once I suffered in your crime.
O that our night of wo might have remembred
My deepest sence, how hard true sorrow hits.
And soone to you, as you to me than tendred
The humble salve, which wounded bosomes fits!
    But that your trespasse now becomes a fee,
    Mine ransoms yours, and yours must ransome mee.

'*Syren* tears' are the tears of sailors yearning for the sweet-voiced Sirens, who lure them to destruction. The tears are in this case Shakespeare's own, distilled from alembics (or stills) that are 'foule as hell within', because Shakespeare's motives were impure; he was driven by worldly ambition and covetousness, not by love, to desert Southampton and seek patronage from others. In putting together the images of 'Sirens' and 'alembics' Shakespeare once again shows how his mind is constantly returning to the years 1592–4. They are used together by Barnabe Barnes in Sonnet XLIX of *Parthenophil and Parthenophe*, sonnet which immediately follows one which Shakespeare summarized in 1593 in his Sonnet 21.*

This is what Barnes had written in his Sonnet XLIX:

> Fool! fool! these labours are inextricable:
> A burden whose weight is importable;
>   A Siren which, within thy breast, doth bathe her;
>   A Fiend which doth, in Graces' garments grath her;
>   A fortress, whose force is impregnable;
> From my love's 'lembic, still 'stilled tears. O tears!
>   Quench! quench mine heat! or, with your sovereignty,
>   Like *Niobe*, convert mine heart to marble!

It is scarcely credible that the coupling of such diverse images as Siren and alembic in the two poems could have occurred by coincidence.[7]

Sonnet 120 takes a different tone. Instead of meekly admitting his own faults as against his friend's perfection, Shakespeare at last sees fit to remind Southampton of his own unkindness on one notable occasion. What the occasion is is not in doubt, because Shakespeare makes his meaning clear by direct quotation

M   * See pp. 30–1.

from the sonnets in which, many years ago, he described his unhappiness over the incident. Here are Sonnets 34 and 35:

> Why didst thou promise such a beautious day,   34.
> And make me travaile forth without my cloake,
> To let bace cloudes ore-take me in my way,
> Hiding thy brav'ry in their rotten smoke.
> Tis not enough that through the cloude thoud breake,
> To dry the raine on my storme-beaten face,
> For no man well of such a salve can speake,
> That heales the wound, and cures not the disgrace:
> Nor can thy shame give phisicke to my griefe,
> Though thou repent, yet I have still the losse,
> Th' offenders sorrow lends but weake reliefe
> To him that beares the stong offenses losse.
>   Ah but those teares are pearle which thy love sheeds,
>   And they are ritch, and ransome all ill deeds.

> No more bee greev'd at that which thou hast done,   35.
> Roses have thornes, and silver fountaines mud,
> Cloudes and eclipses staine both Moone and Sunne,
> And loathsome canker lives in sweetest bud.
> All men make faults, and even I in this,
> Authorizing thy trespas with compare,
> My selfe corrupting salving thy amisse,
> Excusing thy* sins more then thy* sins are:
> For to thy sensuall fault I bring in sence,
> Thy adverse party is thy Advocate,
> And gainst my selfe a lawfull plea commence,
> Such civill warr is in my love and hate,
>   That I an accessary needs must be,
>   To that sweet theefe which sourely robs from me.

Salve, ransom, trespass: there is no reason why these words should crop up in 120 also, except that Shakespeare wished to make reference to the time Southampton hurt him very badly by stealing his mistress. He swallowed the injury then because it happened while he was receiving Southampton's first positive assistance, that over the publication of *Venus and Adonis*, and found ways to excuse it:

> Loving offendors thus I will excuse yee,   42.5-8
> Thou doost love her, because thou knowst I love her,
> And for my sake even so doth she abuse me,
> Suffring my friend for my sake to approove her, . . .

>   * In Q and Willen and Reed: their . . . their.

But 120 shows how deep the hurt really was. It also shows how very different the relationship between the two now is, that Shakespeare could think of bringing up this old matter and throwing it in Southampton's face.

In Sonnet 121 the mood of self-justification becomes stronger:

> Tis better to be vile then vile esteemed, 121.
> When not to be, receives reproach of being,
> And the just pleasure lost, which is so deemed,
> Not by our feeling, but by others seeing.
> For why should others false adulterat eyes
> Give salutation to my sportive blood?
> Or on my frailties why are frailer spies;
> Which in their wils count bad what I think good?
> Noe, I am that I am, and they that levell
> At my abuses, reckon up their owne,
> I may be straight though they them-selves be bevel
> By their rancke thoughts, my deedes must not be shown
>   Unlesse this generall evill they maintaine,
>   All men are bad and in their badnesse raigne.

After fortifying himself with the recollection of Southampton's base act, he decides that there is really nothing very wrong about his own conduct. Although the 'false adulterat eyes' and the frailties of the spies who have criticized him may ostensibly refer to the informers who have blackened his name to Southampton, really the implication is against Southampton himself, whose behaviour over the years has been far from exemplary. Shakespeare may have a weakness for making up to handsome young sprigs of the nobility, but some people have been guilty of much greater acts of faithlessness. With this strengthening thought Shakespeare is able to face in Sonnet 122 the charge of giving away to another the notebook which we have already discussed.

The three last sonnets, 123–125, continue the same train of thought as the preceding three, that Shakespeare has no real need to revile himself, because he is sincerely aware that in his heart of hearts his love and constancy to Southampton have never altered, whatever the appearances may have been. The first line of 123:

> No! Time, thou shalt not bost that I doe change, 123.1

seems to indicate that there is little, if any, time gap between this sonnet and the preceding ones. It is necessary, however, for us to make a little pause in order to look at the background of some important topical references in this final group.

In June 1604 Stephen Harrison brought out the booklet to which I referred earlier about the Seven Arches of Triumph in the City of London, with poems by Dekker, Webster and perhaps others who are unnamed. As well as illustrations of the arches, the text is given of the various poems and speeches which were spoken, or intended to be spoken, as the royal procession passed by on 15th March. Shortly afterwards various other poets who had contributed speeches which they thought should be given to posterity issued pamphlets setting them out, and adding to the official descriptions of the events of that memorable day. Because of James's well-known classical erudition the poets had vied with one another to bring in every classical reference or parallel they could think of, and many mythological personages of surprising appearance had lain in wait along the route in the hope of edifying the King with their laborious prose or verse compositions.

Thomas Dekker's commendatory Ode at the beginning of Harrison's booklet seems to be referred to in Sonnets 123 and 125. Here is what Dekker writes:

> Babell that strove to weare
> A Crowne of Cloudes, and up did reare
>   her forehead hye,
> With an ambitious lust to kisse the skie,
>   Is now or dust, or not at all,
>   proud *Nymrods* wall,
>   And all his Antique monuments,
>   Left to the world as presidents,★
> Cannot now shew (to tell where they did stand.)
> So much in length as halfe the Builders hand.
>
>   The Mausolaean tombe,
> The sixteen curious gates in Rome,
>   which times preferre,
> Both past and present: *Neroes* Theater,
>   That in one day was all gilt o're:
>   Ad to these more,
>   Those *Columnes*, and those *Pyramids*, that won
>   Wonder by height: the Colosse of the Sun:
> Th' *Aegyptian* Obelisks: are all forgotten:
>   Onely their names grown great: themselves be rotten.
>
>   Deare friend! what honour then
> Bestow'st thou on thy Country men?
>   Crowning with praise,
> By these thy labors, (as with wreathes of bayes)
>   this royal City: where now stand,
>   (built by thy hand)
>   Her Arches in new state; so made,
> That their fresh beauties n'ere shall fade:
>   Thou of our English Triumphes rear'st the Fame,
>   Bove those of old; But above all, thy name.

★ i.e., precedents.

Stephen Harrison is as much devoted to the theme of Time, the destroyer, as is Shakespeare himself. In his concluding address to the 'Candid Reader' of his booklet he begins as follows:

> Reader, the limmes of these great *Triumphall* bodies (lately disjoynted and taken in sunder) I have thou seest (for thy sake) set in their apt and right places againe: so that now they are to stand as perpetuall monuments, not to be shaken in peeces, or to be broken downe, by the malice of that envious destroyer of all things, *Time*. Which labours of mine, if they yeeld thee either profit or pleasure, thou art (in requitall thereof) to pay many thankes to this honourable Citie, whose bounty towards me, not onely in making choise of me, to give directions for the intire workmanship of the fine *Triumphall Arch's* builded by the same, but also (in publishing these *Peeces*,) I do here gladly acknowledge to have bene exceeding liberall.

Shakespeare's references to Stephen Harrison's work seem to be tinged with the flavour of sour grapes. His own company of players had a theatre workshop which made scenery, and also such things as the painted devices used by the nobility in their tournaments in the Whitehall Tiltyard.[8] With Shakespeare's poetic skill and Burbage's ability as a painter they might very well have expected some share in the lucrative contracts for preparing the pageants and arches, in which Harrison says the City authorities were extremely liberal. Perhaps this was just one hope in which Cecil and Philip Herbert, if they were the patrons he had recently been cultivating, had let him down. This is what Shakespeare says:

> No! Time, thou shalt not bost that I doe change,   123.1–8
> Thy pyramyds buylt up with newer might
> To me are nothing novell, nothing strange,
> They are but dressings of a former sight:
> Our dates are breefe, and therefor we admire,
> What thou dost foyst upon us that is ould,
> And rather make them borne to our desire,
> Then thinke that we before have heard them tould: . . .

He does not think much of Harrison's antique-style pyramids (perhaps the 70-foot obelisks which had been erected in the Strand, since these were the most striking ones, though several of the other arches also incorporated smaller pyramids. They were not like the pyramids of Gizeh; their shape was similar to that of Cleopatra's Needle). They are no more than a dressing-up of the familiar old streets and conduits of London. Nor does he care for the vogue for the antique; modern designers employed for similar festive occasions would certainly agree with him that contemporary styles would have been more appropriate. Furthermore, the insistence on classical learning as the basis of the pageants may well have been the reason why Shakespeare was not commissioned to write any of the material. It was a field day for the university wits, who could foist old-fashioned material on the public as a substitute for original creative work. In Sonnet 125 Shakespeare refers again to the great procession:

> Wer't ought to me I bore the canopy,   125.1–4
> With my extern the outward honoring,
> Or layd great bases for eternity,
> Which proves more short then wast or ruining?

Now, in his closing letter to the Candid Reader from which I quoted above, Harrison goes on to describe the actual processsion:

> Nor shall it be amisse in this place to give thee intelligence of some matters (by way of notes) which were not fully observde, nor freely inough set downe in the Printed Booke of these *Triumphes*: amongst which these that follow are chiefest.
>
> His Majestie departed from the *Tower* betweene the houres of 11 and 12 and before 5 had made his royall passage through the Citie, having a *Canopie* borne over him by 8 Knights.

It should be noted that in 125 Shakespeare does not say that he had in fact borne a canopy; the verbs 'wert' and 'bore' are in the subjunctive. What he is saying is 'Would it have meant anything to me if I had been sufficiently favoured to be one of the knightly Gentlemen of the Privy Chamber who carried the canopy, paying superficial homage to outward appearances; or by sycophancy had prepared the ground for personal favours, which prove more evanescent than the arches of triumph which I failed to get a hand in?'

It has often been pointed out that the second line of this sonnet recalls Iago's speech in the first scene of *Othello* in which he explains why he follows the Moor.[9] The resemblance is important, as *Othello* was first performed on 1st November, 1604, and is therefore likely to have been written quite close to the time of which we are now speaking. Iago says:

> It is as sure as you are Roderigo,   *Oth.* I.i.57–66.
> Were I the Moor, I would not be Iago.
> In following him I follow but myself —
> Heaven is my judge, not I for love and duty,
> But seeming so for my peculiar end.
> For when my outward action doth demonstrate
> The native act and figure of my heart
> In compliment extern, 'tis not long after
> But I will wear my heart upon my sleeve
> For daws to peck at: I am not what I am.

Not only does the unusual word 'extern' appear, as in the sonnet, close to the word 'outward', but the last phrase, 'I am not what I am', recalls the words, 'No, I am that I am' in line 9 of Sonnet 121. In each case the subject is the same, that of insincere and calculating behaviour to achieve sordid ends, which in the Sonnets Shakespeare is disclaiming for himself and imputing against others: in particular, against one or more of the Gentlemen of the Privy Chamber who bore the canopy on 15th March.

This is how Professor Akrigg describes Sir Philip Herbert, the King's favourite who the following year was to be created Earl of Montgomery:

> All that Montgomery had to commend him was his good looks, though these had a powerful attraction for James who was more drawn to handsome men than to beautiful women. For the rest he was a young boor utterly unworthy of the uncle, Sir Philip Sidney, from whom he derived his Christian name. His interests were hunting and hawking, the bowling alley, the tiltyard, and the gaming table. He did not even take the trouble to cultivate the attentions of the King, treating the royal favours with an offhand neglect even while accepting them. His furious bursts of bad temper made him a man from whom most people had little liking, and a nasty streak of malice and treachery added nothing to his reputation.[10]

It is interesting to set against this a statement that Herbert, by then Earl of Pembroke and Montgomery, is represented by a pamphleteer in the next reign as having made in Parliament in the year 1648:

> I was fed like a Prince at the King's cost, twice every day (long before some of you were born) and this King continued, nay, out-did his Father in heaping favours upon me: yet (for your sakes) I renounc'd my master when he had most need of me; voted against him, hired men to fight against him: . . .[11]

Of course, Shakespeare's Iago is not a direct portrait of Herbert, who did not dissemble his feelings or engage in subtle schemes like Othello's ancient; nevertheless the character of Herbert fits exactly the canopy-bearer of the sonnet, and does have in it more than a hint of Iago's treachery. If Shakespeare was foolish enough to address second-hand sonnets to him in the hope of favour, we may be sure that he would be heartlessly betrayed. Philip Herbert, like his brother William but unlike Southampton, who matured later, was an inveterate womanizer from a very early age, and unlikely to have taken any interest in emotional approaches from Shakespeare.

The dedicatory letter to the Lord Mayor, which prefaces Stephen Harrison's booklet about the arches of triumph, is dated 16th June, 1604, and no doubt the book was on sale shortly after this. On 22nd June occurred an event which is of supreme importance for dating Sonnet 124.

In Chapter XIV I mentioned the voyage to Guiana of Sir Robert Dudley, the bastard son of the Earl of Leicester. He was acknowledged by the Earl to be his natural son, and was left in his will the reversion of Kenilworth Castle after the death of Leicester's brother, the Earl of Warwick. Nevertheless, Leicester named Dudley as a bastard no less than seventeen times during the course of the will. When Warwick died in 1590 Dudley tried to claim his inheritance, but without success.[12]

Robert Dudley was born in 1574, his mother being Douglas, Lady Sheffield. At that time it was not desirable that the Queen should known that Leicester had taken another wife after the death of his first (Amy Robsart), since the Queen had at one time wished to marry him herself and had only refrained from doing so for reasons of state. Whether for this reason or for another, the Earl did not acknowledge any marriage to Lady Sheffield; but soon afterwards he secretly married the widowed mother of the young Earl of Essex. Lady Sheffield then married Sir Edward Stafford, thinking that she had no more to hope for from Leicester.

Dudley, in spite of his illegitimacy, was accepted in society and at court, and in due course was knighted. When James came to the throne he decided to try to establish that his mother had been legally married to Leicester and that he himself was thus entitled to succeed to the earldoms of both Leicester and Warwick. He and his mother therefore commenced proceedings in September 1603 in the Consistory Court at Lichfield. Unfortunately, after nearly thirty years there was very little reliable evidence of the marriage, if marriage there had been, and Dudley and his mother therefore encouraged such witnesses as they had to make their stories more convincing than bare recollection would justify. This gave Leicester's widow, the former Countess of Essex, an opportunity to file a bill in the Star Chamber against Dudley. She naturally had no desire to see her own marriage with Leicester invalidated. The Crown also had an interest in seeing that the earldoms of Leicester and Warwick remained extinct, so that their valuable properties could be retained by the King.

The proceedings in the Star Chamber began on 22nd June, 1604, Sir Edward Coke appearing as usual as Attorney-General. It was a fashionable *cause célèbre*, in the outcome of which many of the nobility had an interest, several of them on Dudley's side. This caused Coke to say that 'it was strange precedent that so great and honourable personages should come to Court to countenance and embrace any cause contrary to the law'. At this, Dudley's half-brother, Lord Sheffield, professed himself very much offended. The case dragged on for nearly a year, and judgment was eventually given against Dudley in May 1605. He abandoned further proceedings and eloped to the Continent with a mistress of nineteen, leaving his wife behind. There he lived for some years, calling himself Earl of Warwick and serving the Duke of Florence as a naval expert.

Now let us examine Sonnet 124:

> Yf my deare love were but the childe of state,   124.
> It might for fortunes basterd be unfathered,
> As subjects to times love, or to times hate,
> Weeds among weeds, or flowers with flowers gatherd.
> No it was buylded far from accident,
> It suffers not in smilinge pomp, nor falls

> Under the blow of thralled discontent,
> Whereto th'inviting time our fashion calls:
> It feares not policy that *Heriticke*,
> Which workes on leases of short numbred howers,
> But all alone stands hugely pollitick,
> That it nor growes with heat, nor drownes with showres.
>> To this I witnes call the foles of time,
>> Which die for goodnes, who have liv'd for crime.

The first quatrain, which has so often been completely misunderstood, can now be seen to refer to the Dudley case. Dudley's father was a very great state personage; in fact Queen Elizabeth had at one time begged the Council to make him Protector of England, with an income of twenty thousand pounds. If he did not quite reach these heights, he was nevertheless made an earl and a Privy Councillor. So 'child of state' is an accurate enough description of his son. If Robert Dudley had been born of a less eminent father he would have stood a much better chance of being legitimatized; as it was, reasons of policy, in Leicester's judgment, made the Countess of Essex a more suitable wife for him than Lady Sheffield. So Dudley had to suffer the swings and roundabouts of fortune, now looking likely to succeed in his claims, now having his hopes dashed. Shakespeare says that his own love for Southampton does not suffer from that disadvantage, but remains constant throughout all vicissitudes.

Two days after the opening of the Dudley hearing there occurred another even more striking event. On 24th June Southampton, Lord Danvers and Sir Henry Neville, all old Essexites, together with Sir Maurice Berkeley, a friend of Southampton's mother, and Sir William Lee, were all suddenly arrested and thrown in the Tower. King James was in a panic that another treason plot was afoot, and could not sleep that night. Prince Henry was ordered not to stir out of his room. After an examination by the Privy Council, all the prisoners were released the following day.[13]

There was no explanation of the incident, though many wild rumours circulated. But with the aid of the second quatrain of Sonnet 124, and of an item in the Salisbury Papers dated 30th July, it is possible to suggest what the real explanation was.

In the second quatrain of the sonnet, Shakespeare continues with examples of the unchanging force of his love. It does not suffer in 'smiling pomp', when Southampton is basking in the royal favour — in April the Queen had acted as godmother to his daughter and he had been appointed joint Lord Lieutenant of Hampshire — or when he is suffering under 'the blow of thralled discontent'. Now the phrase 'the blow of thralled discontent' can surely only mean a blow struck by discontented people who are in captivity; who could that be except our old friends Grey and Cobham, Southampton's inveterate enemies, who with Sir Walter Raleigh were languishing in the Tower on charges of disaffection?

On 30th July comes a report that 'there is some complaining by the principal prisoners in the Tower of the restraints which have been newly laid upon them by the Lieutenant'. Since returning from their trial at Winchester the prisoners had each had two servants, one to attend, and the other to act as messenger. Many visitors came to see them, including their wives and some courtiers. Once or twice Raleigh and Lord Grey had walked and talked together in the gardens: 'but now the Lieutenant has caused locks to be put on their gates, and more straitly prevents too much access, which moves them to complain'.[14] I suggest that these measures were ordered because Grey and his friends had tried to turn the tables once again on their rivals, by spreading rumours that South-ampton and the other survivors of the Essex rebellion had a plot to stage another coup.

Shakespeare can now triumphantly say that this contretemps made no differ-ence to his loyalty to Southampton. His love does not fear the vagaries of policy, which cause swift reversals of fortune when least expected. Political favour is given on leases as short as heretics give, when they wish to sequestrate their property to friends in order to avoid confiscation of it by the state.[15] True love is not like that.

As witness to the steadfastness of his love compared with the fickleness of policy Shakespeare calls the Lords Cobham and Grey. They are 'fools of time' because they were made fools of on the scaffold at Winchester, but also because they did not remain constant to their intentions. 'Time's fools' are those who 'alter when they alteration find', as we were told in Sonnet 116. Cobham and Grey are also prime examples of those who are subject alternately to time's love and time's hate, now up, now down, a fate which Shakespeare in his humble, loyal position has managed to avoid, except when his heart committed the 'wretched errors' of Sonnet 119.

We have already considered the first quatrain of Sonnet 125; the second quatrain continues the train of thought of 124:

> Have I not seene dwellers on forme and favor   125.5–8
> Lose all, and more by paying too much rent
> For compound sweet; Forgoing simple savor,
> Pittifull thrivors in their gazing spent.

Not only is Shakespeare setting out rules of behaviour for himself (to remain humble and loyal), but he is also by implication giving some advice to South-ampton, who has just had a rude reminder that he should not bank too strongly on his recently found royal favour.

The phrase, 'paying too much rent for compound sweet', immediately brings to mind the farm of sweet wines, the revenue on which was compounded to an annual rent payable to the Crown by the person awarded the right to collect it. As we saw in Chapter XVI, it was the refusal of the Queen to renew to Essex the grant of this farm that proved the last straw in pushing him into rebellion. In August 1603 the King had granted this very same privilege to

Southampton, and it was for him an essential means of livelihood, as it had been to Essex. As early as 1606 Shakespeare's apprehensions about it came near to being justified, when the proposal to impose a new tax on sweet wines gravely threatened Southampton's financial position. In 1607 there was another threat from an increase in the standard leakage allowance. But fortunately he was still in favour, and the Crown eventually resumed the farm and gave him £2000 a year in compensation.[16]

Besides Essex, another 'dweller on form and favour' was of course Sir Walter Raleigh, who was suddenly deprived of his London house and of his lucrative monopolies by James, and was thought to have discussed treason with Cobham for these reasons. But one of the most 'pitiful thrivers' was the Earl of Oxford, father of the lady whom Southampton spurned and for whose subsequent marriage to the Earl of Derby Shakespeare wrote *A Midsummer Night's Dream*. He died on 26th June, two days after Southampton's arrest and four days after the opening of the Dudley case. The premier earl in the land and hereditary Lord Great Chamberlain, he wasted his money on every kind of worthless extravagance, including Italian gloves, sweet bags and perfumed jerkins, as well as many more costly items. Having spent his whole fortune he had to be granted a compassionate pension of £1000 per annum for life by the Queen. King James quoted this precedent when refusing to allow any more to Lord Sheffield, another 'pitiful thriver' whom we saw avidly hoping that his half-brother would succeed in his claim to the Warwick and Leicester inheritances, and thus help him to repair the damage he had caused to his own.[17]

Whether because of Shakespeare's advice or because he had by now learned greater wisdom of his own accord, Southampton from now on took little part in the intrigues of the court. In September 1603, on the death of Lord Hunsdon, patron between 1596 and the accession of James of Shakespeare's company, he had been appointed Captain of the Isle of Wight, and from then on he took more and more interest in the affairs of his home territories. It was far more secure and satisfying to be a magnate in Hampshire than a precarious 'dweller on form and favour' in Whitehall. By these tactics he retained sufficient prestige and popularity at court to be given an honourable part in all the state occasions and festivities that were constantly taking place, while his hospitality on the King's many expeditions to his part of England was highly thought of.

Now for the last six lines of Sonnet 125:

> Noe, let me be obsequious in thy heart, 125.9–14
> And take thou my oblacion, poore but free,
> Which is not mixt with seconds, knows no art,
> But mutuall render onely me for thee.
>   Hence, thou subborned *Informer*, a trew soule
>   When most impeacht, stands least in thy controule.

Oblations which were not 'mixt with seconds', like the flour purveyed to the royal kitchens, were not so common in that period of flattery and corruption.

Southampton had just proved himself 'a true soul' who stood least in the control of the informers suborned by his enemies; he had declared to the Council at the enquiry on 25th June that if he knew the slanderer responsible for his arrest he would challenge him to the field, but no attempt was made to substantiate the charges against him. Was he prepared to accept that Shakespeare's heart was, after all that had happened, equally steadfast and true?

CHAPTER XXI

'Now All Is Done'

IN the last chapter we saw that Sonnets 109–125 form one continuous sequence, written in fairly quick succession, with the object of explaining and excusing Shakespeare's apparent disloyalty to Southampton in favour of persons who seemed likely to prove more valuable patrons, probably Sir Philip Herbert and Lord Cecil of Essendon. The dating of the group we established by references in the closing sonnets to events which took place in the latter half of June 1604. If the whole group of seventeen sonnets was written over a period of two or three weeks we may place it with reasonable confidence within that month of June. It is, of course, impossible to tell exactly how long Shakespeare required for the composition of sonnets, but with the knowledge that we have now gained of the dating of the series as a whole this seems a fair enough estimate.

There remains only the twelve-line envoi which is numbered 126, and fortunately the dating of this is very simple to establish, although it seems to have remained unsuspected for the 363 years since the 1609 edition was published. Between 125 and 126 there is an interval of approximately nine months (just time, as it happens, for the Countess of Southampton to conceive and bear a son), and we will take a brief glance at some events that occurred during that time.

In July the King concluded arrangements for fifty-four learned men to undertake a new translation of the Bible, which became the Authorised Version known to us all. As anyone can easily verify for himself, the dedicatory epistle at the beginning of this Bible refers to the apprehensions felt at the death of Queen Elizabeth and the general relief which followed the peaceful accession of James, in very much the same way as Shakespeare does in Sonnet 107.

In August there arrived the Commissioners sent by the King of Spain to ratify the treaty of peace which had constituted James's first and most important article of foreign policy. The leader of the Spanish embassy was Don Juan de Velasco, Duke of Frias and Constable of Castile, and to provide accommodation worthy of him the Queen graciously agreed to vacate her own residence of Somerset House. The whole party of about a hundred persons was fed and waited upon at the expense of the King, and His Majesty's players, in the royal liveries which had been issued to them for the procession of 15th March, were detailed to attend upon the party at Somerset House in their capacity of Grooms of the Chamber Extraordinary. The Earl of Southampton also played a prominent part in entertaining the distinguished visitors.

In October Sir Philip Herbert was betrothed to Lady Susan Vere, another of the daughters of the late Earl of Oxford. In 1597 he had hoped unsuccessfully to become engaged to the heiress of a wealthy kinsman, Sir William Herbert of St Julians in Monmouthshire, and then to the daughter of Sir Arthur Gorges, who had commanded Raleigh's flagship in his abortive expedition with Essex to the Azores. The latest match caused some concern to Lady Susan's uncle, Robert Cecil (now elevated to a viscountcy as Lord Cranbourne), since neither of the parties had any money. King James, however, was delighted; he always took a great vicarious interest in the marital affairs of his favourites. The marriage was celebrated with great ceremony at Whitehall in December, the Council chamber being converted into a bridal bedroom for the occasion. The King joined the happy couple there in the morning in his nightshirt.

In November the Queen's brother, Ulric, Duke of Holst, had arrived in England for a visit that was to last until the following June. The leading courtiers were expected to bear a good share of the sumptuous entertainment thought suitable for him, and so we find Sir Walter Cope writing in January 1605 to Viscount Cranbourne:

> From your library.
>
> Sir, I have sent and bene all thys mornyng huntyng for players Juglers & Such kinde of Creaturs, but fynde them hard to finde, wherfore Leavinge notes for them to seeke me, Burbage ys come, & Sayes ther ys no new playe that the quene hath not seene, but they have Revyved an olde one, Cawled *Loves Labore lost*, which for wytt & mirthe he sayes will please her excedingly. And Thys ys apointed to be played to Morowe night at my Lord of Sowthamptons, unless yow send a wrytt to Remove the Corpus Cum Causa to your howse in Strande. Burbage ys my messenger Ready attendyng your pleasure.[1]

The diplomat Dudley Carleton, in a letter written to John Chamberlain, tells us that Cranborne's party for the Queen and the Duke of Holst was held on 14th January and Southampton's on 12th. We do not know at which one Shakespeare, Burbage and 'Such kinde of Creaturs' eventually performed that witty and erudite piece, *Love's Labour's Lost*, but it is clear enough whose command for their services would take precedence, whatever the Sonnets might say.

On 1st March, 1605, thirteen years after Shakespeare had written those first seventeen sonnets on this very theme, Southampton's wife at last gave birth to a son and heir. The baby was christened James with great ceremony at Greenwich Palace on 26th March, the King, Lord Cranbourne and the Countess of Suffolk standing as godparents.[2] It would have been strange indeed if Shakespeare had let the event pass in silence; what he did was to make it the occasion for a closing poem to crown the great series of 125 sonnets which he had addressed over the years to his respected patron and loved friend:

> O thou my lovely Boy who in thy power,   126.
> Doest hould times fickle glasse, his sickle, hower:

Who hast by wayning growne, and therein shou'st,
Thy lovers withering, as thy sweet selfe grow'st.
If Nature (soveraine misteres over wrack)
As thou goest onwards still will plucke thee backe,
She keepes thee to this purpose, that her skill★
May time disgrace, and wretched mynuit kill.
Yet fear her O thou minnion of her pleasure,
She may detaine, but not still keepe her tresure!
   Her *Audite* (though delayd) answer'd must be,
   And her *Quietus* is to render thee.

The key to the meaning of this little poem, which so many generations of readers have failed to grasp, is in the third and fourth lines, which make a direct reference to the first quatrain of Sonnet 11:

As fast as thou shalt wane so fast thou grow'st,   11.1–4
In one of thine, from that which thou departest,
And that fresh bloud which yongly thou bestow'st,
Thou maist call thine, when thou from youth convertest, . . .

Having at last produced a son, Southampton can at last grow as fast as he wanes, because it is legitimate to call this fresh blood his own, though he has lost his own youth. The same notion was repeated in Sonnet 13:

So should that beauty which you hold in lease   13.5–8
Find no determination, then you were
Your selfe again after your selfes decease,
When your sweet issue your sweet forme should beare.

and again in 16:

To give away your selfe, keeps your selfe still,   16.13–14
And you must live drawne by your owne sweet skill.

The important thing to realize is that for poetical purposes the father and the son are treated as a single entity; but the self that is growing while the poet himself withers is that of the baby, not the father, and it is thus the baby that Shakespeare is addressing as 'my lovely Boy', although in the context of the poetic conceit baby and thirty-one-year-old father are to be regarded as one person. This interpretation cannot be deduced unless the poem is placed against the 'procreation' sonnets of 1592, but once this has been done no other seems to me to be possible.

In order to understand lines 5–8 of this address to the baby in his cradle we must look back at Sonnet 4:

★ In Q and Willen and Reed: skill.

Unthrifty lovelinesse why dost thou spend,   4.
Upon thy selfe thy beauties legacy?
Natures bequest gives nothing but doth lend,
And being franck she lends to those are free:
Then beautious nigard why doost thou abuse,
The bountious largesse given thee to give?
Profitles usurer why doost thou use
So great a summe of summes yet can'st not live?
For having traffike with thy self alone,
Thou of thy selfe thy sweet selfe dost deceave,
Then how when nature calls thee to be gone,
What acceptable *Audit* can'st thou leave?
  Thy unus'd beauty must be tomb'd with thee,
  Which used lives th' executor to be.

Nature only lends beauty on trust, she does not bequeath it outright; and if she allows it to remain much longer than usual, as was the case with Southampton, it is only to discomfort her enemy Time, and to destroy his weapon, 'wretched mynuit'. 'Mynuit' is singular here just as 'hower' is singular in line 2:—meddling editors have usually corrected the text to 'wretched minutes', as if Nature wished merely to kill a few wretched minutes as one kills flies with a fly-swatter. But 'hower' in the abstract is regarded as Time's sickle in line 2, and 'mynuit' in the abstract is similarly to be taken in line 8 as a weapon or accomplice of Time.

Nature will hold her audit and require her quittance eventually, and this can only be satisfied by producing a son to be the executor of his father's beauty. So the new-born baby must not forget that it is his duty to get married in good time and not spend his beauty's legacy upon himself!

Alas, it was not to be. Lord Wriothesley was to die of pestilence in the Low Countries on 5th November, 1624, at the age of nineteen, followed five days later by his father. A second son, Thomas, succeeded to the earldom, but died without a male heir. It was Time that conquered in the end, as far as Southampton's posterity was concerned; but Shakespeare was making no idle boast when he said in Sonnet 19:

Yet doe thy worst ould Time dispight thy wrong,   19.13–14
My love shall in my verse ever live young.

CHAPTER XXII

'I Am That I Am'

If this story is a more or less literal account of events which
actually happened to Shakespeare, it is autobiographical
evidence of a sort which would compel us to believe that
the pessimism of his tragic period, when love, sex, friendship and much more besides were censoriously called into
account, was a personal confession.   M. M. Reese:
Shakespeare, his world and his work, 412.

AT the beginning of this book I set myself the task of examining against the
literary and historical background of the time what seemed to me to be the
most likely hypothesis for the order and dating of the Sonnets and the identity
of the person to whom they were addressed. During the course of this examination much subsidiary detail has been filled in, and a broad picture obtained of
the events and experiences which, in the framework of this hypothesis, seem
to lie behind the Sonnet story. The main items are summarized, with their
dates and the Sonnets that refer to them, in the table which I have added as an
appendix.

If I were a mediaeval astronomer, I should be wise enough not to aim to
establish the actual truth of the workings of the universe; that would be to
attempt to know the hidden mysteries of God. What the astronomers sought
was to find a cosmological theory that would 'save the phenomena', that is to
say, would fit in with the observable facts. When these facts were relatively few,
crude theories of crystalline spheres and epicycles were sufficient to account for
the recorded movements of the heavenly bodies, and even to enable future
movements to be more or less accurately predicted. So with Shakespeare's
Sonnets, when factual information about the historical and literary background
of the time was less ready to hand, those who sought to establish rival claimants
to the title of 'Mr. W. H.' could easily suggest more than one who seemed able
to 'save the phenomena', such as they were; they could even suggest more than
one dating pattern per claimant. As the 'phenomena' become more abundant,
the chances become greater of narrowing down the various hypotheses to one
correct one which fits all the facts. Though I do not claim that this stage has yet
been finally reached, I am nevertheless rash enough to believe that in the story
set out in this book we have come very close to it.

But it would be of little value to establish these bare facts and dates if, at the
end of it all, we found ourselves no wiser as to the effect of the emotional

N

experiences lying behind them upon Shakespeare's personality and upon the great body of creative work which he has left behind for us. In particular, as Mr Reese implies in the quotation with which I have headed this chapter, we should be able to understand something of what lay behind the dramas of his 'dark' or 'tragic' period, when not only love, sex and friendship but all idealism, truth and integrity were cynically and painfully called into account.

'In sonnet after sonnet,' says J. B. Leishman in the course of his outstanding work on Shakespeare's Sonnets, 'we find him declaring what his friend *means* to him, but never (or almost never) declaring what his friend has *made* of him, or may make of him.'[1] My own feeling is that Mr Leishman has not hit the mark, either in this passage, or in a later one in which he tells us that it is Shakespeare's doubt whether his beloved friend is worthy of and responsive to his admiration which is the 'dramatically tragic and tragically dramatic' element in the Sonnets.[2] The real tragedy of Shakespeare's Sonnets, as it seems to me, relates to what the friend makes him discover about himself; that it was Shakespeare who could have been the one who was 'false of heart', 'have looked on truth askance and strangely', and have 'sold cheap what is most dear'. This is the self-torture that runs through the 'dark' series of plays, from *Troilus and Cressida* in 1601 to *Timon of Athens* in 1608, and is responsible for their bitterly pessimistic air. It can surely not be just a matter of coincidence that it is around the time of the publication of the Sonnets, in 1609, that the plays change completely in tone and optimism returns to them once more.

We have seen in the earlier chapters of this book how, in the spring of 1592, Shakespeare found both a patron and a friend in the shape of an idealistic and virginal youth who was at the same time a wealthy aristocrat and a scholarly critic; and how, on the poet's side, friendship rapidly developed into an intense love which could not, in the nature of things, be fully reciprocated by the young man. We have seen also how, just as Shakespeare was publishing a poem on the theme of Adonis's disdain for sexual dalliance, the model for the poem turned the tables on him by accepting the embraces of Shakespeare's own mistress. Unable to admit to himself that his beautiful ideal youth is growing up into a virile and rakish young man, Shakespeare adopts an attitude of exaggerated humility and fondness, intermingled from time to time with an aunt-like tone of reproof over his wild behaviour and of hurt resignation at his showing favour to a rival poet;—all very understandable lines to take, but nevertheless calculated to bring any emotional relationship to the brink of disaster.

In the same wounded but loving spirit, Shakespeare decides in the spring of 1594 to rejoin his company of actors under the patronage of the Earl of Derby, who unfortunately very soon dies. There is nothing for it but to swallow his pride and return to young Southampton for help, bearing his second long poem, now ready for publication. Without any hesitation, so far as it appears, the young man, now reaching his majority and the full control of his inheritance, gives Shakespeare a present large enough to enable him to buy a partnership in his company and to set him on the road to the success which he duly achieved.

While from the end of 1594 onwards Shakespeare's career progressed steadily forward, the young Earl's ran into more and more trouble, until, together with Essex, he was sentenced to death for treason in February 1601. This was the moment for Shakespeare to celebrate in a sublime symbolic poem, *The Phoenix and Turtle*, the death of the two Earls and all the qualities they stood for, after which his own attachment to Southampton would remain ever in his mind as an intensely sweet and sad memory.

But it was not to be; Southampton was reprieved on the somewhat ignominious grounds that he was no more than a foolish young dupe of his friend Essex. This was reason for rejoicing, not sorrow; but I am inclined to feel that Shakespeare may have shamefully caught himself thinking that in some ways it would have been more fitting if Southampton had died after all, and had thus shared in the wave of public sympathy that followed Essex's execution. Perhaps it is this that explains the bitter flavour of *Troilus and Cressida*:

> They pass by strangely: they were us'd to bend   *T&C*. III.
> To send their smiles before them to Achilles; . . .   iii.71–2
>   . . . O! let not virtue seek   169–73
> Remuneration for the thing it was;
> For beauty, wit,
> High birth, vigour of bone, desert in service,
> Love, friendship, charity, are subjects all
> To envious and calumniating time.

As Shakespeare tells us in Sonnet 117, he himself was one of those who passed by strangely after Southampton's downfall. Neither he nor his company could afford to be accused of associating with traitors. Yet, while he was seeking the favour of the opposing party, Cecil and the Pembrokes, and perhaps even the Lords Grey and Cobham, Shakespeare could not get rid of the nagging thought of his own disloyalty to one who, ironically, had been convicted for that very crime. So, in *All's Well That Ends Well*, while belittling Southampton under the guise of Bertram, he belittles himself more in Bertram's misleader, Parolles:

> Rust, sword! cool, blushes! and Parolles, live   *AWTEW*. IV.
> Safest in shame! being fool'd, by foolery thrive!   iii.367–9
> There's place and means for every man alive.

These two bitter plays were all that Shakespeare wrote until after Southampton had been released by the new King. As we saw at the end of Chapter XVIII, the welcoming Sonnets 107 and 108 fell flat, and if we glance back at them it is not hard to understand that Southampton must have felt them to be somewhat patronizing.

Instead of being a penniless actor, struggling to make a name as a playwright, Shakespeare was now the leading dramatist of the day and a partner in the country's leading theatrical company. In 1596 he had obtained the grant of a coat of arms for his father, and the following year had purchased New Place, the best house in Stratford. By adding thrift and hard work to his natural poetic gifts he had become an outstanding member of the prosperous bourgeoisie. Southampton, on the other hand, though still the epitome of renaissance chivalry, was, after all the vicissitudes which he had undergone since the sonnets of 1594, back in the same situation as he was then: a young (if now slightly faded) aristocrat striving to make a mark at court and lacking the ready cash to sustain the generous and extravagant mode of life which he considered proper. The bond of affection was still very much there, but their comparative positions no longer seemed to Shakespeare to call for new flights of flattery, as they had in the old days. A reminder of the changes wrought by the passing years would not be out of place.

If we look again at the remarkable sonnet group 109–125 we can clearly see the state of confusion into which Shakespeare was thrown by Southampton's stinging refusal to be patronized. These sonnets tell us more about Shakespeare and about Southampton's effect on him than all the rest put together. Here is a stark and unsympathetic précis of what they say:

(a) My love for you is undying, and not dependent on your one-time good looks;

(b) To sharpen my appetite for you I have tried out other associations;

(c) Because of economic circumstances I have had to appear to follow others;

(d) When I saw others and followed them, it was because they all seemed to be facets of you;

(e) When I followed others, it was to test your regard for me;

(f) Because I had a surfeit of your goodness, I followed others by way of taking a nasty medicine to cure me of the surfeit;

(g) You were once very unkind to me, by stealing my mistress, so you should not mind my unkindness to you;

(h) I am not so bad as all that, and I do not see why I should be criticized by someone worse;

(i) I gave away your notebook with the fair copy of the Sonnets because I could remember all my love for you without their aid;

(j) My love for you has remained constant and never faltered, unlike that of people who are constantly thinking about the vicissitudes of the court.

Now it is obvious that not all these positions can be reconciled with one another; we feel that Shakespeare, if he wanted to seem convincing about his neglect for Southampton, should have drawn up a more consistent defence. Nevertheless, the inconsistencies are of a very human sort; this is just the way people do argue when they are trying to explain away their past behaviour, especially when they feel that they are more than half to blame for what has resulted.

On page 188 I posed the question whether Shakespeare was successful in bringing about, by means of these sonnets, the renewal of friendship which he sought. If so, his envoi addressed to Southampton's baby son, which was the subject of Chapter XXI, would have been joyfully received and some flash of happiness from this event would surely have illuminated some of Shakespeare's next work, just as the pleasure of his early relationship with Southampton is reflected in *Two Gentlemen of Verona, Love's Labour's Lost* and *Romeo and Juliet.* Instead we have the grim horror and sick disillusion of *King Lear*, where even the humour of the Fool is such as to provoke only wry and uneasy laughter, and the unmitigated gloom of *Macbeth*, in which even the virtuous young Malcolm begins to fear that his own character will be submerged and corrupted by the relentless tide of evil.

In *Measure for Measure* and *Othello*, both written in 1604, it is not primarily the hypocritical Angelo and the villainous Iago who are responsible for the troubles that arise. The fault really lies in the pious but irresponsible Duke, in the one case, and in the noble but morbidly jealous Moor, in the other. Just the same kind of contradictions can be seen running through Sonnets 109–125, written at about the same time, where Shakespeare has to admit his betrayal, while at the same time protesting with full sincerity the undying truth of his love. Southampton's fault has really been no more than to fail to match up to an idealized picture of him which existed only in Shakespeare's mind, yet this is what Shakespeare had found it most difficult to forgive him; having realized this, Shakespeare could not forgive himself for feeling that way. Like Othello, he felt himself to be

> ... one whose hand,   *Oth.* V.ii.345–7
> Like the base Indian, threw a pearl away,
> Richer than all his tribe; ...

In *King Lear*, written, as I think, just after the failure to secure a reconciliation with Southampton, the pearl is thrown away at the very beginning of the play, when Lear says to Cordelia:

> Here I disclaim all my paternal care,   *KL.* I.i.115–18
> Propinquity and property of blood,
> And as a stranger to my heart and me
> Hold thee for ever.

The whole of the bitter tragedy which follows stems from this sentence, which Lear could never withdraw until Cordelia lay dead in his arms. So Shakespeare had been too stubborn to apologize wholeheartedly for the fickleness which prudence had made necessary; he had produced one justification after another, even eventually to the extent of throwing a good part of the blame on to Southampton, and so made reconciliation impossible.

The agony of *King Lear* was not enough to atone for Shakespeare's guilt. The final act of expiation is that other terrifying play, *Timon of Athens*, which has been so brilliantly described by G. Wilson Knight in his book *The Wheel of Fire.* 'Timon's "fault," ' says Wilson Knight, in the course of his essay entitled 'The Pilgrimage of Hate', 'is essential love, essential nobility, unmixed with any restraining faculty of criticism.' This is also what brought Southampton down, and Cecil and the Queen acknowledged as much in commuting his death sentence to imprisonment in the Tower. In a speech given to one of Timon's servants Shakespeare condemns his own behaviour:

> As we do turn our backs   *T of A.* IV.ii.8–15
> From our companion thrown into his grave,
> So his familiars to his buried fortunes
> Slink all away, leave their false vows with him,
> Like empty purses pick'd; and his poor self,
> A dedicated beggar to the air,
> With his disease of all-shunn'd poverty,
> Walks, like contempt, alone.

More than this, Shakespeare even puts himself into the play as the Poet who, with the Painter, opens and sets the tone of the piece as a client in the opulent Timon's hall; and then, in the last act, believing a rumour that, in spite of his strange behaviour, Timon still has plenty of money after all, is foolish enough to let his embittered patron hear him plotting a new approach:

POET.   I am thinking what I shall say I have provided for him: it must be a personating of himself; a satire against the softness of prosperity, a discovery of the infinite flatteries that follow youth and opulency.

TIMON. (*Aside.*) Must thou needs stand for a villain in thine own work? Wilt thou whip thine own faults in other men? Do so, I have gold for thee.

POET.   Nay, let's seek him:
Then do we sin against our own estate,
When we may profit meet, and come too late.

> *T of A.* V.i.31–40

The Poet might well have been describing Shakespeare's last sonnet to Southampton (125) in which he warned him of the dangers of abandoning 'simple savour' for 'compound sweet'. By 'whipping his own faults' in chiding Southampton Shakespeare threw away, as he feels, the chance of re-creating their friendship, and confirmed his friend's impression that his own motives were predominantly venal.

Wilson Knight tells us that 'this play is *Hamlet, Troilus, Othello, Lear,* become self-conscious and universal; it includes and transcends them all; it is the recurrent and tormenting hate-theme of Shakespeare, developed, raised to an infinite power, presented in all its tyrannic strength and profundity, and—killed . . . Timon is the totality of all, his love more rich and oceanic than all of theirs —all lift their voices in his universal curse; Christ-like, he suffers that their pain may cease, and leaves the Shakespearian universe redeemed that Cleopatra may win her Antony in death, and Thaisa be restored to Pericles. . . .' To this I would add but one thought, that the hate-theme is primarily Shakespeare's self-hate at what he feels to be the meanness of his own character, which he then universalizes to pervade the world.

The striking thing is that by the great catharsis of *Timon of Athens* the Shakespearian universe does seem to have been redeemed. Chambers suggests 1607 or 1608 as the date when *Timon* was written, and 1608–9 for the next play, *Pericles*, which is followed in the succeeding years by *Cymbeline*, *The Winter's Tale* and *The Tempest*. Of these four plays A. L. Rowse has said;

> We find these themes re-echoing from play to play: reunion after long division, reconciliation, forgiveness. . . . The recurring myth of lost royalty is curiously sounded. What can it mean psychologically? — a lost authority or control on which life was once pivoted: after much storm and stress one comes back to it by the way of forgiveness and reconciliation?[3]

I do not think it is a coincidence that, soon after the beginning of this change of dramatic mood, there comes the publication of *Shakespeare's Sonnets*, which was entered in the Stationers' Register on 20th May, 1609. It has often been assumed, because of the form of the title and the dedication, and also because of a number of typographical errors which indicate that the author cannot have read the proofs, that this was a pirated edition, published by the printer, Thomas Thorpe, without Shakespeare's consent. But, as we have now seen, Sonnets 1–126, covering the period from 1592 to 1605, seem to be in correct chronological sequence, with the minor exception of 36–39, which should come between 42 and 43. On the other hand, the 'dark lady' series, 127–154, written in the years 1593-4, and the narrative poem *A Lover's Complaint*, also probably written in 1594, are placed after the end of the main series. All this would seem to suggest that the book is printed from a fair copy made not earlier than 1605, rather than from versions which may have been presented at different times to Southampton or any other recipient. It seems unlikely that Thorpe could have arrived at this order, which so many generations of readers have been baffled by, unless he made use of a copy which Shakespeare himself had fairly recently prepared. Otherwise, why should he not have left the 'dark lady' sonnets in their chronological position, that is to say, before Sonnet 107, which was written in 1603?

Almost from the beginning of the series Shakespeare insists that the Sonnets are to be a way of perpetuating the memory of Southampton's qualities and of his own love. He must always have intended that they should at some time be published, yet it is unthinkable that he would have allowed them to be printed against Southampton's wishes, particularly after the protestations contained in 109–125. It seems to me that both the fact of the publication and the change in the mood of Shakespeare's dramatic work indicate that in about 1608 a reconciliation took place between the poet and his former patron, and that Southampton agreed to the Sonnets being published, though in such a way that few people, other than those who already knew, would know that he had been the inspiration of them.

In this context it is easy to understand why Shakespeare might have preferred to leave the manuscript to be published without his direct supervision. If he had taken responsibility for the publication, he would have been expected to contribute a personal dedication and to employ some kind of artistic logic in editing the work, in the manner of the professional poets of the day. Unevenness of style and quality would have had to be edited out, and some poems might have had to be dropped. In view of the highly personal nature of the experience behind all the poems it would not be surprising if he felt he could not undertake this task; better to leave them in the form of a *cahier*, published without any retrospective polishing or selectivity, even though this meant including an undistinguished attempt of fifteen lines, like Sonnet 99, or two alternative versions of a Greek original, like Sonnets 153 and 154.

If I am right about the reconciliation between Shakespeare and Southampton, we may imagine that it was with a tranquil heart that Shakespeare was able to leave London about 1610 and move into his fine mansion at Stratford, New Place. From time to time he visited London to deliver plays to his company and to conduct other matters of business, and there is some reason to believe that he remained in touch with Southampton. The Earl had become a member in 1609 of both the Virginia Company and the East India Company, and it has often been remarked that *The Tempest*, written in 1611, is based partly on the mis-adventures of one of the Virginia Company's ships, the *Sea-Adventure*, in 1609, off the Bermudas. Some passages in the play seem to derive directly from a letter written by one William Strachey, secretary to the Governor of Virginia, to an anonymous 'Excellent Lady' in London. This letter was not published until 1625 (in Purchas' Pilgrims)[4], so it is not unlikely that Shakespeare obtained sight of it in 1611 from someone who was in close touch with the Virginia Company, perhaps Southampton himself. At any rate, the choice of this theme for the play would seem to indicate that the Virginia Company held no unpleasant associa-tions for Shakespeare at this time, as it must have done if the estrangement from Southampton were still continuing.

Shakespeare died in 1616, a prosperous and respected member of the proper-tied middle class with a shrewd head for business, yet at the same time an artist of unsurpassed poetic sensitivity. From the Sonnets, and from them alone, we learn that his ability to portray in drama the whole range of human emotional experience was not mere professional skill, but derived from a temperament which was itself capable of the most intense personal emotion, and, eventually, of attaining the most merciless self-knowledge. This is the heart that lies unlocked when at last the key to it has been found.

Notes

General Note

In order not to make these notes unnecessarily voluminous I have refrained from giving references for well-known historical facts, unless they relate directly to the interpretation of a sonnet or seem otherwise to be of particular interest. Where I have not noted them, the references for background events or for incidents in the lives and careers of William Shakespeare and the Earl of Southampton may be found in one or more of the following works:

G. B. Harrison, *The Elizabethan Journals* (1591–1603). London: G. Routledge & Sons, 1938. New York: Macmillan, 1939.

—— *A Jacobean Journal* (1603–1606). London: G. Routledge & Sons, 1941. New York: Macmillan, 1941.

E. K. Chambers, *William Shakespeare. A Study of Facts and Problems*, 2 vols. Oxford: Clarendon Press, 1930. New York: Oxford University Press, 1930.

—— *The Elizabethan Stage*, 4 vols. Oxford: Clarendon Press, 1923. New York; Oxford University Press, 1923.

C. C. Stopes, *The Life of Henry, Third Earl of Southampton, Shakespeare's Patron*. Cambridge: Cambridge University Press, 1922. New York: AMS Press, 1970.

The Dictionary of National Biography.

The Complete Peerage.

Of the Sonnets themselves there are a vast number of editions, of which I have found the following most useful:

H. E. Rollins (ed.), New Variorum Edition of Shakespeare, *The Sonnets*, 2 vols., Philadelphia and London: J. B. Lippincott Company, 1944.

Facsimile of the 1609 Quarto. Menston, Yorks.: The Scolar Press, 1968.

G. Willen and V. B. Reed (eds.), *A Casebook on Shakespeare's Sonnets*. New York: Thomas Y. Crowell Company, 1964.

J. Dover Wilson (ed.), The New Shakespeare, *The Sonnets*. Cambridge and New York: Cambridge University Press, 1967.

W. G. Ingram and T. Redpath (eds.), *Shakespeare's Sonnets*. London: University of London Press, 1964. New York: Barnes & Noble, 1965.

Martin Seymour-Smith (ed.), *Shakespeare's Sonnets*. London: Heinemann Educational Books Ltd., 1963. New York: Barnes & Noble, 1966.

For reference to other works of Shakespeare I have relied mainly on:

W. J. Craig (ed.) *The Complete Works of Shakespeare*. Oxford: Clarendon Press, 1892.

J. C. Maxwell (ed.), The New Shakespeare, *The Poems*. Cambridge and New York: Cambridge University Press, 1966.

But use has also been made of a number of other editions.

Introduction

[1] The reference is, of course, to Wordsworth's ' . . . with this key/Shakespeare unlocked his heart. . . .' (*Misc. Sonnets* II. 1)

CHAPTER I

The Framework

[1] Rollins II, 166.
[2] Stopes, *Life*, 291.
[3] Harrison (*T.L.S.* 1928), qu. Rollins I, 264.
[4] Wolfgang Keller, 1916, qu. Rollins I, 264; followed by A. L. Rowse, *William Shakespeare* (1963), 183.
[5] See, for example, Rollins II, 232–9.
[6] Leslie A. Fiedler in *The Riddle of Shakespeare's Sonnets*, ed. Edward Hubler (1962).

CHAPTER II

'The Worlds Fresh Ornament'

[1] The biographical facts about the Earl of Southampton are taken from Stopes, *Life*, and G. P. V. Akrigg, *Shakespeare and the Earl of Southampton* (1968).
[2] G. Gorer in the *Sunday Times*, London, 15th March, 1970.
[3] C. Plummer, *Elizabethan Oxford*, Oxford Historical Society VIII, 294.
[4] J. C. Clapham, *Narcissus, sive Amoris Iuvenilis et Praecipue Philautiae Brevis atque Moralis Descriptio*, London, 1591 (British Museum).
[5] There is no evidence that Southampton was ever other than normally hetero-sexual in his erotic activities except for a passage in an informer's letter, sent to Sir Robert Cecil after the Essex debacle in 1601. This alleges that he was on terms of undue familiarity with his Corporal-General of Horse, Captain Piers Edmonds, a follower of the Earl of Essex. Since all the Essex faction were in disgrace at this time they were obviously fair game for any kind of malicious gossip, and little reliance can be placed on this unsupported assertion. (See Ak-rigg, *Shakespeare and the Earl of Southampton*, quoting *Cecil Papers* 83, 62.) On the other hand, there is plenty of evidence about his heterosexual propensities.
[6] E. K. Chambers, *The Elizabethan Stage*.
[7] *Greenes Groatworth of Wit* (London, 1592).
[8] This sentence appears to be derived from Diotima's speech in Plato's *Symposium* (See Jowett 208d).
[9] Gerald Massey, qu. Rollins II, 119.
[10] Lansdowne MS. LXXI. 72, qu. Stopes, *Life*.
[11] J. B. Leishman, *Themes and Variations in Shakespeare's Sonnets* (1967), 149 ff.

CHAPTER III

A Rival Poet and a Fallen Favourite

[1] Wilson, *Sonnets*, 126.
[2] cf. Stopes, *Life*, 60.

[3] Sidney Lee (after Arber), *Elizabethan Sonnets*, 2 vols. (London, 1904). Reprinted New York, 1964), I, 165 ff.

[4] Plummer: see note 3 to Chapter II.

[5] Rowse, *William Shakespeare*, 146–7.

[6] E. K. Chambers, *The Oxford Book of Sixteenth Century Verse* (1932), 476 ff. See also *The Poems of Sir Walter Raleigh*, ed. Agnes M. Latham (1951).

[7] Qu. Stopes, *Life*, 237.

[8] cf. C. T. Onions, *A Shakespeare Glossary* (1953 edn.), under 'Worth'.

[9] John Nichols, *The Progresses and Public Processions of Queen Elizabeth*, 3 vols. (London, 1823. Reprinted New York, 1968.)

[10] Historical Manuscripts Commission, 7th Report, 522.

CHAPTER IV

The Death of Marlowe

[1] Stopes, *Life*, 137.

[2] J. L. Hotson, *The Death of Christopher Marlowe* (1925).

[3] cf. Rowse, *William Shakespeare*, 175–7.

CHAPTER V

Venus and Adonis and an Anagram

[1] Wilson, *Sonnets* 137. (The line endings for Sonnet 38 are incorrectly given in his New Shakespeare edition.)

[2] cf. George Chapman's clumsy anagrams on the names of Henry, Prince of Wales, and Robert Cecil, Earl of Salisbury, at pp. 389 and 397 of P. B. Bartlett's edition of his *Poems* (1941). Another example is 'Here I see many worthies lye', an anagram of Henry James Wriothesley, made by Rev. W. Jones of the Isle of Wight in 1624. (Stopes, *Life*, 469.)

CHAPTER VII

'And Strength by Limping Sway Disabled'

[1] See G. B. Harrison, *The Life and Death of Robert Devereux, Earl of Essex* (1937).

[2] See Catherine Drinker Bowen, *Francis Bacon, The Temper of a Man* (1963).

[3] See C. D. Bowen, *The Lion and the Throne* (1953).

[4] See Thomas Birch, *Memoirs of the Reign of Queen Elizabeth*, 2 vols. (London, 1754); also Martin Hume, *Treason and Plot* (1901), and the D.N.B. under 'Lopez'.

[5] Anthony Standen's letter of 3rd Feb., 1594, qu. Birch I, 152, tells us that the committal was the previous Tuesday (29th January). Harrison in his *Elizabethan Journals* quotes the date as 5th February.

[6] See *Elizabethan Journals* under 3rd and 6th February, 1594.

[7] Bowen, *The Lion and the Throne*, 59.

[8] *Idem*, 24.

[9] Birch's *Memoirs*, I, 129. Birch thought the 'late recover'd man' was Lord Keeper Puckering.

CHAPTER VIII

The Shadow of Atheism

[1] For the suspicions about Raleigh's alleged atheism see Rachel Lloyd, *Dorset Elizabethans* (1967), 233–92, from which I have taken the quotations from Father Parsons and Sir John Harington.

[2] Akrigg, *Sh. and S'ton*, 179.

[3] Thomas Nashe, *Works*, ed. R. B. McKerrow (1904).

[4] A. Acheson, *Shakespeare and the Rival Poet* (1903).

[5] The text of all the Chapman quotations is Bartlett's with *i* and *j* and *v* and *w* modernized.

[6] *Reliquiae Wottonianae*, qu. Akrigg, *Sh. and S'ton*, 47.

[7] M. Seymour-Smith, *Shakespeare's Sonnets*, 149.

[8] Ovid's *Metamorphoses*, the Arthur Golding Translation (1567), ed. J. F. Nims (New York, 1965), 383.

CHAPTER IX

'A Better Spirit Doth Use Your Name'

[1] Thomas Nashe, *Workes*, ed. McKerrow.

[2] Stopes, *Life*, 57.

[3] J. L. Hotson, *Mr. W. H.*, 260, says that the Friend's eyes have conferred a second degree on the already-graced Rival Poet.

[4] See the *Oxford English Dictionary*.

[5] *Elizabethan Sonnets*, I. 28.

[6] J. Bakeless, *Christopher Marlowe* (1938), 110.

[7] M. C. Bradbrook, *The School of Night* (1936).

[8] See Rollins II, App. X, for a summary of the earlier speculation on the identity of the Rival Poet.

CHAPTER X

'Farewell Thou Art Too Deare For My Possessing'

[1] M. M. Reese, *Shakespeare, His World and His Work* (1953), 408n.

[2] C. F. E. Spurgeon, *Shakespeare's Imagery* (1935), Chapter X.

[3] Martin Hume, *Treason and Plot*.

[4] Sir Simonds D'Ewes, *Journals* (London, 1682), 599–600 (27th October, 1601).

CHAPTER XI

A Wintry Summer

1 John Stow, *Annals*, 766–7.
2 Chambers, *William Shakespeare*.
3 Henry Foley, *Records of the English Province of the Society of Jesus*, IV, 49. cf. Stopes, *Life*, 86.
4 Stopes, *Life*, 86, followed by A. L. Rowse (*Shakespeare's Southampton Patron of Virginia*, [1965], 103), says, without quoting any evidence, that the child turned out to be a girl.
5 Chambers, *Elizabethan Stage*, IV, 164.
6 Leishman, *Themes and Variations in Shakespeare's Sonnets*, 191–2.
7 G. Massey, qu. Rollins I, 245. Constable's poem is at II, 83 of *Elizabethan Sonnets*.
8 G. Wyndham (ed.), *The Poems of Shakespeare* (1898), 244–6.
9 Wilson, *Sonnets*, intr. lxxxiii–iv.

CHAPTER XII

'Oh Blame Me Not If I No More Can Write!'

1 D. M. Main, *A Treasury of English Sonnets* (1880), qu. Rollins I, 261. cf. Claes Schaar, *Elizabethan Sonnet Themes and the Dating of Shakespeare's Sonnets* (1962), 90–2.
2 Akrigg, *Sh. and S'ton*, 235.
3 Nicholas Rowe, 1709, qu. Chambers, *William Shakespeare*.
4 J. Dover Wilson, *The Essential Shakespeare* (1932), 66–7.
5 Wilson, *Sonnets*, 202–3.
6 Stopes, *Life*, 69 and 80 ff.

CHAPTER XIII

'Darkning Thy Powre To Lend Base Subjects Light'

1 See the discussion of theories about 'Will' in Rollins I, 345–7.
2 Rowse, *Shakespeare's Southampton*, 95.
3 Thomas Nashe, *Works*, ed. McKerrow.
4 Schaar, *Elizabethan Sonnet Themes*, 105–7.
5 Ingram and Redpath, *Shakespeare's Sonnets*, 337–8.
6 See Onions, *A Shakespeare Glossary*, under 'Base'.
7 Hotson, *Mr. W. H.*, 244.
8 e.g. Sonnets 127, 132, 134, 135, 136, and *L.L.L.* III. i. 199, and 214, V. ii. 378.
9 Akrigg, *Sh. and S'ton*, 218–9.

CHAPTER XIV

An Interval

[1] For the sources of historical facts not otherwise annotated, see General Note above.

[2] H.M.C. Report XIII, I. 321.

[3] e.g. Rowse, *William Shakespeare*, 205.

[4] J. C. Collins, *Sydney Papers* (1746), I, 348 and II, 61.

[5] James Spedding (ed.), *The Letters and The Life of Francis Bacon* (London, 1861–72), I, 370–3. (Reprinted New York, 1968.)

CHAPTER XV

Southampton and Essex

[1] Salisbury Papers, VIII, 371, qu. Stopes, *Life*, 133.

CHAPTER XVI

Rage and Rebellion

[1] Spedding (ed.), Bacon's *Apology*, qu. Harrison, *Journals*, for 15th September, 1599.

CHAPTER XVII

'Death Is Now The Phoenix' Nest'

[1] Elegie or Friend's Passion For his Astrophill, by Matthew Roydon, is included in Spenser's *Colin Clout* and in a collection entitled *The Phoenix' Nest*. My text is from Spenser's *Poetical Works*, ed. J. Payne Collier, London, 1891, V, 138–45.

[2] cf. J. C. Maxwell (ed.), *The Poems*, Cambridge New Sh., 221.

[3] S. P. Venetian, X, 81.

[4] Akrigg, *Sh. and S'ton*, 128, quoting Stow.

[5] Clara Longworth de Chambrun, *Shakespeare: A Portrait Restored* (1957), 244–5.

CHAPTER XVIII

The End of a Reign

[1] See Harrison, *Elizabethan Journals*, for 5th February and 26th April, 1601.

[2] cf. Rowse, *William Shakespeare* 353, and Akrigg, *Sh. and S'ton*, 256.

[3] Harrison, *A Jacobean Journal*, under 28th April, 1603.

[4] Stopes, *Life*, 263.

[5] Akrigg, *Sh. and S'ton*, 255.

CHAPTER XIX

The New Era

[1] In addition to the works quoted in the General Note, in the next two chapters useful background material has been obtained from G. P. V. Akrigg, *Jacobean Pageant, or The Court of King James I* (1962).

[2] Salisbury Papers, XI, 40, qu. Stopes, *Life*, 277.

[3] T. Birch, *The Court and Times of James the First* 2 vols. (London, 1848. Reprinted Philadelphia, 1969.)

[4] T. B. Howell, London 1816, II, 54. Letter from Dudley Carleton to John Chamberlain, 11th December, 1603.

[5] Akrigg, *Jacobean Pageant*, 47.

[6] Stow, *Annals*, 833.

[7] Quoted in Chambers, *William Shakespeare*.

[8] J. Nichols, *The Progresses, Processions, and Magnificent Festivities of King James I*, 4 vols. (London, 1828), 396. (Reprinted New York, 1967.)

[9] Akrigg, *Jacobean Pageant*, 89 and 370.

CHAPTER XX

The Jacobean Sonnets

[1] cf. H. McC. Young, *The Sonnets of Shakespeare: A Psycho-Sexual Analysis* (Menasha, Wisconsin, 1937), 101, qu. Rollins, I, 277, who says that the reference is to inserting a gore into a clown's breeches to give them fulness.

[2] Rowse, *Shakespeare's Sonnets* (1964), 231.

[3] Onions, *A Shakespeare Glossary*, under 'Abysm'.

[4] T. Tyler (ed.), *Shakespeare's Sonnets*, (London, 1890), 271.

[5] C. C. Stopes (ed.), *Shakespeare's Sonnets* (1904), 213.

[6] Onions, *Sh. Glossary*, under 'Hallow'.

[7] cf. S. Lee, *A Life of William Shakespeare* (London, 1898), 152n. Barnes's poem is in *Elizabethan Sonnets*, I, 197.

[8] Chambers, *William Shakespeare*, quoting the account for the payment of 44 shillings each to Shakespeare and Burbage for painting an impresa for Lord Rutland for a royal tilt on 24th March, 1613, the King's Accession Day.

[9] George Steevens in 1780 was the first to point this out.

[10] Akrigg, *Jacobean Pageant*, 51–2.

[11] qu. Sir Tresham Lever, *The Herberts of Wilton* (1967), 114.

[12] Harrison, *Jacobean Journal*, under 22nd June, 1604. See also the Introduction to 'Voyage of Sir Robert Dudley to the West Indies', ed. George F. Warner, Hakluyt Society Series 2, III, 1899, xxxix-xlvii, and D.N.B.

[13] Akrigg, *Sh. and S'ton*, 140–2.

[14] Salisbury Papers, XVI, 137, qu. Harrison, *A Jacobean Journal*.

[15] Stopes, *Shakespeare's Sonnets*, 222.

[16] Akrigg, *Sh. and S'ton*, 135.

[17] Harrison, *A Jacobean Journal*, under 26th June, 1604 and the note on p. 369.

CHAPTER XXI

'Now All Is Done'

[1] Salisbury Papers, XVI, 415.
[2] Stopes, *Life*, 290–1.

CHAPTER XXII

'I Am That I Am'

[1] Leishman, *Themes and Variations . . .*, 132.
[2] *Idem*, 230.
[3] Rowse, *William Shakespeare*, 418.
[4] Samuel Purchas, 'Purchas His Pilgrimes' (London, 1625), Part II, Book 9, Chapter VI.

Table of Main Landmarks for Dating the Sonnets

SONNET No.	LINE(S)	TOPICAL REFERENCES	LIKELY DATE OF SONNET	PAGE
1	10	References to Spring and April.	Spring 1592	22 and 110–2
3	10		(Year deduced from S. 104)	
10	7–8	Letter from Southampton to Burghley's secretary about repairs needed to Beaulieu manor house—26th June 1592.	June–July 1592	22–3
21	Whole	Allusions to Barnabe Barnes: *Parthenophil and Parthenophe* (registered 10th May 1593).	First half of 1593	29–32
25	5–12	Allusions to Sir W. Raleigh: 11th and last *Book of the Ocean to Cynthia*, probably written in latter half of 1592.	First half of 1593	33–8
26	Whole	Presentation to Southampton of *Venus and Adonis* (registered 18th April 1593).	First half of 1593	27–8 and 38
30–1	Whole	References to death of Christopher Marlowe, 30th May 1593.	June 1593	41–3
36	9–12	References to publication of *Venus and Adonis* with dedication to Southampton (probably a few weeks after registration).	June 1953	39 and 44–9
38	Whole			
39	1–4			

o

SONNET NO.	LINE(S)	TOPICAL REFERENCES	LIKELY DATE OF SONNET	PAGE
53	5–8	Reference to modelling of Adonis on Southampton and to intention to write a poem about a beautiful woman with same inspiration (*Venus and Adonis* in April 1593 and *Rape of Lucrece* in May 1594).	Latter half of 1593	53
66	Whole	Allusions to rival candidacies of Bacon and Coke for post of Attorney-General (January 1594); Essex's rebuke by the Queen (24th January 1594); closing of theatres (6th February 1594); attempts by Chapman to obtain sponsorship of Southampton for *The Shadow of Night* (registered 31st December 1593); rumours of impending investigation of atheistical beliefs of Raleigh's circle.	February 1594	56–64
67	1–4	Allusion to risk of involvement of Southampton in the investigation into Raleigh's atheism held at Cerne Abbas, 21st March 1594.	March 1594	66–8
69	Whole	Allusion to aspersions on Southampton in Chapman's *Shadow of Night*, published March/April 1594.	March 1594	69–72
78	3	Mention of 'Alien pen' picked up by Nashe in his dedication to Southampton of *The Unfortunate Traveller* published some time after 25th March 1594.	March 1594	78–9

SONNET No.	LINE(s)	TOPICAL REFERENCES	LIKELY DATE OF SONNET	PAGE
90	2 and 7	Allusions to theatres having been closed since 6th February 1594 and to the storms of wind in March 1594.	March 1594	96
96	5-10	Allusion to trial of Dr Lopez for treason, 18th February 1594, and to the jewelled ring which he had offered to the Queen.	March 1594	94
97	1-5	Reference to bad weather of spring and summer 1594.	Autumn 1594	97-100
	6-10	Reference to the Countess of Derby having been left pregnant when her husband (the patron of Shakespeare's company) died on 10th April, 1594.		
98	13	Further reference to wintry spring and summer of 1594.	Autumn 1594	101
100 103	Whole Whole	Acknowledgement of sponsorship by Southampton of *The Rape of Lucrece*, (registered 9th May 1594 and published some time that year).	Late autumn 1594	105
104	Whole	Reference to Southampton's 21st birthday, 6th October 1594, and to the three revolutions of the seasons since they first met.	October 1594	111-2

SONNET No.	LINE(s)	TOPICAL REFERENCES	LIKELY DATE OF SONNET	PAGE
107	Whole	References to release of Southampton from the Tower (10th April 1603); Death (24th March 1603) and funeral (28th April 1603) of Queen Elizabeth; Coronation of James I (25th July 1603) and his policy of peace with Spain.	Between April and July 1603	156–8
123	1–9	Allusion to Procession through London (15th March 1604), with pyramids and classical arches of triumph, as described in Stephen Harrison's booklet published June 1604.	End of June 1604	166 and 179–81
124	1–4	References to arraignment of Sir R. Dudley, bastard son of the Earl of Leicester, before the Star Chamber (22nd June 1604).	End of June 1604	183–5
	6–7	Reference to arrest of Southampton on suspicion of treason (24th June 1604).		185–6
	13–4	Reference to reprieve of Cobham, Markham and Grey (9th December 1603).		160–5 and 185–6
125	1–4	Further reference to Procession of 15th March 1604 and echo of first scene of *Othello* (first performed, November 1604).	End of June 1604	182–3
126	Whole	Celebration of birth (1st March 1605) or christening (26th March 1605) of James, Lord Wriothesley, son and heir to Southampton.	March 1605	190–2

Sonnets 127–54 (the so-called Dark Lady sequence) contain no topical allusions to act as dating landmarks. Those which refer directly to this lady, however, can be placed by reference to Sonnets 33–5, 40–2 and 100 3–4 in the years 1593 and 1594. (See pp. 113–120.)

Index of Sonnets referred to

Index

As a general rule, historical figures are entered under the designations by which they are most commonly referred to in the text, often with cross-references under other names or titles by which they were known.